ABOUT THE

Xandria Williams began her career with degrees in chemistry from Imperial College, London University. From there she moved via biochemistry to the study of human nutrition, naturopathy, homoepathy and botanic medicine. After some years in private practice she extended her studies to Neurolinguistic Programming, Time-Line therapy, Voice Dialogue and many other aspects of psychotherapy and counselling.

She has lectured extensively at many colleges of chiropractic, osteopathy and naturopathy, at conferences and to private groups. She runs seminars on a range of aspects of physical, mental and emotional health care.

She is the author of several hundred articles on health and nutrition, is often heard on radio and television and has published eight books.

Xandria Williams' unique and highly effective approach to helping people tackle life's problems has evolved over more than two decades of research at her clinics in Sydney and London, as well as through her writings and lectures.

She sees clients in both London and Sydney and can be contacted for advice or consultations as follows:

LONDON
By phone on   (44) 0171 824 8153 or
By mail   c/o Hodder and Stoughton
                    338 Euston Road, London NW1 3BH

SYDNEY
By phone on   (61) 02 953 4771
By fax on   (61) 02 953 4714
By mail   P.O. Box 117, Cremorne,
                    NSW 2090, Australia

Also by Xandria Williams

Living with Allergies: (Allen & Unwin, Australia)
What's in Your Food: (Nature and Health Books, Australia, 1988)
Osteoporosis
Choosing Health Intentionally: (Simon and Schuster, Australia,
1990; Charles Letts, London, 1992)
Choosing Weight Intentionally: (Simon and Schuster, Australia,
1990; Charles Letts, London, 1992)
Stress – Recognise and Resolve: (Charles Letts, London, 1993)
Beating the Blues – A Guide to Avoiding and Lifting Depression:
(Heinemann, London, 1995)

LOVE, HEALTH AND HAPPINESS

Understanding yourself and your
relationships through
THE FOUR TEMPERAMENTS

Xandria Williams

Hodder & Stoughton

First published in 1995 by Hodder and Stoughton
A division of Hodder Headline PLC

10 9 8 7 6 5 4 3 2 1

A CIP catalogue record for this title is available from the British Library

ISBN 0 340 62857 X

Typeset by
Phoenix Photosetting, Chatham, Kent
Printed and bound in Great Britain by
Mackays of Chatham PLC

Hodder and Stoughton
A Division of Hodder Headline PLC
338 Euston Road
London NW1 3BH

This book is dedicated to all people, of all temperaments, who provide the endless variety of human personalities that make this world such a fascinating place, and to the ancient Greeks for elaborating the concept.

ACKNOWLEDGEMENTS

I would like to thank all the many authors whose hundreds of books I have read over the years, for the ideas they have shared; all my patients for the examples they have given me of the different possibilities of human personalities, and all my friends and relations who have further added to my understanding of the different temperaments.

CONTENTS

Publisher's Note

Xandria Williams' study of the four temperaments began in the 1960s. Her first introduction came through reading about the ancient Greeks and their beliefs, including their assessment of the human temperament and personality. Just as they believed their physical world was made up of different combinations of the four elements – fire, air, water and earth – so they believed that the characteristics and behaviours of people were a combination of the four basic temperaments: Choleric, Sanguine, Phlegmatic and Melancholic. As explained in this book, the Greeks thought of people as being either dominantly a single temperament or a blend of two, three or possibly even four identifiable and different temperaments.

After further research into this field, she moved beyond thinking of the temperaments as a stationary set of attributes and characteristics and recognised the developmental patterns and differences between the temperaments and the different needs of each temperament as people strive to mature, reach their potential and achieve their goals.

Initially she focused on the concepts in her daily life and soon discovered she was an introverted Choleric. In the early 1970s she changed profession to the health field and her studies of the four temperaments found immediate application. Her new-found knowledge gave her an added tool with which to relate to and help her patients and clients to deal with their physical and emotional health.

She began writing and lecturing about the temperaments in 1982 and her interest has continued ever since. She believes it has given her a better understanding of people and relationships.

She has spent more than twenty-five years considering the subject and its application to her own and other people's lives in the family, work and social spheres. Over the past twenty years she has studied and used these ideas in relation to thousands of patients and clients and helped them in her role as naturopath, psychotherapist and seminar leader. But most importantly – and the key to this book – she has developed an understanding of what each temperament needs to do and to have in order that they can develop their character to the fullest and in the best possible way.

Xandria has now written several books on personal growth and development aimed at assisting people in dealing with the mental and emotional problems and challenges they face in life in regard to both their physical and their mental health and well-being. Through all of them runs the common thread that she feels is so important: that of helping people to find ways to grow and progress in their journey through life, to develop their positive attributes and avoid their negative possibilities. This theme is continued here.

Other books describe the temperaments and personality types. But this book is unique. Here you will learn not only about your temperament in general and gain overall understanding of other people, but also how the temperaments manifest in a wide variety of life situations and stages. Further, you will learn how to use the four temperaments to understand yourselves and others as well as to make positive changes in your life.

PART I:

Introducing the Four Temperaments

CHAPTER 1

The Four Temperaments: A Useful Guide

I work every day with clients and patients, people who have come to see me because of health or emotional problems. Many health problems have a physical cause or basis. Many others come about as a result of mental and emotional stress and distress. Much of this arises because people either fail to understand themselves and to achieve their best, or are intolerant of themselves and berate themselves for not being different to the way they are. Much of the stress is also caused by difficulties in relationships. People have difficulty relating to people and situations and in knowing where they want to go and how to get there.

Time and again I am saddened at the way in which people can interact and yet never really communicate. One person says and means one thing; the second person hears it but gives it a totally different meaning. They may even pass this on to a third person, who reinterprets it in yet another way. The result of this is often much confusion, suspicion and misunderstanding: it may be overt, or it may be hidden and festering. It may show up, ultimately, not only in problems with relationships but also in a variety of health problems, both physical and mental. You have almost certainly had the experience yourself of finding that what you have said or tried to express has been totally misinterpreted.

It's not only at the level of communication that relationships can break down. You may look at someone who other people like and yet find that you are only aware of their faults. You may fail totally to understand why they are so popular. Or you may like someone and admire them, and fail to understand why so many people do not get on with them. You may try to cheer someone up only to find they claim you are heartless and that you don't realise how serious their problem is, or you may try to make a fuss of someone when things go wrong only to find they brush you off as a fusspot and accuse you of making mountains out of molehills. Perhaps you do someone a good turn and then cannot understand why, instead of being grateful, they shun you.

Poor communciation does not just occur on an interpersonal level. People may also communicate incorrectly with the world in general. They build up appearances that deny their inner emotions and character. Their lives seem wonderful on the outside and they appear to be in control and healthy and happy. Yet prick this bubble and you can often find much distress inside.

The trouble comes in part from assuming there is such a thing as the average person and that other people think and feel the way you do. If you interpret other people's words and actions on this basis you have a one in four chance of being approximately right and a three in four chance of being totally wrong, as we shall see.

One way to help reduce this problem of communicating with and understanding other people is to come to a better understanding of some of the major ways in which people differ. Understand the ways in which their words and deeds have different meanings to the ones you might give them, and different meanings to the meanings they would have if you said or did the same things. An aid in this process is to come to an understanding of the four temperaments, the four personality types, labelled by the early Greeks and still so labelled by psychologists today: Choleric, Melancholic, Phlegmatic and Sanguine.

You have to communicate with a lot of people in your life, some of them casually, some of them intimately. These days most of us live in cities or other urban societies and this necessarily means that you are in very close proximity to a lot of people. Some people you know well; most are strangers. Yet at some level you have to interact with a large number of them, often in very compressed circumstances in both time and space. And all the time you are drawing conclusions based on what you perceive in the world around you, conclusions which affect your state of happiness and your assessment of yourself and others.

In many of the interchanges between people there is little or no time to establish a rapport, or to get to know the other person sufficiently to relate to them productively and smoothly. It is all too easy to assume that the other person thinks, feels and behaves in the same way that you do, and you may then be surprised when, as frequently happens, they don't. The assumption that they would respond in the same way as you would can lead to much pain and frustration, as can the assumption that they would like to be treated in the same way as you would like to be treated. The dictum 'do unto others as you would have them do unto you' is not always a wise one.

CHAPTER 2

History of the Four Temperaments

The concept of the four temperaments is ancient. The early Greeks loved dividing their world into four. They believed the physical world around them was made of up four elements: fire, air, water and earth. They believed the health of the human body was dependent on maintaining the correct balance between the four fluids: blood, phlegm, black bile and yellow bile. Their year followed four seasonal changes. Their calendar contained twelve months which they related to the twelve signs of the zodiac and in turn divided this into four groups: the fire, earth, air and water signs. And they divided people's characteristic make-up into the four temperaments.

Hippocrates, often thought of as the founder of modern medicine, spoke of the four temperaments as far back as 400 BC and Galen, a Greek physician in 180 AD, classified people as being made up of a blend of the four temperaments. The Greeks thought of Choleric people as having an excess of yellow bile, Sanguines an excess of blood, Phlegmatics an excess of phlegm and Melancholics an excess of black bile.

Much of twentieth-century psychology has been based on the premise that people are fundamentally similar, a belief that fits in well with our democratic principles that include the concept that we are all equal and should all have the same opportunities. If people are fundamentally similar and yet behave differently then there should be a solution, and many have thought that there should be just one solution and that it should fit all and should explain all aberrant behaviours. Freud sought this solution in sexual and maternal relationships. Adler focused on people's relationship to power, others on other basic instincts. Then began the Existentialists' search for the Self.

In contradistinction to this, the concept of fundamental differences and that of the four temperaments continued among those who disagreed with the notion that people are essentially the same. Among those who recognised differences among people, four still seems to have been the magic number.

At the beginning of this century, in 1907, Adickes divided people into four categories based on whether their view of the world was dogmatic, agnostic, traditional, or innovative. A decade or so later Adler described people as being differentiated by the goals they had – whether they desired recognition, power, service or revenge – and Spranger by their values: religious, theoretic, economic or artistic. Kretschmer divided people by their abnormal behaviour, whether it tended to be hyperaesthetic, anaesthetic, melancholic or hypomanic.

Jung was convinced that people were fundamentally different and that these differences were healthy, not abnormal. He developed the concept of psychological types, recognising that each person has their own set of drives, desires, needs and characteristics. Not only did he not see these differences as problems or abnormalities, he recognised all the types as being of equal value, no one type being better than or worse than another, merely different. He also suggested that these types, since they existed, could be classified, described and understood.

A number of questionnaires have been devised to enable the practitioner to better understand the personality of their clients based on the recognition of the existence of different types.

Eysenck considers that people's personalities can be assessed according to whether they are introverted or extroverted, stable or unstable. In other words, they can be placed somewhere along a single scale, with introverts and extroverts at the extreme ends and, on a different scale of neurosis, ranging from stable to unstable. If you place the introvert to extrovert scale horizontally going from left to right and the neurosis scale vertically going from stable at the bottom to unstable at the top you have four quadrants. Eysenck pointed out a possible correlation between these four quadrants and the four temperaments, putting Cholerics in the top right-hand quadrant, Sanguines in the bottom right, Phlegmatics in the bottom left section and Melancholics in the top left (see Chapter 14).

The questionnaire which he uses to place people at a point within this circle produces some interesting results, although I have found that some people, myself included, are unconvinced by the result they get when they do it. This is possibly because the basis of the groupings and differentiations consisted of the two scales referred to rather than a fundamental assessment of each of the temperaments.

Some psychologists and psychotherapists work simply with the four temperaments; others work with more detailed subdivisions. Myers and Briggs returned to the ideas of Jung and others who had worked on the basis of fundamental differences in the 1930s. By the 1960s they had formulated and tested a questionnaire according to which people were divided into sixteen categories, four within each temperament. This questionnaire is too lengthy and detailed for our purposes here but a shortened version, based on four questions, is given in Chapter 16 and can be used as a guide when you are determining your own temperament.

So the history of these concepts is a long and varied one. The idea of four sub-types of people stretches back 2,500 years and probably more. Even when it seems to have disappeared it has re-emerged. This can encourage us in our belief that an understanding of the temperaments is both valid and useful. It is also fun, so come with me and develop an increased understanding of yourself and your fellow beings.

CHAPTER 3

The Four Temperaments in Brief

By now you will have gathered some of the basic ideas behind this book. The next step is to find out about each of the temperaments individually. As you work through Part II you will learn about each temperament in detail and as a separate entity. First you will learn about each temperament in general terms and about the way it matures, and then you will learn about the temperament in different settings: childhood, adulthood and old age, at work and play and so forth. You will also learn about it in relation to different aspects of life, such as love, health, money and hobbies.

Here is a very brief thumb-sketch of the four temperaments: Choleric, Melancholic, Phlegmatic and Sanguine. You will learn much more as you work through the book but this outline will give you a working framework. As you read on you can fill in the details.

Cholerics are strong, extrovert leaders. They are intellectual, intelligent and have a desire to understand the world, particularly the physical world. They are confident. They can be impatient and arrogant or they can be a source of strength and inspiration. You are likely to find them in business and the sciences. They make up 12 per cent of the population.*

Melancholics are soulful, often but not always pessimists, searching for the meaning of life and trying to find their true inner identity. They can be self-involved and easily depressed, or wonderfully caring people who put the needs of others above their own, responding to pain and suffering with succour and support. You are likely to find them in the arts, in caring professions and in religion. They also make up 12 per cent of the population.

Phlegmatics are slow and thoughtful traditionalists. They are the pillars of society and like to serve others and do their duty. They may seem dull but they are willing to do the routine jobs others may find boring, they offer quiet stability and make excellent peace-

---

* Population statistics taken from *Please Understand Me* by David Keirsey and Marilyn Bates (Prometheus Nemesis Book Company, 1978).

makers. You are likely to find them doing routine work in factories or offices, and as teachers. They make up 38 per cent of the population.

Sanguines are fun and want, above all, to enjoy themselves. They bring light, joy, sparkle and interest into life. They have multiple interests, may be superficial but are great storytellers and are excellent at all types of the arts and crafts. You are likely to find them in the arts or where there is physical movement and activity, and in jobs with a variety of activities. They make up 38 per cent of the population.

For simplicity's sake, each temperament will be described as if you are dealing with an individual who is 100 per cent the temperament under discussion. You will, for instance, learn about the Choleric as if he or she is all Choleric with no Sanguine, Melancholic or Phlegmatic temperament; you will learn about the Melancholic as if she or he had none of the Sanguine cheer or the Phlegmatic calm.

In real life, in real human beings this, of course, is not necessarily the case. The easiest way to understand some of the individual variations is to consider the people you know and meet as being made up of a combination of temperaments, with one or two dominating.

Are You Only One Temperament?

To divide the world into four types of people is a big task. Obviously there are many more differences than that would suggest. To resolve this situation there are many questions we could ask. Is an individual, such as yourself, necessarily all one temperament or all another temperament, or can you be a combination? Do you stay the same or can you change from one temperament to another over time? Can you change your temperament with your circumstances? Let's start to answer these and some other questions that will occur to you as we go along.

Most people are made up of a combination of characteristics from all four temperaments. Yet in very few people is there an equal balance of them all. It is possible that the truly balanced person is an equal mixture of all four, progressing from the immature Stage I to the mature Stage III quickly and easily in each phase of their life and living smoothly through their three score years and ten, but if this were so and if we were all like this, then the world would be a very dull place.

Instead we find that some people are dominantly one temperament and that the other three play only a minor role in their make-up. Other people have two temperaments that are strongly displayed and the other two are minor. Still others find that they have three temperaments well represented and that the fourth is conspicuous by its absence most of the time.

One Temperament

If a person is dominantly one temperament you will find it relatively easy to 'read' this and determine which one it is. There is little possibility of confusing a true, 100 per cent Choleric with a complete Phlegmatic, or a full Melancholic with a pure Sanguine.

These people are likely to behave consistently and in line with their temperament most of the time. Do not be confused by occasional displays of behaviour that you think are out of character. If they occur only rarely you are dealing with someone who is dominantly a single temperament.

Two Temperaments

It is also relatively easy to isolate two temperaments in a person. They will oscillate from one to the other and you will probably be able to pick them both out relatively easily. The changes may occur in different settings, or when the individual is faced with a variety of different circumstances. It is possible for the chaotic and impulsive Sanguine to have alternating periods of Phlegmatic relaxation and calm. It is possible for the dynamic, strong and positive Choleric to switch to a moody Melancholic when things don't go their way.

Three Temperaments

It is more difficult to identify the make-up of someone who is normally a mixture of three temperaments. They may seem to you to fit into no particular category. One solution is to look for a temperament that is missing. You may find someone who is a dynamic mixture of Choleric and Sanguine extroversion mixed with some Phlegmatic calm and a willingness to fulfil the dull and routine aspects of their life when needed, yet they show little signs of the Melancholic temperament and are never sad, depressed or off with the fairies and dreaming for long. Or you may know a quiet and reserved person who shows the characteristics of the Melancholic and Phlegmatic plus some of the Choleric strength and assertiveness, yet is rarely the light-hearted Sanguine.

If a person seems to be a mixture of all the temperaments and you cannot 'sort them out', check to see if one is missing. You will find this the easiest way. If no temperament is missing then obviously you have indeed found someone who is a mixture of all four.

Four Temperaments

It is rare to find someone who is a mixture of all four temperaments, certainly not a balanced mixture. They do exist, but usually there is some imbalance and you already know how to discover this.

CHAPTER 4

How the Temperaments Change with Time

As you read this book you will have great fun recognising the different temperaments in your friends and family and in the people you meet. You may feel confident that you have established their dominant temperament. Then suddenly you find that there are times when you or they act out of character. Their basic make-up can seem to change with time and you may find this confusing. In fact, their basic temperamental mix generally stays the same but different parts of it can be emphasised or brought out in different or unusual circumstances.

Eighty or ninety per cent of the time an individual may show their normal, consistent pattern, but this can change. The positive Choleric can be Melancholic when a close friend dies; a butterfly Sanguine can get sudden urges to organise their life; a steady Phlegmatic is sometimes capable of letting their hair down and having fun, and Melancholics can laugh, look on the bright side and focus on being frivolous and having fun occasionally. However, for most people these less common behaviours are likely to be mild and short-lived and a reversion to their normal temperament status is usually fairly rapid. Knowing your basic mix and that of other people can help you to understand them better.

Apart from these changes related to circumstances, you do in general remain the same temperament throughout your life. There is little chance of converting an introspective, pessimistic Melancholic into an extroverted, optimistic Sanguine, or an insecure Phlegmatic into a dominant Choleric. On the other hand, if you are, for instance, poised with somewhat similar amounts of Choleric and Melancholic in your make-up, you can practice focusing on being more Choleric than Melancholic, or the other way around, if that is your wish and, in time, you can bring about at least some of the desired changes.

Rather than trying to alter your temperament, it is wiser to focus on encouraging your development through the stages, from Stage I through Stage II to Stage III, showing ever-increasing maturity and bringing out the best in your temperamental make-up.

As You Mature

We have already mentioned the stages of development through which people progress. It is now time to consider this aspect further.

Everyone goes through a life experience, and for each of us it is a unique and individual experience. You start out young and innocent, taking the world at face value, observing and learning rather than applying judgements. However, things begin to happen pretty quickly and you soon start to make assessments and draw conclusions about the world you have entered. These assessments and conclusions then become your filters and when further things happen you take them in through these same filters. Not only are your interpretations of the world around you gradually affected to a greater and greater extent by the filters you establish, but these filters too change with time, as your experiences grow.

As a baby you might, for instance, have found that in general being hugged and kissed was pleasurable but then found that when a man with a beard kissed you he squashed you as well. Your filter might then become a belief that people with beards hurt you. You probably found that when you cried you got fed and so another filter became that you needed to cry to get what you wanted. Inevitably hundreds and thousands of these situations and filters become established. They are part of learning about and adapting to the world you have entered. As the years go by this pattern develops further and maturity comes.

In the beginning you, the newborn baby, are totally egotistical. You feel yourself to be the centre of a world that revolves around you. As you observe the world around you, you find out more about this experience of life. You are totally unselfconscious, you have no awareness of the fact that, just as you are observing others, so they are observing you. In fact you have little or no sense of self, as distinct from the world around you.

Consider the little child, how it gazes at you with wide open eyes, staring at you, quite unselfconsciously, observing what it can see. Children are neither boastful nor modest; they have not yet learnt these traits. If they do something well and enjoy the experience they may be excited and want to share it with you. They will then say something like, 'Look Mummy, I did this. Aren't I clever?' The wise mother will agree and share in the child's pleasure in the experience. All too often, however, the child is told 'Yes, I see it, but don't boast, dear.' Thus begins the process by which the child learns to belittle his or her own achievements and, in turn, to belittle and doubt themselves. It also begins the process from immaturity to a stage of developing maturity as the individual learns to differentiate between self and non-self and to build, either positively and constructively or negatively and destructively, on the characteristics with which they were born and the environment in which they live.

As you grow from childhood through to early adulthood your experiences accumulate and you gain a wider perspective on life. This experience forms the basis of understanding, both of yourself and of others, and of personal growth and development that occurs along the way from childhood to full adulthood. With maturity you have a greater awareness of other people and their rights and needs and an understanding of the ways in which you can bring out and develop the best of yourself.

At full maturity you have a wide experience of the world, of other people and of yourself. You have, hopefully, learnt to enhance your best qualities, leave your less admirable qualities behind and to share your own experience to help and encourage others. Sadly, some people develop what is worst in their nature, or fail to develop at all.

Three Stages of Development

These development patterns apply to everyone and to each temperament and so we will be considering each temperament in three stages. It is important, however, to understand that each stage is a continuum, that, in fact, all three stages are really one long continuum. It is simply for convenience that we divide the process of maturation into three.

Just as there is no exact dividing line between each of the four temperaments, so there is no exact dividing line between the three stages. With time and personal development most people make a gradual progression from one to the next. It is also possible to move from one stage to another and back again under changing conditions. At certain times of stress a mature Stage III adult will feel overwhelmed by life and revert to an immature Stage I, or a young Stage I will suddenly show Stage III maturity in a crisis.

In Stage I you are young and egocentric, the temperament and characteristics are undeveloped and relatively instinctive. This is followed by a more mature Stage II as your awareness of yourself versus others and your relationship to the people around you develops. During Stage II you are developing and metamorphosing your temperament. The third stage, the fully mature Stage III, shows the culmination of your experience, the best possible development of all that is best in you, whatever your temperament.

As with the temperaments, knowledge of the three stages can help you to understand and relate to other people and to have a greater understanding of yourself and be more tolerant in your own self-assessment.

The Three Stages and Time

The three stages do not occur during any given period of life. It is impossible to say that Stage I takes a certain number of years, Stage II lasts from this age to that age and Stage III occurs after a given length of time. Some people develop rapidly through all the stages to Stage III and are mature in their early twenties, others develop so slowly that even at sixty they may be in Stage I. There is no guarantee that you will reach Stage III development, many people don't.

Further, you often find that people go through these three stages in all the different phases of their life: a microcosm of development within the overall macrocosm. For instance, a child may be an immature Choleric when they start in school. By the end of their school life they may have developed to the extent of showing Stage II or even III maturity. Yet when they go out into the world they may clash with the adults they find and revert to behaving like Stage I Cholerics all over again. The Sanguine child who has learnt to settle down and apply themselves may, on release from school, become a Stage I social butterfly. The steady Stage II Phlegmatic may leave university and, faced with the complexities of a new job, revert to a Stage-I need to be guided closely in what they do. The Stage I Melancholic child may become a nurturing Stage III in junior school, only to revert to Stage I self-absorption and depression when being sent away to boarding-school.

Each of the temperaments matures in its own particular way. Not only that, but there are different needs for each temperament as it matures. Other people can help you to mature, and you can do the same for them. Assistance that is appropriate for one temperament is not necessarily appropriate and certainly not the best for another temperament. In the chapter covering each temperament in general and the overall development you will learn the best way for each temperament to develop and the best type of help to give it.

CHAPTER 5

The Temperaments and the Zodiac

It is worth taking a moment to compare the signs of the zodiac to the temperaments. The twelve signs can be divided into four groups: the four elements, fire, earth, air and water. Thus there is an implied correspondence with the temperaments, as shown below.

ELEMENT	FIRE	EARTH	AIR	WATER
ZODIAC SIGNS	Aries	Taurus	Gemini	Cancer
	Leo	Virgo	Libra	Scorpio
	Sagittarius	Capricorn	Aquarius	Pisces
TEMPERAMENT	CHOLERIC	MELANCHOLIC	SANGUINE	PHLEGMATIC

In many ways these associations are too simplistic and fail to take into account a number of factors. Not all those people with their sun in Leo are necessarily Cholerics, although they often are, and not all those with the sun in Aquarius are Sanguines, although again, they often are.

In astrology there is a great deal of input from rising signs, the planets and so forth, and all these have to be taken into consideration. You will find that you know many people with Aries, Leo or Sagittarius as their sun sign yet who are not Cholerics and many Geminis, Libran or Aquarians who are not Sanguine. I personally have six close Phlegmatic family members who have their sun in Aries, Gemini, Cancer, Virgo, Scorpio and Aquarius respectively.

Do not be tempted to throw the baby out with the bathwater and decide that all these concepts are nonsense. All that is really being said here is that if your sun sign is Aries, Leo or Sagittarius you have a stronger than average tendency to be a Choleric; if your sun sign is Taurus, Virgo or Capricorn you have a bias towards being Melancholic; if your sun sign is Cancer, Scorpio or Pisces you have a tendency towards being Phlegmatic; and if your sun sign is Gemini, Libra or Aquarius you have a tendency to be Sanguine. The typical characteristics of these signs do have a relationship with the temperaments and you may find it instructive to explore this.

The date you were born is a fixed event in your life. If you were born a Libran, then a Libran you stay. Astrologers would argue that the aspects under which you were born dictate the way you handle whatever events occur in your life and that the differences that occur between, for instance, one Leo and another reflect the other aspects of the charts.

There is a difference between the assessment of the four temperaments and your relationship to them and your sign of the zodiac, and I think it is a very important one, namely that the date of your birthday does not predetermine your temperament. You are free to recognise and acknowledge the temperament that best seems to fit you, the way you were when young and the way you are now. You are then free to use this knowledge for maximum benefit in so far as it helps you to understand yourself and to grow. Similarly it can help you to understand the people you meet, as they are, rather than on the basis of their birth date. None of this is intended to be a negative comment about astrology, which does have much of value to offer.

In addition, of course, there are twelve signs of the zodiac and only four temperaments so that three sun signs, all of them different, fall within each temperament. Equally, if you refer to the last chapter of this book, you will see that each temperament can be divided into four sub-temperaments on the basis of specific characteristics and these give greater detail.

As always, I am interested in what is most useful. In my work with patients I find a knowledge of their temperament, specifically their sub-temperament, considerably more easy to identify than the details of their birth chart, and much more useful than a knowledge of their birth sign.

CHAPTER 6

How to Use the Temperaments to Help You Know Other People and Yourself

Other People

When a practitioner starts in practice there is a lot to remember and there are a lot of new habits to form. When I started, my mind was focused on all I had learnt, about physical symptoms, treatments and so forth, and I didn't always focus on the personality of the patient, sometimes to my, and their, cost. I remember two clear examples of this from my early days in practice.

The first was an extremely confident-looking career woman in her mid-thirties. She told me that she got frequent and prolonged migraines and that she wanted me to get rid of them. I assured her that I would be able to help and would do everything that was required. Wanting to demonstrate my new capabilities and determined to convince her that I would be thorough and get a positive result, I said I would work with her for however long it took and that I was sure we could help her. I was a little surprised when she got impatient with that and demanded to know what I could do to fix it right away.

Aware that I had seemed to make too much of her problem, I was more encouraging with the next patient, a quiet man in his twenties who took thirty minutes to describe in considerable detail the variations of pain he had in his chest before and after a meal, pain that many other people would simply have called mild heartburn. I assured him as cheerfully as I could that I understood his problem and that if he made a couple of changes in his diet and took two remedies he would find the pains would disappear almost at once. He left muttering to my secretary that he hoped I understood the full seriousness of his problem and would be willing to put in the time it would undoubtedly take, in his mind, to treat his condition.

Had I recognised that the woman was Choleric and got impatient with her body and its health when it let her down I would have been able to say something like 'No problem, a quick allergy test, avoiding certain foods and you'll be as right as rain in no time.' The Melancholic man I would have treated differently. I would have commiserated with his pain, assured him that I realised the full gravity of the situation, and promised to take all the time it needed to ensure he not only got healthy but stayed healthy.

Once I realised that different temperaments required different treatment, I was able to be more effective with patients. Recognizing their temperament allows you to relate to and understand people in a more productive way, right from the first moment of meeting them.

Practise from this moment on. As soon as you start reading about any one of the temperaments start to look for these characteristics among the people you meet. You might choose to read the four general sections first, outlining each of the four temperaments. Then you can 'temperament watch' wherever you go. Practise using this awareness and knowledge to add to your communications with people. Surprise them by how much you know about them within only a few minutes of meeting, or how much you understand about someone they have just started to describe to you.

In couple counselling for relationship problems, when I am able to see only one of the people concerned, I have often used the four questions in Chapter 16. I ask the person in front of me how their partner would respond to these four questions. In this way I am able to estimate the absent partner's temperament, the way they will behave and how the person in front of me will respond to them. Sometimes this seems like magic, yet really it is very simple. What it does do is give my client more confidence and it enables us both to reach some positive solutions much faster than if I had no or little knowledge of the missing person.

Consider some common situations in your life. You wake up in the morning and have to relate to your spouse, your family, your flatmates, room-mates, or whoever it is you live with. On your way to school, college, work or the shops you meet people. You meet them on public transport, buying tickets, buying the paper, waiting in queues or sitting in the seats around you.

You already know there are early birds and night owls. When you have learnt and understood the temperaments you will realise there are the Sanguines, whether early birds or night owls, who are chirpy once they get going and the quiet Melancholics who will probably never get excited about a new day whatever time they wake up.

If you drive you 'meet' people in traffic jams. The Choleric driver will charge straight ahead, often but not always ignoring the speed limit or the needs of other motorists, the Sanguine will dart from lane to lane and will ignore the speed limit, certain that the rules don't apply to them, while the Phlegmatic will plod steadily along in their current lane, even if it is the slowest and you, a sparkling Sanguine passenger are gritting your teeth in frustration, wishing they'd swap lanes and get going. The driver who is going slower than the rest, lost in their own inner world is probably a Melancholic.

During your working day you meet people in the office, in the factory, in the shops. Some you see regularly. You have to relate to the boss, to the people you work with and to the people who work for you. Others, such as casual customers, you may meet only once. In social situations you have to relate to the friends you know well, to the casual friends you meet and to strangers.

You may flirt with the tall slim blonde (Sanguine) and come to the conclusion you have found someone who truly appreciates you, only to find, days later, that she can barely remember where she met you, and as a result you feel personally hurt and slighted. Had you known you were dealing with a Sanguine you would have enjoyed the moment with her and placed little reliance on tomorrow, willing to be pleasantly surprised if she did follow through.

Or you may struggle valiantly and unsuccessfully to make conversation with a tall, solid-looking (Phlegmatic) man at a social gathering, and, getting nowhere, leave feeling depressed and unpopular, only to get a call from him a week later, when he has finally gathered his courage together, inviting you out. Had you recognised that he was a Phlegmatic you would have known that he would appreciate a few hints of encouragement from you to reduce the risk he felt he was taking in issuing the invitation at all.

The soulful (Melancholic) type with whom you discussed Shakespearean tragedies may turn out to be a crashing bore on your next date when he discovers you are a nurse and insists on telling you every one of his health problems, past and present, imagined or real. Had you recognised his temperament you would have been better prepared and known how to draw him out of himself (as you will discover later).

If you had recognised that the customer who came into your business was a proud Choleric you would not have been so foolish as to risk crossing swords with them by even daring to suggest that they were not the most important person present, and you would have known that you should give them immediate service and treat them with respect or to watch out for fireworks. You would not have been worried if a Phlegmatic customer had been kept waiting until the impatient Sanguine was served, knowing that the Phlegmatic was content to wait but would need time when you did serve them as they, indirectly, sought your advice on what to choose. You would have laughed and joked with the Sanguine and commiserated with the Melancholic.

As in my situation in the practice, in these and other interactions there is often too little time for you to get to know the person well enough to have the best possible relationship with them. If you can understand, from the few clues you can pick up at the first meeting, a lot more about the person concerned you can have a much smoother and more rewarding relationship.

When it comes to relationships, particularly that very important one in your life, your relationship with your partner, you will have an easier time if you understand what you yourself want and have to give, and if you understand your partner and what they want and what they have to offer. You can then decide to enjoy their differences, the ones that attracted you to them in the first place, instead of trying to change them into your own temperament, something many people spend their entire married life trying to do ... usually unsuccessfully.

Instant Impressions

There is something else to ponder on. Sometimes when you meet someone you have the instant feeling that you know them, that you can relate to them and that you know how they are going to think and behave. In the vernacular, you 'click'. Perhaps it is a new soul mate, someone it was your destiny to meet, or someone you have known somewhere before, even possibly in a past life? Do you make such assumptions? Or perhaps it is simply that you have just met someone with a similar temperament to yourself. When you understand this you will be able to avoid rushing into something that seemed to be, but wasn't, ordained.

At other times you meet someone and can be almost overwhelmed by the confusion that results when they behave in ways that you simply can't understand or relate to. Perhaps this is indeed someone with whom you can never work or be friends, someone who is antipathetic to you and with whom you should have nothing to do. Do you make such assumptions? Or perhaps it is just that you have met your opposite temperament type. When you understand this you will be able to explore the possibility of getting to know them better and you will be able to enrich each other's lives as you realise that the apparent discord is not personal.

Wouldn't it be nice if people wore little labels telling you what sort of person they are, what their dominant characteristics are and how they liked to be treated, what their responses mean and how you can expect them to react? In fact they do. All that is needed is to be able to read and understand the signs. This skill, of understanding the four temperaments, is one you will have acquired by the time you have read this book and integrated the ideas into your life.

Getting to Know People

In their looks and in the way they speak and move people often, unconsciously, announce which of the four temperament types are dominant in their nature. So do you. If you learn to understand and to pick up on these clues right at the start of your relationship with people, you will then be able to relate to them much more smoothly and to understand them and yourself better. This is true of the five-minute relationship you may have with a shopkeeper or your life-long relationship with relatives.

Some of the quick clues you get will be visual. There is a different build and body shape for each temperament and a different way of moving. For instance most Cholerics are short and chunky, most true Sanguines are long boned, often slender and delicate. The typical Phlegmatic is somewhat flabby with poor muscle definition, and the Melancholic droops. However, these are by no means hard and fast rules. Further, the temperament has to be blended with the physical genes and in a tall family the Choleric may still be relatively tall. A Sanguine who comes from a family that eats big meals, or emphasises food for solace, can overeat.

Other quick clues come from the early behavioural signs they show and the way they react in different situations. Are they impatient (Sanguine) or relaxed (Phlegmatic), do they push themselves forward (Choleric) or get lost in a daydream (Melancholic)?

In the chapters ahead you will learn about the four different temperaments in detail. You will learn how to pick up on the clues they give you, quickly and easily, and how to apply this knowledge to your relationships. Once you understand the basic temperament types and apply this knowledge, it will be like applying a lubricating oil to your relationships and will add enormously to the richness and smoothness of your life.

Yourself

You can use the same skills to improve your self-understanding and self-knowledge. Do you often judge yourself by other people's standards and find yourself wanting? Are you timid compared to some, irritable and aggressive compared to others, careless and lacking the patience of yet others, or less understanding than you should be of other people's problems? Do you criticise yourself on all these counts as you measure the worst of yourself against the best of each of the other temperaments? Would you like to understand yourself better, learn to recognise and appreciate your good points and know what tools you need to change some of the things you would like to alter? All this is about to happen.

You can learn more about yourself. You may have wondered why you are so much quieter than other people and berate yourself for your lack of initiative. If you come to recognise yourself as a Phlegmatic you can take heart that this is typical of your temperament. You can also acknowledge and appreciate your other qualities: your willingness to take on, for instance, the routine and monotonous jobs that other people hate to do, your reliability, your steadiness and the fact that you are always there for other people to rely on.

You may berate yourself for your Choleric temper. Now you can come to terms with this and recognise the other powerful qualities of leadership and courage that go with this. If you are a butterfly Sanguine and get frustrated because you don't stick at things, remember the fun and joy you bring into other people's lives. If you hate waking up depressed and feeling like a wet blanket—Melancholic—you can focus instead on the wonderful caring you provide for other people.

By learning more about yourself and recognising that there are others like you, you can come to terms with your negative traits and learn to appreciate your positive ones. You will also learn how to make the most of your temperament and how to develop through the three stages.

Many, many people have told me that it was a relief to recognise and identify their own personality type. They valued the understanding this gave them of their good points and positive attributes, and allowed them to develop a greater tolerance of what they felt had been their weaknesses. Another frequent comment was that they felt free now, without the need to live up to the standards or behaviour of other, quite different, temperaments.

If you are scatterbrained, intent on having a good time and often criticised for being flighty it may be a comfort to you to know that this is all part of your Sanguine temperament and that you have a lot to offer other people. By your own nature you can bring fun, cheer and excitement into their lives. You can also show them the delights of things that would otherwise have passed them by.

If you feel sad and despondent, and are often told not to be so dreary and negative, it will help you to recognise that this is part of the Melancholic temperament and that other people value your warm sympathy and the care and concern you offer. Other of your positive traits may include the ability to be organised and to do things well, if not perfectly.

Do you berate yourself for being dull and wish you had more get-up-and-go? You may see yourself as the dull person in a crowd of people who are all doing interesting things with their lives while you stick in your routine day after day. It helps to know that this is the Phlegmatic temperament and is accompanied by great reliability and steadfastness. Far from finding you dreary, other people may see you as the diplomatic peacemaker, a stabilising influence in their hectic and erratic world, and be grateful for your presence in situations of conflict.

Or perhaps you have a quick temper and believe you are too strong and dominating? You may even think you're a pretty nasty sort of person and that you should learn to be softer and more gentle. This is easier to work with if you realise you are Choleric and that other people see you as a strong and independent leader, someone they like to have around when they feel unsure of themselves.

A word of warning is appropriate here. A knowledge of the temperaments, and your own in particular, can be used as an excuse for your faults if you blame your temperament rather than yourself for your behaviour. It is not enough for an angry Choleric to blame his temperament rather than himself when he flies off the handle in a rage; his temper should still be controlled. The knowledge gained here will give him a tool that will enable this to be easier. The flighty Sanguine still has a responsibility to learn to distinguish between truth and fantasy. The Melancholic cannot blame her negativity on her temperament for continuing to be a wet blanket and the plodding Phlegmatic cannot refuse to make decisions for ever. *The purpose of discussing the temperaments is to give you a tool to enrich your life, not an excuse to avoid personal responsibility for the way you are and the way you behave.*

The best way to obtain the love, health and happiness you want is to understand yourself better than you do now. Discover your strong points and the best possible way to develop these to their maximum potential. Learn about your weaker points and how to strengthen these and avoid the pitfalls your personality can lead you into. Make the most of yourself. Find out how to grow and how to get the help that will make your path through life easier. Come to terms with who you are and build on what you have. Explore your own temperament and find out what you can do to bring out the best in yourself.

The Purpose of Understanding Your Temperament

If you do not fully understand your make-up your response to certain circumstances may disturb you and leave you feeling confused.

Martin, a positive Sanguine businessman, told me he had loved his wife dearly and had been devastated when she was killed in a car accident. However, within a short while he had reconciled himself to the fact of her death and reorganised his life. Not only that, but he was taking out other women and, in spite of his sadness over the loss of his wife, enjoying social freedom. His concern, deep down, was that somehow he was callous and uncaring, as some of his friends had hinted, and he felt he should have been depressed for longer.

'After all,' as he told me, 'Bob was really in the dumps for months when his wife left him, yet the funny thing is, he wasn't all that fond of her, he said things hadn't been good between them for a while. Whereas Clare and I were a great couple, we were very close and I do miss her. But you do have to get on with life, don't you?'

Martin's mistake was to assess the degree of loss experienced by the amount of mourning that was demonstrated. He was instinctively a positive and optimistic Sanguine, prepared to make the best of things, to put tragedies behind him and get on with the rest of his life. Bob, on the other hand, was a Stage I Melancholic and revelled in the bad and the depressing: being down in the dumps was second nature to him. Neither behaviour was an objective evaluation of the way either man had felt about his wife while she lived, or how he felt about her loss. Once Martin understood this he was reconciled to his own response and stopped feeling self-critical.

Categorising People

There are many ways of subdividing people into groups and describing these subgroups. The four temperaments is one method, and the one we will be exploring here. People can also be divided into the twelve signs of the zodiac. They can be labelled as optimists or pessimists, as introverts or extroverts. They can be subdivided by several other lesser-known ways of categorising people. All these have their uses. However, there are also potential traps and pitfalls.

It is important to understand that, at least at some level, all these groups are intellectual concepts. We can divide the world into these subgroups, yet in reality there is a continuum from one extreme to the other, from one type to the other. Dividing people into different types does not mean there is a clear distinction between each type and that individuals are all-or-nothing – one type or the other.

In reality, people are blends and combinations. You can be a pessimist who is optimistic in certain situations. You can be an introvert who comes out of their shell at late-night parties. You can be on the cusp of two signs of the zodiac or have your sun sign affected by your rising sign. You can also be a blend of the temperaments.

Nevertheless, if we describe the archetypal pessimist or optimist, the archetypal fire, earth, air or water sign, the archetypal Leo or

Aquarius or the archetypal temperament, we have a starting point.
You can then consider the possible blends and combinations and
what would result, and can soon reach a better understanding of
yourself and the people you meet.

Use – Don't Judge

Back to the temperaments. There is one very important characteristic about this form of naming or pigeonholing people. No moral or
value judgements are applied or implied. No one temperament is better than another. We are not subdividing people on the basis of education, skills, achievement, status or standing, although such
judgements are made frequently in other situations. Within each
temperament there is the opportunity for good and the opportunity
for bad. Each temperament has its strengths and its weaknesses.
Each temperament can mature and develop or fall into decay. Each
temperament can succeed, and each temperament can go mad. It is
up to you as an individual to make of your life and your temperament what you choose. Ultimately only you, the individual, can
know and decide what is best for you.

The objective here is to be very practical, to provide you with specific tools to help you in your daily life. Put the ideas into practice as
you read. Be observant of the people around you, and as you learn
more about each temperament consider which temperament is dominant in them in general and which is dominant at any one time.
Practise treating people according to their temperament so that you
can relate to them better than you have in the past. This way you
can offer them the gift of a truer understanding, and give yourself
the benefits of achieving these goals.

Sub-Temperaments

Earlier I alluded to the fact that there are questionnaires that divide
personalities into sixteen types. This is done by subdividing each of
the temperaments into four sub-types. Another way of looking at

this is to say that if you take those sixteen types you can group four of them with similar characteristics into Cholerics, four into Sanguines and so forth.

This is a useful concept for psychologists, psychotherapists and other practitioners, and for people who need this level of detailed analysis. For general purposes, and for our purposes here, it may be somewhat overwhelming and unwieldy and not nearly so practical as using the concept of the four major temperaments, blended in different combinations.

However, it can happen that you have trouble in identifying your own temperament, even after you have done the questionnaire. Or you may have identified your temperament by the questionnaire but have difficulty relating to the descriptions of it given in each section. If this happens I recommend that you go to Chapter 16, answer the four questions given there and find out which of the sixteen types you are.

The more introverted Sanguine, of whom there are relatively few, may not relate fully or comfortably to the overall picture of the typical Sanguine. In an attempt to 'find themselves' they may look for, but fail to find, similarities with Phlegmatics or Melancholics who generally are more introverted. As an introverted Choleric myself, of whom there are also relatively few, I used, from time to time, to search the other temperaments for a more convenient home, but failed to find one.

As you will have gathered, one of the subdivisions used in establishing the sixteen types relates to whether a person is an introvert or an extrovert. Once you understand the types better it may surprise you to think of an introverted Sanguine or an extrovert Melancholic since they are usually the opposite, but there are ranges of introversion and extroversion within a single temperament. The introverted Sanguine may still be more extroverted than the introverted Melancholic, but the idea does have its usefulness. We will allude to this occasionally as we discuss each of the types and, when we do so, it should be remembered that the terms are being used in a relative sense.

Whether you choose to stick with an understanding of the four temperaments or to read further, you will find this assessment of the four basic personality types enormously useful. We will be focusing our attention on the four basic types in Part II. The first section of each temperament will cover the basics of each one as it progresses through life.

CHAPTER 7

How to Find Love, Health, Wealth and Happiness

Love

When you first meet someone you may find you have been attracted to your opposite temperament, drawn by the appeal of the many ways in which the other person has the attributes you may feel you lack. Now you have to consider whether or not you want to live with that type of person throughout the years ahead: someone who not only has a different temperament to you but will develop through the three stages in a different way.

On the other hand you may be attracted to someone you recognise as a soul mate, someone of the same temperament as you. In the light of your new-found knowledge you will soon be able to assess what this could mean for the rest of your life.

There are no ideal partners. With the signs of the zodiac you might say that someone of one sun sign should marry someone of this or that sign and avoid people with other sun signs. That is not so appropriate when you consider the temperaments, or even the sixteen sub-types.

Wonderful marriages exist where people have married their opposite temperament and continued to treasure the differences. The extroverted and happy Sanguine can find their life enriched by the idealism and depth of the Melancholic, who in turn is drawn out of their introspection by the varied interests of their Sanguine partner. The strong and restless Choleric can find peace when their home is run by a contented Phlegmatic, who in turn can value the courage and decisiveness of their Choleric partner.

The problems usually start when each of them tries to change the other. The differences that attracted you in the first place can become uncomfortable to live with when the novelty has worn off.

The Melancholic may be embarrassed by their Sanguine partner's exhibitionism, as they come to term the outgoing behaviour that they initially admired. The Sanguine may get restless with the lengthy periods of introspection and inactivity that accompany the Melancholic's depth. The Phlegmatic may become afraid of the arrogance and aggression of their partner as they learn this side of the Choleric strength, and the Choleric may eventually find the routines of the Phlegmatic boring and stultifying.

Do you want to live with your opposite, or do you want to find someone of a similar temperament to your own? Do you want the interest and excitement of living with someone who is different to you and has complementary characteristics, or do you want to live with someone with whom you can be comfortable and share experiences?

It is an interesting irony that the characteristics that are appropriate for courting – the fun, the new, the interesting and the different – are often not the attributes you want to live with for the rest of your life.

Two Melancholics can have a wonderfully romantic, emotional and spiritual relationship as they work together to make a difference in the world, helping the needy and the suffering, or developing their artistic talents. Alternatively they can fail to find in their partner the interest in their own problem that they demand. Two Phlegmatics can have a close, quiet, predictable relationship, not necessarily saying a lot to each other but living a peaceful life of shared interests and quiet companionship. On the other hand they may get bored with each other. Two Sanguines can have fun together and set the world alight or get lost in a sea of adultery as each surveys the scene and searches for variety. Two Cholerics can unite and go after common goals or they can fight as each strives for dominance.

If couples of different temperaments divorce it is often because they couldn't convert their partner into their own temperament. If a couple of the same temperament divorce it is probably because they are being attracted to the characteristics they lack in themselves.

So, I'm sorry, but even a thorough knowledge of the temperaments cannot tell you who will be your ideal partner. What it can do is help you to make a much wiser decision for yourself. First you have to decide what you want – variety or similarity – and, if you do want a different temperament, which one will give you what you seek.

By knowing more about the other person as you see them right now, and by knowing the way in which they are likely to develop, you can gain a better idea of what is likely to be ahead, than you would have had without this knowledge of the four temperaments.

If you are already married and are doubtful about the relationship, then a knowledge of your partner's temperament can give you a more realistic idea of what is ahead. Better than living in the blind hope that they will change in the ways you want them to and thus, in your view, improve the relationship.

By knowing the positive attributes of the other person of a different temperament, you can enrich a relationship. Such a relationship may have been foundering in a morass of differences, especially when your partner does not live up to or conform to the way you do things, or demonstrate the attributes you value in yourself.

We will consider love and compatibility in much greater detail in Chapter 14.

Health

Health seems relatively unimportant when you are young. Unless your health is bad you probably take or took your good health for granted.

Some temperaments are more likely to take their health for granted than others. If you are one of these and you finally become sufficiently aware of some warning twinges or pains, you would do well to listen to them, to overcome your natural impatience, and have a check-up.

Other temperaments are more likely to worry about any tiny sign or symptom, often ones so small that other people would consider them normal variations. If this applies to you, you can now recognise this and realise that you are probably worrying unnecessarily.

You will learn more about the attitude to health of each of the temperaments in Chapter 10–13. You will also discover some of the health problems to which your temperament is particularly prone.

Wealth

Also in Chapters 10–13, you will learn more about your attitude to wealth and what it means; whether it means money or power, assets or savings, or whether it means other, far less tangible, things.

Once you realise what is important to you, and how that fits in with your temperament and make-up, you can aim for what is truly important and not worry about what other people are doing. You can pursue your own goals, not those of other people or the society around you. And when you have achieved them, you can relish and value them, and not have that vague feeling of dissatisfaction many people experience when they judge themselves and their achievements through the eyes of other people.

You may have felt you should have provided as well for your wife as your Choleric neighbour and come to realise that she married you for your spiritual values, knowing that money was never going to be a sufficient motivating force for you.

You may feel you should criticise yourself for your irresponsibility and for not having any savings in the bank, but realise that with Sanguine carelessness you have spent it on looking good, and thoroughly enjoyed every minute of the active lifestyle you have led.

As a Phlegmatic you may not have a lot in the bank, and may have been in awe of the commercial risks some of your wealthier friends took as they built their wealth. Now you can congratulate yourself on the solid and sensible nest egg you have acquired by careful saving and be pleased that, in your old age, you can continue to live the lifestyle to which you have been accustomed.

Happiness

Peace, contentment and happiness come from a full understanding of yourself, from recognising both your good points and your less good, from learning to enjoy and appreciate the former and accept, yet work on, the latter. The knowledge of the four temperaments will enable you to do this with greater effectiveness. You will also know how to search out someone who can help guide you in the best way: the way that is the most suitable for the development of your temperament.

CHAPTER 8

Personality Quiz

Now to the big question –

Which temperament are you?

There are several ways of determining which temperament is dominant in you, and I have shown one here and one in Chapter 16. You can either do the following questionnaire now or wait until you have read the book. This is not a trivial decision.

You may want to read the book first, with an open mind and no bias on the basis of the temperament you have discovered to be your dominant one by using the questionnaire. In this way you will be able to relate freely to each temperament and find out how closely you feel it describes parts of your make-up. This has another benefit: you are more likely to read all four sections rather than focusing solely on your own.

One purpose of this book is to help you to learn more about yourself and how to develop your strengths and alter your weaknesses. A second and equally important purpose is to help you to understand other people better. You will do this more easily if you read about all four temperaments first, without having a particular bias towards the one to which you feel you belong. You can then find out which one is yours according to the questionnaire and reread various sections as appropriate. After all, this is meant to be a practical book to which you will refer often, not just a once-only read.

Alternatively, you may be impatient to do the questionnaires, or even have found and done them already. Here we already have a clue about you. Are you the steady Phlegmatic who reads a book sequentially from start to finish and who has reached this point without yet having encountered the questionnaires? Or are you the happy butterfly Sanguine who has skipped around until you found the point where you can get a quick fix on what temperament you are?

Self-assessment is not always easy. I thought initially that I was a Sanguine and I even answered the questions accordingly. Then, as mentioned before, I recognised myself as an introverted Choleric and learnt to value and appreciate the positive aspects of this temperament, which initially had not attracted me, and work on the less positive aspects. Many people are not nearly as objective about themselves as they think. I have had a Melancholic patient assure me she was a Choleric, and I know a Phlegmatic accountant who insisted he was a Choleric until we discussed the subject further. Many Melancholics have gone through these and other questionnaires many times, trying to be a different temperament.

There are many ways of determining your temperament, some simple and some complex. Ultimately it is not a matter of doing a questionnaire and then believing in the answers unquestioningly; it is a matter of understanding the types in greater depth and learning to recognise yourself.

By reading the full descriptions of each temperament you will soon recognise which category you fall into. If you have any doubts, answer the four questions in Chapter 16.

There are several reasons for doing questionnaires. First, they are quick and simple and they give you a starting point. Secondly, it is helpful to look at the characteristics that do not describe you. Frequently these are traits or attributes to which we give little thought. Thirdly, by looking at them from time to time, particularly the one below, you get a potted description of each temperament with which you can refresh your memory.

Here is a very quick and simple test to help you in your search for greater self-knowledge.

The Questionnaire

Consider your strengths and decide which of the following four groups of words best describes you. One way to do this is to tick or circle each of the words you feel applies to you. When you are doing this, at least in the first run-through, tick only the words that generally and commonly apply to you. Leave out the adjectives that apply to you only occasionally, or in certain circumstances. You may enjoy public speaking but be quiet in a social crowd: this does not make you an extrovert. You may be very patient most of the time but get angry if seriously provoked or if someone is hurting a person you love: this does not qualify you to mark angry as a consistent attribute.

If all or most of your ticks fall in one group, then clearly that is your dominant temperament. The more ticks you have in it and the fewer you have in the other groups, the more likely it is that you are essentially this one temperament only.

If it is not immediately clear which group you fall into, then tick off the words that do apply, count the number of ticks in each group and pick the group with the most ticks. That is your dominant temperament. The group with the next highest number of ticks is your second temperament.

The following section appears twice so that you can mark one copy and keep the other one clean.

A. When you consider your positive attributes, which of the following apply to you?

1. Adventurous, ambitious, autocratic, capable, competitive, courageous, daring, decisive, demanding, forceful, independent, outspoken, persuasive, positive, resourceful, ruler, self-assured, self-reliant, strong-willed, tenacious.

2. Analytical, calm, caring, considerate, deep, detailed, even-tempered, helpful, idealistic, intuitive, loyal, organised, perfectionist, persistent, psychic, respectful, self-sacrificing, sensitive, understanding, visionary.

3. Adaptable, balanced, calm, content, consistent, dependable, diplomatic, friendly, helpful, inoffensive, mediator, patient, peaceful, organised, reserved, self-controlled, shy, steadfast, submissive, tolerant.

4. Amusing, animated, cheerful, convincing, delightful, demonstrative, entertaining, extrovert, gregarious, imaginative, lively, optimistic, playful, popular, positive, refreshing, sociable, spirited, spontaneous, talkative.

B. Consider your weaknesses and decide which of the following four groups of words best describes you.

1. Angry, argumentative, arrogant, bossy, cold, domineering, frank, headstrong, impatient, impulsive, intolerant, manipu-

lative, proud, rash, short-tempered, stubborn, tactless, tyrannical, unsympathetic, workaholic.

2. Critical, depressed, detached, difficult, fussy, hypochondriac, insecure, introverted, loner, masochistic, moody, negative, pessimistic, resentful, sceptical, self-absorbed, suspicious, touchy, unforgiving, withdrawn.

3. Afraid, dull, hesitant, indecisive, indifferent, lazy, monotonous, nonchalant, over-compromising, reluctant, self-righteous, shy, slow, sluggish, stubborn, timid, uncreative, unenthusiastic, unmotivated, worrier.

4. Careless, changeable, dilettante, disorganised, embroidering the truth, exaggerates, flighty, forgetful, haphazard, inconsistent, interrupts, repetitious, restless, scatterbrained, seek limelight, show-off, superficial, undisciplined, unpredictable, unreliable.

Scoring

If your ticks or circles are dominantly in the first category for both Section A and Section B you are Choleric, in the second you are Melancholic, in the third Phlegmatic and in the fourth Sanguine.

A. When you consider your positive attributes, which of the following apply to you?

1. Adventurous, ambitious, autocratic, capable, competitive, courageous, daring, decisive, demanding, forceful, independent, outspoken, persuasive, positive, resourceful, ruler, self-assured, self-reliant, strong-willed, tenacious.

2. Analytical, calm, caring, considerate, deep, detailed, even-tempered, helpful, idealistic, intuitive, loyal, organised, perfectionist, persistent, psychic, respectful, self-sacrificing, sensitive, understanding, visionary.

3. Adaptable, balanced, calm, content, consistent, dependable,

diplomatic, friendly, helpful, inoffensive, mediator, patient, peaceful, organised, reserved, self-controlled, shy, steadfast, submissive, tolerant

4. Amusing, animated, cheerful, convincing, delightful, demonstrative, entertaining, extrovert, gregarious, imaginative, lively, optimistic, playful, popular, positive, refreshing, sociable, spirited, spontaneous, talkative.

B. Consider your weaknesses and decide which of the following four groups of words best describes you

1. Angry, argumentative, arrogant, bossy, cold, domineering, frank, headstrong, impatient, impulsive, intolerant, manipulative, proud, rash, short-tempered, stubborn, tactless, tyrannical, unsympathetic, workaholic.

2. Critical, depressed, detached, difficult, fussy, hypochondriac, insecure, introverted, loner, masochistic, moody, negative, pessimistic, resentful, sceptical, self-absorbed, suspicious, touchy, unforgiving, withdrawn.

3. Afraid, dull, hesitant, indecisive, indifferent, lazy, monotonous, nonchalant, over-compromising, reluctant, self-righteous, shy, slow, sluggish, stubborn, timid, uncreative, unenthusiastic, unmotivated, worrier.

4. Careless, changeable, dilettante, disorganised, embroidering the truth, exaggerates, flighty, forgetful, haphazard, inconsistent, interrupts, repetitious, restless, scatterbrained, seek limelight, show-off, superficial, undisciplined, unpredictable, unreliable.

PART II:

The Temperaments

CHAPTER 9

The Development Pattern of Each Temperament

In the four sections ahead, one on each temperament, you will learn about the individual temperaments as they grow from birth, through childhood and into adulthood. You will learn how they plan and design their lives, the jobs they are likely to choose and be good at, and how they handle their finances. You will discover how they develop relationships, their attitude to love, sex and marriage. After that you will learn about them as parents and as they move on into the latter years of their life. By the time you have read this you will have a clear understanding of each of the temperaments, based on the assumption that they have matured and developed in an average or normal way. In general, we will be assuming that the individual has trod a mid-line path in the full range of that temperament.

The first section of each temperament is slightly different. It is important to keep in mind that people mature at different rates and that the stages can in no way be linked to certain years or ages. As I said earlier, you will meet some very young people who have already developed to Stage III, some very old Stage I people, and all possible variations in between. You will also think you have a friend who is a mature Stage III, then find that in certain circumstances they revert to behaviour that you associate with Stage I.

It is also possible to consider the relative development of the individual at each stage of life: childhood, adulthood and old age. By this I mean we can see signs of the three stages as they relate to the various ages. A child who shows some of the mature characteristics of Stage III may possibly, when they become an adult, revert to Stage II or even Stage I behaviour. It all adds to the fun, as you try to understand people better. It also emphasises the variability of human behaviour and human nature.

For these reasons the first section on each temperament takes a brief look at the general nature of the temperament, and then what it is like at each of the three stages, and how people of different ages behave when they are at each stage. You will find this useful as an introduction to each temperament. You will also find it illuminating to reread the first section on a temperament once you have read the whole chapter.

CHAPTER 10

The Choleric Temperament

Main Characteristics

Cholerics are strong, positive and relatively outgoing, although not as extrovert as the Sanguines. They can start out as little tyrants, demanding their own way and insisting on being the leader. Gradually, with maturity, they will learn to respect others and eventually they can become the strong but gentle rulers and leaders. There is much that is good in their make-up, once they have learnt to channel and control it. They are independent and self-sufficient, unwilling to submit to authority unless they feel that the authority has been well earned. They can be critical of others but also set high standards for themselves, drive themselves to achieve and are self-critical if they don't, but they are rarely willing to accept the criticisms of others.

They are intellectual, intelligent, with a strong desire to learn and to understand the intricacies of the world within which they live. They want to achieve, to be good at things, to be competent, and they do so with a drive and a passion that leave the other temperaments somewhat breathless. They can, however, become lost in the rarefied world of scientific abstractions and lose touch with their feelings.

Cholerics are natural leaders, knowing what to do, taking control and having the strength and endurance to see things through. They have great courage, physically, mentally and morally. They live in the fast lane, are usually found where the action is and are often creating it, yet they do not attempt to be in the limelight for its own sake, as the Sanguine does. They do, however, thrive on recognition and acclaim.

They have a strong code of honour, to which they adhere. They do not lie, break promises or fail to keep agreements. Nor do they like to show weakness or be seen to be vulnerable. In general they expect others to behave in the same way and, unless they develop a patient and sympathetic understanding, can have contempt for lesser mortals who prevaricate or show weakness. Do not try to get them on your side by beating them in a show of strength: competition only spurs them on, it doesn't break them. Equally, you will not win them over by being weak and trying to appeal to their better nature. Show them what you can do and that you are doing your best. That they understand. They can then be the rock on which you depend for further advice, support or strength, so that you, too, can become strong.

Wrongly used, their strength can allow them to become bullies, their confidence can become arrogance and they can be sarcastic with a biting wit. As with all temperaments, it depends on how the individual uses and develops their attributes and characteristics.

Life Path

The Path of the Choleric involves many steps. They know their own strengths, and they need to learn about the strengths of others, strengths that may manifest themselves in ways unfamiliar to the Choleric. They need to learn respect for other ways of doing things than their own, and to recognise the qualities of people who are quieter than themselves, more subtle and less confident.

They can be helped along this path by one or more heroes, people they can look up to and respect. They may never meet these people; these people may even be dead. Cholerics are self-masters and will drive themselves to achieve. All the Choleric needs is a suitable role model; they will track their own progress in developing along their chosen lines. The Choleric can also be helped by people who assume they have already developed the character traits towards which they are striving. The developing Choleric will recognise this person's confidence in them and do all they can to live up to it.

So, now let's take a look at this exciting, and sometimes frightening, temperament in more detail and see how the progression occurs.

Stage I

The young Choleric takes the lead easily and naturally – unless they choose to march ahead on their own, leaving the others far behind.

As babies and children they have a confidence and sense of purpose not seen in the other temperaments. They are brave and adventurous. They have initiative and the imagination and capacity to carry out their ideas and achieve their goals. Their natural confidence comes from a firm belief in themselves. They expect both their mind and their body to do their bidding. They will get into scrapes when they overestimate their strength, yet somehow they also have the tenacity and capacity to get out of them.

Stage I strength, however, is often foolhardy. It is also obstinate. You will see this in children who, rather than toe the line and use their strength constructively, use it to resist authority, to fight when they are being punished, to insist that the blame belongs to others and that they are being wrongly punished.

Stage I Choleric children can become bullies, they can be boastful or arrogant. They may grab toys from their weaker or younger siblings. They may be little tyrants and monsters, often with a temper that flares up when they are thwarted or don't get their own way.

In general, Stage I Cholerics are quick-tempered and impatient with other people. They are sure of their own strengths and worth and may seem brash and boastful. This, since they still have a lot to learn, can get them into a considerable amount of trouble, but they learn as they go – and they go faster than most. They demand freedom for themselves, not the airy, even irresponsible freedom to move and change direction for the sake of it, in the way the Sanguine wants freedom, but to get on, to be themselves and do what they want to do unfettered by what other people want for or of them. Yet in this stage they are rarely willing to give other people the freedom they want for themselves: after all, they say, they are the leaders and they know what's best, not only for themselves but for everyone else.

The Stage I Choleric is intolerant of stupidity. Anyone who is slow or thoughtful, preferring to make decisions or act only after careful consideration, is assumed to be dumb, stupid or cowardly and not worthy of time, attention or friendship. If forced into association with such a person the Choleric is likely to treat them harshly and get angry and impatient with them. The more inward the Phlegmatic turns, in self-defence, the angrier the Choleric will become. The solution is for the Phlegmatic to stand up to the Choleric, but if this is not in their nature they are in for a rough time.

If Cholerics enter adulthood without maturing they can become troublemakers. The trouble they cause is likely to be due to their confidence and arrogance, their need to lead combined with their lack of maturity and experience and their dislike of criticism or authority.

They may become hot-headed hooligans. They may get a job and be the cheeky junior who refuses to obey the rules and fit in, telling everyone what a fool the boss is. They are quick on the trigger, easily annoyed, particularly if opposed, and all too ready to steamroller over other people's opinions and ideas. They may even look for a fight as the best way of proving their dominance. Choleric Stage I women are likely to be called pushy or aggressive and to frighten off the men.

Cholerics are also likely to be impatient at what they perceive as unnecessary caution in others. In fact, they are likely to confuse caution and care with fear and cowardice. The teacher in a rock-climbing class who takes hours checking all the knots may well be called a coward by the foolhardy Stage I Choleric, who would have taken off up the rock face with no rope at all. The woman who listens to complaints of a junior with sympathy and an attempt at understanding is likely to be thought weak by the new Stage I Choleric employee, who would have used the authority of her position to let the junior know who was in charge.

Stage I Cholerics are disinclined to listen to the opinions of others and more likely to march over them, confident that their own opinions are better, and, aggravatingly for the other people concerned, they often are. If not, there are ructions, since immature Cholerics hate to be criticised or found wanting. In fact, all Cholerics hate to be criticised, but the immature ones handle it badly, feeling it is a direct attack on them and quite unwarranted. They are sure they are correct. If they do come to realise that they were wrong, they find it very difficult, if not impossible, to apologise.

The phrase 'The best committee is a committee of two, with the other person absent' was surely coined by a Stage I Choleric. They will be on committees, but only as the chairperson. Why would they accept any other role when they know they can lead better than anyone else?

Jane headed the local mothers' group at her son's school. Everyone said how efficient she was: meetings only took half the time they used to and so much more was accomplished. Then gradually, as one by one the other mothers brought up a point or made a suggestion that was important to them, they came away feeling that they hadn't been heard or listened to, they hadn't had enough time to put their case. Jane was so sure she knew what was best that she pushed decisions through when she was in favour of them and quashed ideas she thought would fail. The fact that she was often right did little to appease the by then unhappy group. With maturity, Jane would learn to take more time to listen to other people's opinions, even if, in the end, the final decision was the one she had wanted to make all along. She would also learn that social interaction and the time for people to air their views were just as important as getting to the final decision and implementing it. People count too.

Many is the time people have tried to do something for a Choleric, even to curry favour with them, in the hope of a better relationship, only to find that things immediately get worse. Cholerics hate to be under an obligation to anyone, particularly in Stage I, and every time they see the person concerned it reminds them of a time they needed and accepted help, a time they were not invincible and totally capable of looking after themselves.

Frank came from a wealthy home and always had money in his pocket. Most of the students looked up to him as a natural leader of their group, none more so than Peter. He was more slightly built than Frank and less good at sports or in the class-room, yet he desired, above all other things, to be included in the small elite group known as Frank's friends. One day, Frank arrived at college without any money. Peter happily seized the chance to lend him enough for the day's visits to the canteen and the pub after class, even forgoing his own needs in his desire to show his friendship for Frank and thinking, 'In future, surely, he'll remember this and count me a friend.' To his dismay, Peter found that, on the contrary, in the days that followed, Frank, showing his Stage I immaturity, actually avoided him. And since the others copied Frank's behaviour, Peter was eventually excluded from group altogether. He didn't understand that Frank was mortified at having been seen, for once, as being in need, as not being able to take care of himself or buy whatever he wanted. Every time he saw Peter he was reminded of that painful day. A more mature Choleric, while not liking the situation, would be better able to receive and acknowledge such support.

Cholerics thrive on opposition. This can also affect the young Stage I adult Choleric, many of whom have done things simply because they have been told not to. This can take the form of skipping classes or driving over the speed limit. A young female Choleric may go out with a man who is dangerous simply because she is determined to show she is not afraid. Cholerics will accept all sorts of ridiculous dares with this same motive in mind. As they mature, however, this courage and determination, this willingness to accept a challenge, can become a positive attribute.

Maturing

To mature, Cholerics need to control their temper, to be willing to learn from others and to learn respect for others. Some Cholerics mature automatically, but for others it is more difficult. On the whole, as for the other temperaments, it is easier for a Stage I Choleric to reach and develop into Stage II if they have some outside help.

The Choleric benefits from having a hero to emulate. It is not necessary for the Choleric to know the hero: they can be a character from history, someone in the public eye, in another country or otherwise out of reach. The hero can also live within the orbit of the Choleric, but they don't have to do anything. Nor do they have to know that they are the hero concerned. They simply have to be the sort of person whom the Choleric admires, looks up to and would like to emulate. It goes without saying they must remain on their pedestal; if they are seen to crumble, even once, they are no longer a satisfactory hero for our evolving Choleric.

If there is someone the Choleric admires they should not only *wish* to be like them but actively strive to *be* like them. They should find out all they can about the person, how they behave in particular situations, how they relate to people, how they have learnt to control and discipline themselves. If the person is dead or is a public figure, they will be able to read about them in books or find out about them via the media. If they are known personally to the Choleric student then the individual can observe them in their daily life.

Role models are helpful in all walks of life, but they must be chosen wisely. Choose a Churchill rather than a Hitler; choose a wise and mature Stage III Choleric rather than a brash and arrogant Stage I. Indeed it will often be another Choleric that is chosen as the role model: a strong leader, someone in a position of power or authority.

James was new in the company and as yet had no special duties or clients. He was to assist the other consultants and do whatever was asked of him. For a Choleric this was an intolerable situation. After all, he was newly qualified and knew he could do the jobs better than the others: you only had to look at them and see the time they took to get things done, the amount of time they spent talking to the other consultants, the time they spent reading boring old financial reports. So he fretted and fumed, waiting for his chance.

Thomas, a Phlegmatic, was his main target. He was the most senior consultant yet he seemed to be a real old ditherer. Every time he asked James to do something he sounded so weak that James wanted to scream. When he wasn't busy, James found ways of criticising, laughing at or annoying Thomas, as if by showing up Thomas's weaknesses he could in some way display his own brilliance. As a result James was becoming known as a trouble-maker. It was ridiculous, thought James as he became aware of this: all they had to do was give him a senior position and he'd soon show them what he could do.

Eventually, Thomas was promoted to another department and David came in as head of the section. David was a strong and mature Choleric. He took the same amount of time and consideration over the projects as Thomas had done but he exuded an unmistakable air of command and competence and would brook no nonsense from others. All of a sudden James became ashamed of his past behaviour. He looked up to David, tried to be like him and soon gained in popularity and confidence as he was successful first in minor roles and then in major ones.

To help a Choleric to mature, give them someone who is strong and cannot be bullied, someone they cannot browbeat. As the Choleric matures they will oscillate between being strong and being a bully. Give them staff who are confident and good at their job and the Choleric will be an excellent boss. Give them staff who are weak, shy or lacking in self-confidence and the Choleric can quickly become a bully.

Mary had a large house and a busy career so she had a house-keeper to look after her home. The problem was, she could never get anyone who was any good. One after another they were tried, found wanting and fired. They did a poor job, they did too little, they complained at the lack of equipment or of polishes or cleaners, they took too long to get the job done. It was all tentative and nervous requests for things that Mary, unaware of the details of domesticity, thought totally unnecessary. In an area where work was hard to get they hung on for as long as they could, which only made Mary more impatient.

Eventually she hired Betty. Betty was in her fifties, mature and full of self-confidence. The moment Mary suggested she hadn't achieved very much in a day Betty had no trouble in telling her just how much she had done and all that needed doing, and what a poor state the house was in. Mary, right from the start, stood in some awe of Betty, who obviously knew far more about running a house than she did. She learnt to listen to Betty's home-grown wisdom and came to value her. Afraid that Betty might suddenly up and leave, Mary began to treat her with respect and the two worked out an excellent relationship.

Stage II

Cholerics tend to know what they want to do early in life, and once they have made the appropriate decisions they get on with their chosen career with determination and energy. They are clever, bright, capable and independent and so can do most things they set their mind on.

By Stage II they are coming to have a greater respect for other people and learning to tone down their strengths and extreme independence and to control their temper and their impatience. They will be working hard to achieve their goals and be more willing to cooperate with others to do so. They develop warmth and are easier to get on with, though they are often unaware of their own strength and may still crush or hurt others without meaning to.

Their excellent characteristics of strength, determination, initiative and leadership can then start to come to the fore. They develop a recognition of the worth of others and a respect for their, often very different, way of doing things. In time there are fewer biting comments, less impatience and a greater willingness to listen. It is not that the Choleric, at any stage, is necessarily cruel or thoughtless on purpose, it is rather that they are strong, impatient and unaware of their own strength or the fragility of others. In time they become more gentle and develop a greater degree of affection for others.

If they are employed they have probably worked themselves into a position of authority, if a minor one. At home they are taking control of the family and providing wise guidance and security.

The Choleric wants to rule unconditionally. They have to learn that this right only comes with time and further maturity: the right to rule is not theirs automatically but has to be earned as they demonstrate their growing wisdom.

While they are happy to stand in isolation at the top, they do need and appreciate recognition from those they command. They thrive on the praise and obedience of those that follow and will work very hard to achieve success and gain this praise. However, they see through false praise, viewing it as the flattery of the weak and faint-hearted; they think little of the giver and are scornful of tears and wimps.

Many a Choleric grandfather, of whose anger the whole family is terrified, has been coaxed into good humour by a dimpled grandchild who climbs into his lap when he is in a rage and says, 'Grandpa, you do look funny when you go bright red and get those funny lines on your forehead.' He would be furiously intolerant of someone nervously trying to cajole him into a better temper but is impressed by the courage and precocity of the little minx on his lap. Similarly, just as they are scornful of false tears they can be profoundly moved by real and deep sorrows.

By this stage the Choleric is becoming chivalrous and will respond to expectations that he take care of others, in the warrior sense rather than in the nurturing sense. If you indicate your high expectations, the Choleric's pride and sense of their own total capability of doing anything that is expected of them will lead them to live up to these expectations. In this way you can help them to mature.

Conversely, criticising them and telling them they should do better will bring trouble and conflict. In fact, so sure is the Choleric that he or she is capable of all things that they will be staggered when they attempt something and fail. If their company or their department is involved in the failure they will often be convinced it is others who have caused the problem, demonstrating a fall back to Stage I. Their conviction that they are all-powerful will demand – if they have reached Stage II or if there is no one else who could have caused the failure – that they try again, and that this time they must and will succeed.

The Choleric female, who has been battling her way through life as she tries to deal both with her own strengths and with the weakness of those around her, has a tougher time than her male counterpart. She faces an additional hurdle: the automatic disadvantage simply of being female. The Choleric characteristics are admired in a male but generally considered inappropriate or unsuitable in a female.

In a job she not only has to fight the competition, she also has to deal with seeing men promoted over her, simply because they are men. This is likely to make her even more aggressive and determined and may make it difficult for her to become firmly Stage II. If she does mature she will be sufficiently sure of herself and her own position to afford to relax and let her accomplishments speak for themselves. Like her male counterpart, she responds to challenges.

Rachel was in her last term at school and wanted to be a chemist. She had applied to several training colleges and universities and was waiting to hear the outcome. One day the headmistress passed her in the corridor and asked what she planned to do. Rachel told her which colleges she had applied to and asked, almost as an afterthought, if there were any others.

'Oh yes,' she was told, 'there's Imperial College, but you'd never get in there. What you've already done is quite appropriate. Good luck.'

Well, this was quite enough for Rachel. She set her mind on doing all that had to be done to get into Imperial College – and she made it. All she needed was the suggestion of a challenge.

Maturing

It is very difficult for a Choleric to reach Stage III, but if they do the effort is worth it. Of all the temperaments, the Stage III Choleric is the noblest and one of the most admired. In a world of uncertainty, of people who are frightened, unsure of themselves or looking for something or someone to rely on for help or support, the Stage III Choleric is a source of strength and wisdom, providing a port in the storm of life. This is in sharp contrast to the Stage I Choleric, who is difficult for most people to handle, particularly as they grow older.

You can help a Choleric to reach this third stage by careful guidance. Even more than before, let them know that you recognise their worth, that you admire their best attributes, their tolerance, their patience, their understanding of other people and their desire to encourage and support them. As you create the image for them that they would, deep down, like to achieve, and as you indicate that you think they are already there, they will do all they can to reach this stage and to live up to your belief in them. Again, the use of role models is helpful, provided they are chosen wisely.

Stage III

It is as exciting and delightful to deal with a mature Stage III Choleric as it can be difficult and bruising to deal with a Stage I.

The third stage can come at any age, and you may well find some young Stage III Cholerics. When you do they will stand out as extraordinary people. More often, Stage III develops over time and requires many changes and many levels of self-development. Stage III Cholerics are wonderful matriarchs and patriarchs. They are staunch friends, showing great interest in and appreciation of others. They support those around them and are willing to help and train others, passing on to them the achievements of a lifetime.

The young Stage III Choleric will look after younger brothers and sisters, and even those somewhat older than themselves, taking on the role of leader and guardian as if by birthright. They have more tolerance for wimps and whiners than they used to have, but will encourage them to become independent and take responsibility for themselves.

The mature Choleric has developed respect for other people and has learnt to recognise that, whereas their ways of doing things may not be the Choleric's way, they are valid ways. They have learnt to take an interest in other people and discovered that other people do have things to contribute to the common good, that their ideas are worth listening to and that they can even teach the Choleric a thing or two. They have also developed the generosity and security that enables them to show their appreciation of others freely and easily.

Control, tolerance and discipline have all been developed by the mature Choleric. They have become big enough and generous enough to deal fairly with lesser mortals. They become the compassionate ruler, the benevolent patriarch or matriarch, the older friend who is looked up to, respected and admired. They willingly give improved conditions and better pay to their staff. They pass the credit on to others rather than taking it for themselves and want to help others fulfil their own potential.

They are not hurt by attacks or criticism, for they are quietly sure of their worth and are more intent on nurturing and promoting the growth of others. They are the strong leaders who rule by example rather than by bombast, who are delighted when others overtake them and who are respected because they have earned the respect of others rather than because they demand it.

The mature Choleric will, with age, give way gracefully to younger people and allow others to take over the reins. They are the professors who hand their research grants over to their bright students, the company directors who make way for others and stand down from positions of leadership when the time is right, the grandmother who gracefully gives way to the daughter-in-law, or the chairman of the family company who gives way to the next generation.

Cholerics and Their Appearance

Like all temperaments, you can often tell a Choleric simply by their looks, their body language and their demeanour. They have a very strong presence, they are strong and demanding, they are sure of themselves and their stance lets you know this. They expect to be taken as the leader of the group, not because they want it particularly, but simply because that is the way it is. The Sanguines may dominate the room by their life and vitality, Phlegmatics may be larger, but the Cholerics display an aura of power and substance.

They may not be tall; indeed, they often aren't. But they have a way of throwing their shoulders back, of holding their backs straight, and lifting their heads, and especially their chins, that makes them seem taller than they really are. They may even tilt their heads back so that they seem to be looking down their nose at you from a great height. If you are taller than them they still achieve this effect, simply by the way they hold their body and by leaning backwards slightly. After you have left them, as you think back to the occasion, you will feel sure they were indeed taller than you. You will almost certainly estimate their height to be greater than it is.

Their stance is masculine. Young Choleric girls will often be seen as tomboys and told to act in a more ladylike way. Women will act more like men, standing at the bar rather than reclining gracefully in an easy chair. When wearing jeans or trousers they will often sit in positions more typical of a man than of a woman. They will cross their arms, or have their hands on their hips and their feet apart, or sit with one foot on the other knee.

Unlike the Phlegmatic, whose body tends to be flabby and without definition, the Choleric is muscular and well shaped. The body is there to do their bidding. The mind assumes control of the body and the Choleric is both surprised and dismayed if their body lets them down. The Second World War pilot, Douglas Bader, who lost both his legs and was determined to master his (then crude) artificial ones, showed just this sort of determination. His physical body was jolly well going to do as his mind dictated. Nor was he going to let people know his legs were false – all pride and no time for sympathy, that's the Choleric. The modern-day paraplegics who fight every inch of the way to reactivate their damaged bodies are showing a similar Choleric tenacity.

You are left in no doubt that Cholerics are strong. They have strong muscles and strong joints. These are clearly defined in men, less so in women. But in a female gathering it is the Choleric woman who will have the extra strength needed to open difficult containers or lift heavy loads.

Cholerics are tough mentally as well as physically and have great endurance. This is of the active rather than the passive kind. They can exert their strength actively and put up with a great deal, particularly when challenged. Phlegmatics, on the other hand, demonstrate endurance simply because, once there, they hang on rather than changing what they are doing. It is a more passive and uncomplaining form of endurance. Cholerics won't complain either, but that is because they are too proud.

In gymnastics, the Sanguine would do the graceful floor routines, the Choleric would be on ropes and pummels. The Sanguines demonstrate length and grace and the Cholerics chunkiness and strength. Phlegmatics and Melancholics are less likely to be doing anything so active.

Cholerics are high chested and have good lungs, which adds to their physical capabilities as well as to the impression they create of size and strength.

In their walk, Cholerics stride over the ground as if they own it. They don't dance over it like the Sanguines or walk on it as the

Phlegmatics do; rather they stride over the top of it. They do not get out of other people's way since they know they are the chiefs, the rulers, the leaders and it is the duty of lesser mortals to give way to them. All the movements of a Choleric are energetic and tense, with a compact and concentrated strength to them. You may get the impression of a tiger waiting to spring, possibly at the graceful Sanguine gazelle.

The head of a Choleric is relatively large and solid boned. Their skull is strong and can withstand much – and it may have to, for the males get into fights easily and willingly, sure of their greater power and their ability to beat any opponent. Their hair is usually dark, sometimes red, and there is plenty of it. They have strong brows and often thick eyebrows.

Their eyes tell you who they are. They are strong and unwavering. Cholerics look you straight in the eye, not to play with you and communicate and laugh as the Sanguine does, but in a way that is both commanding and searching. You don't need to know about them – their looks will tell you – but they wish to know who you are and whether you are worth spending time with. They will decide whether or not to deal with you. There is not necessarily an implied criticism in this. It is simply that they make the decisions about what they want in their life and they don't waste time on people that don't interest them or match up to their standards and ideals. In so far as they are immature and lacking in understanding, Cholerics may miss out on many delightful people in this way, people who are quieter than they are, for they measure other people by their own Choleric yardstick, and often miss out on the subtleties of the other person's personality. By Stage III they are more perceptive.

Their desire for action is clearly seen in their eyes and may sometimes even be taken for anger. It isn't, or only rarely so, and when it is you will know about it in other ways as well. It is simply that Cholerics don't know their own strength, in many different ways, and this applies to their strength of character and the strength of their emotions and the way they express them, as well as to their physical strength. They may trample on you with their gaze, their glance may cut through you like a knife, but they will be staggered if you tell them so: they were simply being themselves, looking and thinking, and then getting on with what was important to them and the task in hand. They make it plain they want to get on with things and get into action. They are likely to intimidate the faint-hearted, but this need not be so if you understand that they are not angry, just strong and fearless.

The Choleric has a strong and often large nose. Their mouth is firm, they may clench their teeth and clamp their mouth shut when active but not speaking. Their voice is firm and strong. It is usually deeper than the Sanguine's, stronger than the Melancholic's and louder than the Phlegmatic's. It carries well – so does the Sanguine's, but that is because it tends to be light and clear. You are left in no doubt about what a Choleric is saying or what they want, even at some distance. Not for them the quiet whisper, self-conscious about what they are saying and worried that others may overhear.

All their facial features are strong and well defined. They may be considered good looking or beautiful, but that is more because their character shines through and because of the way they present themselves rather than their inherent good looks. The Sanguine men can be devastatingly handsome and the Sanguine women are either pretty or elegantly beautiful. Choleric men are more often thought of as the strong rugged types and the women are more usually described as good looking, striking or even possibly handsome, rather than beautiful or pretty.

When seen in the early morning, before shaving or make-up and without the advantage of clothes or uniform, you may be surprised to find they are less good looking than you thought.

Their complexion is either pale, if they have a quiet and self-assured strength, or the typical red and bucolic expression and colouring you see in people who can fly into a temper when provoked.

The rest of their body is likely to be short and chunky. It's as if, as babies, they were so keen to get on with their life that they put all their energy into doing things and didn't give their bones time to grow to full length. They have good muscle definition, provided they exercise. In this they are unlike the Phlegmatic, who may aspire to be a bodybuilder but will always look flabby by comparison.

Their hands and feet are usually square with short but strong fingers and toes. The finger tips and nails, too, may be square.

Being in fashion or wearing the correct clothes is not important to Cholerics, though they like their mate or partner to be well dressed and admired so they can be proud of them. For themselves they are likely to adopt an individual style, one they like and with which they are comfortable, rather than follow conventions or the latest fashion. Their clothes say a lot about them and their own self-confidence.

Cholerics enjoy sports, particularly contact sports or those requiring physical strength and stamina. Their lung capacity gives them great endurance. They have courage and are not afraid of being in the thick of things. At the same time they can be gentle when gentle strength is required.

There is an air of compact and concentrated energy about them, and they dislike sitting still and doing nothing. Even while waiting they are likely to be pacing the floor rather than sitting quietly. In the old days, before men were allowed in the delivery room, the Choleric husband in the maternity wing would be pacing the corridors while the Melancholic sat dropping in a corner, the Phlegmatic sat stolidly waiting and the Sanguine darted around, flirting with the nurses.

Yet, for all their energy, you feel they know exactly where their limbs are and what they are doing. The larger Phlegmatic, although less energetic, may well have you worrying about the safety of your porcelain; the Choleric, you feel, will only break things by intention, not through carelessness.

By their gestures Cholerics also show their strength and self-confidence. They do not waste their gestures or use them almost as a form of speech as does the Sanguine; all the movements they make are strong and firm. They tend to be upwards or outwards, denoting a positive or challenging attitude. If downward, it is likely to be in anger or to emphasise a point and not to indicate depression, like the downward movements of the Melancholic.

Not all Cholerics are physically violent, yet many of them do feel that violence is a suitable way of dealing with difficult situations. They may strike their fist on the table, kick the cat or slam the door when angry, or they may physically attack another person. They may throw things, confident in their power to replace them later, if they choose to, when the mood has passed.

Cholerics like to be the centre of attention: they expect people to look up to them and to look to them for leadership. Where things are happening that is where they want to be, either because they have initiated the events or because they want afterwards to be remembered as having been there, and to be thought of as the leading light. So look for them in a dominant role at the centre of the action. The presence of rivals for this position will only spur the Choleric on. He or she likes a challenge and will rise to it every time, expecting to conquer.

The Choleric Child

Choleric babies are born with a rush and a roar. They come out fighting, scream loudly at the world they have entered and proceed to dominate it. Right from the start there is a challenge when they are thumped on the back – how dare they? What a welcome! Even at this young age they will assert their authority and be demanding. Soon they will find out how to get their own way and will quickly and automatically exercise these new skills. The Choleric twin will do all it can to be born first, unless the Sanguine slips out gracefully before the Choleric notices. The Phlegmatic twin will come out when pushed and the Melancholic is sure the new world will be even worse than the one they have been in.

Stage I Choleric babies are cheeky delights when they get their own way; when thwarted they are little monsters. They are quick-tempered, expecting and demanding their own way at all times and likely to throw a tantrum if frustrated. They will attack the breast with vigour, sucking and pummelling, determined to dominate it and get all they need from it as they make their presence felt right from the start. If they don't get what they want there will be angry screams of rage as the 'little darling' turns bright red in anger and frustration. If they get what they want they will crow with delight and grace the world with their smile. If other people are slow to understand their needs, or slow to do their bidding, all hell will break loose. They will not necessarily cry a lot but they will howl with rage if unhappy, and continue to do so until their needs are met. At this point they will again smile happily at you, knowing that they have the control they crave and consider to be their right.

They are strong and sturdy babies. As toddlers they will walk early, showing their physical strength, but will do so when they want to and when it is necessary for them to get their needs met, rather than when they are encouraged to by others. Their strong desire to explore and command will have them on their feet early. While the Sanguine will walk quickly for the sake of it, for the delight they experience in their limbs and their dexterity, the Choleric will learn to walk so they can get on with life and do what they want. 'What they want' is an important phrase. Woe betide other toddlers or children, even other adults, if they thwart the Choleric. If the Choleric child wants a toy the Choleric child will have that toy ... or else. When they have finished with it, it will be discarded or graciously passed on to others, who can then play. The Choleric's attitude is 'what's yours is mine and what's mine's my own – and least for as long as I have a use for it. After that I may be willing to pass it on to you if you're good.' This is not selfish, it is simply their assumption of their rightful place in the universe.

As children they are the leaders among their peers, mostly leading their friends into all sorts of adventures and misadventures, confident of their supreme ability to do and achieve anything they want. They bang the drums loudest, fight the hardest, make the most insistent demands for your time or attention when they want it and have no hesitation in boasting of and affirming their achievements. This is not done with surprise or pleasure at their achievement, but as a simple statement of prowess, a prowess Choleric children take for granted.

Young Cholerics like to be in the front of things, not because they want the limelight for its own sake as a Sanguine child does, but because they simply have to play a leading role. The Choleric child will be the teacher in the play school, the leader of the team, the 'mother' when playing families; they will be the king in the royal family, the leader in the war gang, the director in the production. Either the Sanguine or the Choleric child will have the ideas; the Choleric will decide what the group is going to do and the others will follow. Since neither the Choleric nor the Sanguine is troubled by details it may be left to the Phlegmatics to make sure their games work out. The female Choleric child will seek to dominate not only the other girls but also the boys of the other three temperaments, and she will often succeed. When it comes to a Choleric boy she will give as good as she gets.

If, for some reason, the Choleric is excluded from the group, or if they have a mean streak and others fail to stand up to them, they can become the bullies and terrorise the other children.

> Little David, a typical Choleric, was always leading his brother and sister into trouble. Susan, a slim Sanguine, was often the one who dreamt up impossible ideas, but David would take them over, or else produce his own, and lead. Susan would then dart along with him, often trying to change their plans midstream as new ideas and distractions occurred to her, and always infuriating him by refusing to do as she was told. Phlegmatic Jonathon plodded along behind, obedient but slow and always holding the other two back, which infuriated David.

Melancholic Jane would frown or cry, aware of all the things that could, and probably would, go wrong.

When the inevitable trouble occurred and they returned home covered in mud they had different stories to tell. David would boast of his achievements, expecting his mother to understand the heroic nature of the way in which they had invaded the orchard next door and got past the neighbour's dog. The mud, the result of a fall down a wet bank, seemed of little consequence to him and he couldn't understand why his mother was so put out by the dirt and a tear on his new trousers. Susan would spin the most fantastic story. They had only been going for a walk, then this man passing by in a cart had sprayed them with mud. Then an old woman had told them how hungry she was and they had only collected the apples to give her food. The fact that her story in no way agreed with either the facts or David's description did not faze her. She was genuinely surprised when accused of telling fibs. Jonathon would stand silently by, looking and feeling both guilty and out of his depth as he slowly pondered on what had gone so badly wrong and what would happen next. Jane knew what would happen next: it would be a punishment of the worst kind.

The Stage I Choleric is likely to overlook all kinds of details. Margaret, aged twelve, was wildly excited when taken out on the river for the first time in a friend's rowing boat. She was determined to repeat the experience, to have a boat of her own and to be its captain. Thwarted by parents who refused to understand the importance and the urgency of such a purchase, she purloined a small table, dragged it to the river and, with its four feet pointed skywards and a pole for propulsion, set off. Details, such as its seaworthiness and manoeuvrability, were not considered. Fortunately, as a true Choleric, she was strong and determined and managed, after the table sank, to swim back to the bank and clamber out. Also like a true Choleric, she took her beating without a whimper and swore that she'd do it again – and that next time she'd be more successful.

When angered they are apt to lash out, but if their friends are in trouble it will be the Choleric's strength and resourcefulness that saves or holds them while the fleet-of-foot Sanguine runs for help.

Clearly these are dominantly male characteristics, and boys make the more appropriate Cholerics. Female Cholerics have a harder time of it. They may be told that they are not behaving as little girls should, that girls don't fight, and other such gender benders. Female Choleric children often have toys more suited to boys and are likely to spurn the dolls of their friends. They may be labelled as tomboys, preferring jeans and trousers to skirts or dresses, and doting mums will hope they grow out of it.

School

Cholerics expect to shine at school and often do, academically or in sports. They will either achieve automatically through their innate skills, or they will achieve through determination and hard work as they strive to live up to their image of themselves as being the best. Mathematics and the sciences are favourite subjects. They will train hard physically in order to win, and are also willing to train mentally. They come at or near the top of the class either naturally or, since to do poorly is not part of their self-image, because they force themselves to study and learn. They hate to be criticised and they hate to have people – teachers, parents or others – checking up on what they do. They know they are right and have done things correctly and they take checking up as a criticism and a negative reflection on their ability to perform as required.

If they simply cannot do well in class they will let it be known that this is not their forte and that sports, business or some other area of interest is much more important.

Choleric girls will often choose subjects more suited to boys, such as maths and the sciences rather than languages or literature; they will choose woodwork over embroidery, and cricket or football rather than netball or rounders. They enjoy sports as a way of releasing their physical energy.

The temperament shows itself in the way sports are played. In tennis, Cholerics are likely to serve and volley rather than baseline rally. In team sports they are more likely to be on the attack than in defence. In cricket they are more likely to bowl than wicket-keep and they'll certainly be at the head of the batting line.

Stage I Cholerics have absolute confidence that they know what to do and that their way is the best. They will not be told; instead they have to learn from their mistakes, and they do this quickly and successfully. If the Choleric child has transgressed or done something stupid they should be chastised or corrected in private and not made to look foolish among their friends. Do not tell the Choleric child (or any child for that matter) that they are bad; tell them simply that there is a better way of doing what they want to do, or point out the harm in what they have done. Let them understand that what they have done is not worthy of them or of someone of their temperament and character. They will then strive to live up to this image of themselves, once they know that you recognise they are little rulers in the making and that they, you assume, want to be benevolent rulers rather than tyrants.

If they do not respond to this treatment, do not be tempted to punish the Choleric child by a show of force. Cholerics thrive on opposition. If you set out to subdue them they will take up the challenge. You may impose tougher and tougher punishments but it is you who is likely to crack first and refuse to impose more, rather than they who will acknowledge defeat. You cannot beat a Choleric child into submission, either physically or mentally. Instead you can appeal to their sense of honour, their responsibility, their role as a leader and their desire for praise and recognition. If you continue to try to subdue them by force, either physical or mental, you are likely to turn them into belligerent rebels more determined than ever to show their strength and to dominate.

School, in many ways, is a miniature version of life and many children go through a relative version of the three stages in school. Thus as Choleric children mature they become the responsible prefects and heads of school.When they move on into adulthood, however, they may be a relative Stage I again and have the real business of maturing to do.

In fact, there are several traumatic moves in the life of the Choleric child to which they have difficulty adapting. In junior school they gradually mature from the first class to the most senior class. Even if they haven't matured to any great extent, simply by the right of age and being in the most senior class, they are able to assume some of the power and authority they crave over the younger children. When they move on to senior school and again become part of the youngest class, the most junior student group and the bottom rung on the ladder, they have great difficulty adapting to their new, reduced, status. The same rise then happens up through the senior school years until they are prefects and accept the authority they feel to be theirs by right. Often it is, yet they normally still have a lot of maturing to do. The next step may be university or some training institute where the process is repeated. The first year at university can be a severe trauma for them as they have to find their feet again. Finally they are out in the adult world and, older now, yet again they find themselves at the bottom of the hierarchies, the most uncomfortable place for the Choleric to be.

The more rapidly the Choleric can mature, the more comfortable their life will be.

The Choleric Adult

Cholerics tend to be career oriented. They know what they want to do in life and where they want to go. They want to achieve, they want to feel they have accomplished something and to be satisfied with what they have accomplished. They also want respect for who and what they are and the recognition and admiration of those around them. Not for them the show of the Sanguine – they want recognition for their solid worth. In Stage I they feel and assume that this is theirs by right. By Stage III they have earned it.

They may seem selfish, but would be surprised if you told them so. They simply feel that the best belongs to them. They want the best jobs, the most attractive sexual partners, the largest slice of the cake all round.

Men may choose careers in sports, in business or in the sciences. The military also appeals to the Choleric. Here, under the guise of fighting for their country, they can use their strength and their desire to dominate to create a niche for themselves.

Women are likely to be career rather than home oriented. They may see the home and marriage as a place where they will be dominated by a man and where they will lose their freedom to do things their way. At work they will be frustrated if expected to be secretaries or work in a serving role. They will want their own status and their own position.

Cholerics, when they leave school, will also want to leave the nest and explore the world. Sanguines may go on an extended travel tour, working simply to pay their way, but the Choleric is more likely to want to come to grips with each new country and place. They will work to be more involved.

Cholerics will want their own home because they will need their freedom: the freedom to do as they want when they want. They also want to rule, and staying at home means they stay where their parents rule. In their own home what they say goes – and that suits the Choleric very well.

Cholerics have great confidence in themselves and their abilities. This new adult world into which they are entering holds few fears for them. Rightly or wrongly, they are confident that they can conquer and get the best of it.

As a result they will often throw themselves into ventures with little thought for the practicalities, confident that they will be able to get themselves out of any trouble that occurs – and they often can, though not always. A Choleric buying a business will not be put off by the fact that it has been losing money. They will be confident that all it needs is the Choleric's unique skills and abilities to pull it into a profitable position. A dilapidated house is meat and drink to the Choleric, who is convinced that they will be able to restore and repair it where others have failed.

A Choleric, offered a job for which he or she lacks the qualifications, will take it, confident that they can bluff their way through and pick up the necessary skills fast enough to avoid detection.

The Choleric can be foolhardy. Maturity turns this into well-thought-out and well-placed displays of courage and a willingness to face challenges.

When things do go wrong in the Choleric's life, they assume first of all that someone else is to blame. If there is no one around to blame and the Choleric is forced to realise that the problems are of their own doing, they will learn quickly and not make the same mistake again. In the process, Cholerics have to deal with their own fallibility; a tough lesson for Cholerics but one that, if handled well, can lead them on to further maturity.

Veni, vidi, vici – I came, I saw, I conquered – could well be the motto of the Choleric. Cholerics like to be perfect, be the best, to have their own way. They also like freedom – freedom for themselves – yet deny it to others who, they feel, must do their bidding.

Friends

Cholerics are staunch friends. Once you have won their friendship they will be loyal and constant. Their code of behaviour leads them to stand by their friends, to stand up for them when required, and to be available for support. Do not, however, play games with them. Do not pretend to be in need to get their attention. They will see through this and will think the less of you for that. They like to have respect for their friends, so be careful not to lose this. Be honest with a Choleric; never lie to them. So long as you are honest a Choleric will forgive your mistakes or unwise actions. Cholerics are not cruel and will not hurt you when you are down. But if you lie to cover up an action or weakness, if you lie to them or cheat on them, you will have lost their respect and probably their friendship permanently.

Do not box the Choleric in. The friend or lover who hints at a permanent relationship will send the Choleric running. The colleague who draws a commitment from the Choleric to go into business together can set the Choleric in search of reasons not to go ahead. Once a Choleric has agreed to a commitment, even one they wanted, they are likely to start looking for problems and reasons why they should get out. Persuade them to commit themselves to a holiday with you or a social event and they will soon want out. Until they have matured they can feel hemmed in by outside restrictions and commitments.

Even if they have planned the situation themselves all may not go smoothly. Many a Choleric has begged and pleaded for a job, only to feel trapped when it is offered and to wonder what other and possibly better opportunities they might be missing. The Choleric woman longing for a proposal may, soon after accepting it, start thinking of reasons why she shouldn't get married.

To get a Choleric to want something, commit to it and stay committed to it you should keep trying to take it away from them. Tell them there is this wonderful opportunity ... but you're not sure they'd get it (red rag to the Choleric). Tell them you're not sure they could do it (Cholerics love the challenge, and will do it simply for the sake of doing it and winning). Tell them that you're not sure they have the staying power, not sure that the other person will want to stay within the agreement, that finances may not be available, that there are other people determined to beat them to get the house they're looking at. In these circumstances the Choleric will focus on winning rather than on the possible loss of freedom.

The clever lover will never let the Choleric feel sure that they have won, that the other person has been mastered and is committed to the relationship. Keep the challenge alive and the relationship with your Choleric will flourish.

The Choleric has all the qualities of a 'toughie'. They are so strong and independent it is easy to think of them as hard, and without feeling. They are not: they do have a heart, a big heart. But they also have enemies and are reluctant to let their feelings show for fear of being caught at a disadvantage or of showing weakness and vulnerability. They hate to show weakness and may feel that showing their feelings is soft.

The usual wheedling or manipulation will get you nowhere with a Choleric. They are critical of weakness and determined to be the boss. This may hold true at home and with their spouse, yet a delightful child who is totally immune to their towering rages and only laughs with them can often win anything they want. Equally, they admire strength in others. The employee who shows they are not scared of the boss will earn their respect. Kindness and tact will go a long way when dealing with a Choleric.

Cholerics are unmoved by calculated grief but can be strong, magnanimous, gentle and understanding in times of real tragedy or need. When being their aggressive selves they can cause others pain. If the other collapses in a heap of fear or tears the Choleric will only get more impatient. But Cholerics also know themselves, at least to some extent, and they do know they can be tough. If you try to stand up to them and not show weakness they will respect you. If inadvertently they see how they have hurt you, they will be filled with remorse and bend over backwards to make amends.

Cholerics will tend to live up to your expectations, provided these are something that the Choleric admires. If you want them to be generous, let them know you think they are generous. If you want them to be magnanimous, let them know you think they are already magnanimous. If you want them to be chivalrous rather than chauvinistic, let them know you think they already are chivalrous. Provided they are happy with the goal you are setting they will strive to live up to it as part of their desire for recognition and admiration. The Stage III Choleric has these characteristics already. If this stage has not yet been reached then providing this impetus is one way to help them reach it.

Cholerics are capable and competent, often more capable than the people around them. When other people do things less well or more slowly than the Choleric then the Choleric's patience, of which there is only a little, is sorely tried. If they have not matured they are likely to get angry and push the other person aside with a comment such as 'Let me do that, you're too slow, I haven't the time to waste.' Or 'Give it to me, it's quicker to do it myself.' Your best answer is to stand up to them: do not shrink back or show weakness or you will create further problems for yourself in the future.

The Choleric, being capable and strong, expects other people to be the same and considers them weak and failures if they do not live up to this expectation. There is little point in chiding or blaming the Choleric for this, or calling them intolerant. It is better to let the Choleric know that with his or her great strengths, wisdom, skill and intelligence it is within their power to understand and make allowances for lesser mortals. This way they can mature.

The Choleric at Work

The Choleric's approach to work is as important as the type of work. They want to be the boss, to rule, to tell others what to do. They do not want to take orders, to have their work inspected, to accept criticism or to do things other people's way. Work is also a very important part of their life and, if they are not careful, some Cholerics can even find it takes over, to the detriment of their home, family and social life. Such Cholerics would do well to strive for a better balance.

Cholerics thrive on admiration and appreciation for what they are and what they can do. However, though they feel this is theirs by right, one of the most valuable lessons they can learn is that they have to earn this appreciation. They can do this by maturing and showing their best qualities – which are many. They set high standards for themselves and are rarely content. The more they accomplish, the more they raise their own self-expectations.

By instinct they want to be at the head of the organisation, but they have to learn to start at the bottom and earn their way up. On the way, Cholerics must learn tolerance and appreciation for their superiors, or they will be labelled troublemakers, and for their staff, or they can become bullying bosses and ruthless taskmasters.

Cholerics are empire builders and can do well in business. They can create a concept, visualise the outcome and make it happen. Power appeals to them. They are good administrators and planners, they work efficiently and logically rather than relying on emotion, and they keep their departments running smoothly. They are innovative, but in this they may also be helped by the imaginative ideas of Sanguine friends or colleagues and be dependent on the Phlegmatic's and Melancholic's role in making things happen, by attending to the detailed work and taking care of the people. Their empires may be large or small, but the Choleric will be at the top. They may work for themselves or be part of a larger concern.

They can work within organisations and structures, within governments, big business or teaching organisations. They make good and firm administrators and can rise rapidly through middle management to the top. All the time they are carving out a niche and a career path for themselves. When they first join an organisation they are likely to rise quickly, heading first small sections and then large departments with ease and authority, but they do need to feel there is room for them at the top. If progress is blocked they are likely to leave and to look for some other company or situation in which their skills will be appreciated. They can handle responsibility and are willing to make tough decisions when these are called for.

Cholerics do have respect for authority, provided they feel it is deserved; they don't have respect for someone within the structure simply because of their title. They have to feel that the individual deserves to be where they are. A Choleric faced with a boss who has been employed because of the strings they can pull rather than on merit will soon let their feelings show.

All this can make life difficult for the young Choleric starting out in their first job, especially if they have just graduated from a school, university or training programme where they were one of the leaders. They have to learn to fit in, and fast. Too often a Choleric will arrive in the office sure that they can do things without being told, sure that there are better ways and that they, bright and newly trained, have just what the place is looking for. They can be reluctant to listen to advice, unwilling to recognise that they still have a lot to learn.

Provided they *can* learn, can fit in yet again as a junior at the bottom of the ladder, they have a lot to offer their employer.

Cholerics will put a lot into their work and usually have strong career drives. They are willing to work long hours, to get to work early and to stay late if necessary. Their homes and families may suffer as they focus on the goal of achieving their career aims. However, because they are usually healthy, fit and strong, they are commonly able to meet the demands placed on them by a heavy work schedule and a busy home and social life. They can do without much sleep when they have to, and have the energy and stamina to meet the challenges they encounter. You are unlikely to find the Choleric sloping off early to the pub or spending time chatting in the ladies' room while they debate the merits of different lipsticks.

Cholerics love a contest and will rise to meet on-the-job challenges with alacrity. They are logical and pragmatic and prefer to make decisions devoid of emotion. In this they can at times seem hard and cold, yet they have their eyes fixed firmly on the final goal and the most efficient way of getting there. They are loyal, but their loyalty is usually to the company rather than to individuals.

The more they are told something is impossible, the more determination they can put into doing it. Faced with a possible bankruptcy they will be the last to give in, will pull out all stops, prune costs, sack inefficient staff, work tirelessly and usually avoid disaster.

If you work for a Choleric boss, do not show weakness or uncertainty. If your Choleric boss is inspecting your work and you look apprehensive, they will find fault with it even if they are not sure of their ground. This is partly to show who is in charge and their desire to dominate, and partly because they assume that since you are nervous you must know you have not done a good job. Since they would be proud of their work and stand up to anyone, they have difficulty realising that you could be nervous of them, no matter how good you think your work is. Stand up to your Choleric boss and they will respect you.

The Choleric's own stamina can lead them to make heavy demands on their staff and colleagues, expecting them to have a similar amount of strength and stamina and calling them weak and lazy if they don't perform as well. As they mature they must learn to understand the relative strengths and capacities of others.

Business appeals to the Choleric, as do the sciences, mathematics and engineering. As scientists they are driven to learn, to understand whatever they are studying: they want to be able to explain what it is and how it works and predict what will happen next and, of course, they want to control it. Their innovative ideas, their appreciation for logic and their ability to think things through makes them good researchers and interesting teachers. The more introspective Cholerics may write, either about factual and technical information or, if fiction, books with action. Melancholics will write about feelings and people. As teachers, Cholerics are better with mature than young students, and with the bright rather than those who have difficulty learning. They tend to be hard taskmasters, expecting much from their students and setting difficult exams, but they provide a wonderful challenge and inspiration for the bright students.

It is important for Cholerics to keep a clear eye on the final goals. Some Cholerics, if they are not careful, can let the ideas take over and follow them for their own sake, debate for the fun of it and in order to beat the other debaters, make a project work simply for the achievement. Other Cholerics have no trouble keeping on course and will seem ruthless in their ability to discard what is not immediately required and valuable.

Again, female Cholerics may have difficulties. They will almost certainly want a career, but many of the chosen career paths are typically thought of as male. Nowadays, however, as women are increasingly entering a wider variety of jobs, there are opportunities in the sciences, industry and big business, and in the armed forces. The idea of men working for a female boss in a position of power and authority used to be hard for any man to deal with. Now this is becoming more readily accepted than in the past.

If the female Choleric can mature fast, it will help her in her desire to achieve all she wants without having to fight too many men and gender prejudices along the way.

The Choleric and Money

Cholerics are normally successful in life, and this means financially as well as in other ways. They are not particularly inclined to save money or squirrel it away for a rainy day, but are usually well off or safely and adequately provided for when they retire. Money, for them, is a measure of their achievement; it is also an instrument, a tool, something to be used. They are not so much interested in money in the bank, as in what they can do with it. Money, for a Choleric, can mean power, the ability to bend the world to their wishes. Having money also means that they are able to look after themselves; they do not have to depend on someone else or on state benefits, both anathema to the Choleric.

Cholerics like to succeed and money is a symbol of success, yet for many the drive towards wealth can be intermittent. They need to be motivated by something for which they need money rather than by the money itself. If they wish to buy more property or a business, send their children to better schools, provide more leisure for their family or more time for themselves, then they will strive towards greater wealth.

They enjoy possessions, but do not have to possess something to enjoy it and thus are relatively unacquisitive. When insufficient money is available for their needs they will go out and get it, usually very successfully, but the urge to riches may fade once they have achieved what they want.

Cholerics are generous. They are generous with money and they are generous with their possessions. They are less likely to be generous with their time and their patience. Being generous and distributing largesse is part of the Choleric's way of showing status and the ability to provide.

The Choleric male will spend generously on his wife, on furs and jewels, on clothes and other expensive presents. His wife is his showpiece, one of his prized possessions. The Choleric female will also use her money, possibly in a slightly quieter way than her male counterpart, but still to demonstrate her independence and her ability to provide for herself and others.

Choleric men like to be breadwinners. If his wife goes out to work, earns money of her own or is wealthy in her own right, the Choleric man is likely to insist that she keep that money for herself, that they will live on what he earns. If he is particularly immature or vulnerable in this area he may insist that she doesn't go out to work at all, or may try to ignore the fact if she does, refusing to discuss her work or her income with her, or he may belittle what she does and what she earns.

Choleric women are likely to insist on paying their way, certainly with other women and almost always with men. The Choleric woman may well feel uncomfortable if her husband is the sole breadwinner. She does not like being dependent so she is often happier if she, too, is working and bringing in a salary. The exception is when a Choleric woman finds a Choleric man who is stronger than her and whom she can admire and respect. Then, and only then, is the Choleric woman inclined to relax and let herself be taken care of.

The person in the restaurant loudly insisting on paying the bill for the group is likely to be a Choleric, probably an immature Choleric, especially if there is no particular reason why they should pay it. The mature Choleric will still pay the bill but will do it with such quiet authority that everyone will accept that it is their right to do so.

The person contributing most to the new local school building is probably a Choleric, and they will also want to control the project. The Choleric's generosity is more likely to be overt than covert. It is also likely to give them some authority, status or reflected glory.

The Choleric needs to be generous to show his or her ability and power. Cholerics can also afford to be generous because they are sure of their ability to provide, to make more and to come out on top. They will spend on their home and its contents. They will spend on a good car. Their wealth will show, more or less ostentatiously depending on how much they have matured.

The Choleric and Time

Cholerics have mixed responses to time. In general they will expect other people to be on time in their dealings with them. They may see it as a mark of disrespect from the other person if they are kept waiting. Stage Is certainly will, Stage IIIs probably will although it won't bother them all that much; they will also see it as a reflection of the manners of the other person. On the other hand, Cholerics may not always be on time themselves. In Stage I this is a reflection of their arrogance and their assumption of a leading role: they simply consider that they are the more important and that the other people can and will wait for them. By Stage III the Choleric probably has too much respect for the other person to keep them waiting, and too much respect for themselves to behave so badly as to turn up late.

If the Choleric is late it is probably because they feel that what they are doing is important, too important to leave, since they know they are indispensable. They may feel that the next person will be willing to wait for them since what they have to offer is valuable and their company is appreciated. Often this is true.

The Choleric couple who arrive late at a dinner party will tell you loudly and confidently what they had to do on the way as you announce their presence. They will then let you know, subtly, that the evening can now commence. Because they are so sure of themselves and perhaps because you are in awe of them or nervous of their disfavour, you will accept this. There will also be a general feeling from the other guests that this is true, everyone responding to the fact that two strong, confident and probably popular people have now arrived and will give the event a certain style.

Cholerics rarely waste time. There is a lot they want to do in their lives and they like to get on with it. They are too full of energy to hang around wondering what to do next: they are more likely to get on with things, to act first and think later. They may feel that to think something through in detail is a waste of time. Instead, they first assume that they already know what they need to know and so are willing to charge straight ahead. If that fails they then assume that they will be able to do whatever it takes to right the situation or get out of the mess. Either way, why waste time thinking about it, let's get going!

It often seems as though the Choleric can dominate time, can bend it to their will. They will fit more into the day than those of any other temperament. They instinctively move and do things quickly and effectively and can do more than one thing at a time. They are practical rather than dreamers and, unlike the Melancholics, do not need to spend time smelling the roses or in quiet contemplation; instead they are active and get on with things.

The Choleric in Love

Cholerics may, and do, experience deep emotions, but they rarely express them. To many they may seem cold, hard and unemotional, except perhaps when they are angry. Only to a few close friends will they show just how deep and strong their emotions can be. They do not wear their heart on their sleeve, nor do they like to participate in public displays of emotion.

They are more likely to have a few serious love affairs than many light flirtations. They themselves will choose to have it this way, not wanting to waste time on trivial dalliances. Others will contribute to this outcome, for it takes considerable time and energy to get close to a Choleric and not everyone is willing to invest this in such a strong partner, and one of whom they may be slightly afraid. Cholerics are complex people and the closer you get the more surprises you may find, which can be unsettling for someone who wants a predictable relationship and outcome. They are also self-contained, self-sufficient and willing to take responsibility for their own actions. Thus they are less easy than others to manipulate, which in turn can be somewhat daunting for someone who wants mutual dependence.

The Choleric will give thought to the prospective partner and decide ahead of their actions what outcome they want. They will then pursue this wholeheartedly. Once settled on their goal, Cholerics are single-minded.

If you become involved with a Choleric you will know where you stand, but you will have to take their word for it that if they do not repeat their sentiments nothing has changed. If they tell you they love you once, they will consider that to be sufficient; you should not need to hear it every day. Having to repeat this each day could mean that there was a doubt, and of course there isn't, they're steadfast. Cholerics do hate to be doubted. If your Choleric is mature, and unless they tell you otherwise, the relationship will be a long one. If they are interested only in a short-term romance they are likely to tell you – and you had better believe them and act accordingly, or you could get hurt.

Cholerics are more interested in the goal than in the process of getting there, unlike the Sanguine for whom the romance and the chase are all important. Young Cholerics, particularly those at Stage I, consider sex a challenge as much as an act of love; the love comes later, often with ownership or possession. On the other hand, the degree of sexual satisfaction is commonly a reflection of the depth of the relationship and not purely physical.

Young and single Stage I Cholerics are not essentially faithful. Just as they feel they are the boss, even when new in the job, so do the men feel, like the lord of the manor, that they can pick and choose who they want for an affair. They give no one the right to tie them down, so if they feel like having two or more women 'on the go' they feel they have the right to do so without having to explain themselves. Yet because in their mind the woman in their life belongs to them, they can be outraged if she has another man or, as the Choleric would view it, if another man trespasses on his territory and takes his woman. Although this analogy fits the men more than the women the attitude is the same for both sexes. She too will feel she has the right to choose, but woe betide any other woman who trespasses on the Choleric woman's territory.

The net result of this is that Cholerics of both sex desire freedom and feel that they have the right to their own way and to have the lovers they want, although they may not be so willing to let one of their partners have the same freedom, a characteristic we have already met. At the same time they do not really like promiscuity, finding it messy, inconvenient and looking on it as unworthy of them. So, on the whole they are more likely to have a sequence of affairs one after the other than two or more at a time. Since they are selective and do not meet many people they feel are worthy of them, and since they are often heavily involved in careers and other pursuits, they are unlikely to have as many relationships as the Sanguine.

In general they will not discuss their relationships. He is not interested in boasting of his conquests to his friends in the pub or club unless he is seriously stuck in Stage I. She will not share her secrets with her girl friends. Neither of them will share information about past lovers with their current partner. Nor do either of them like dirty or sexy jokes or smut.

Cholerics are relatively uninterested in conforming to the rules of society simply because they exist. They are more likely to make their own rules and then stick by them. Provided they have lived up to their own code of behaviour they can sleep sound in bed at night and be comfortable. In general, they consider sexual boasting unworthy of them, and their affairs to be of no concern to anyone but themselves. Similarly they are uninterested in group sex, wife swapping, or any other more public sexual activity.

The more introverted Cholerics often are completely faithful, tending to have one affair at a time. Once married, all Cholerics tend to be loyal and the pillar of the family, at least for as long as their partner has their respect and for as long as they are recognised in their role as leader and provider. Cholerics desire freedom but also want to be liked and admired; they do not want empty adulation but recognition by other people of their true worth. As this develops, Cholerics will do all they can to continue to deserve this recognition and this frequently includes being a stalwart and faithful member of the family.

Unlike the Melancholics, the Choleric does not die for love. They have a lot more in their life than the current partner and if an affair ends they are likely to shrug it off and get on with other things. This may be their career or hobbies and other interests, or they may look for a new partner. The *mature* Choleric is unlikely to blame their ex-partner for the failure of the relationship, as they tend to take responsibility for themselves. At the same time they usually have sufficient self-confidence to be able to move on without feeling inadequate or a failure. If they have been deeply hurt that is where it will stay – deeply buried. They will grit their teeth, come to terms with it and get on with their life.

Men

The young male Choleric is likely to be the chauvinistic stud, chasing after women or, better yet, having them chase after him. In affairs of the heart the young Choleric male is truly the conquering hero. He will stand at the edge of the party surveying the scene. He will choose the woman he wants and then go after her with a single-mindedness that leaves little room for the competition. Sure of himself, he is also sure that he can win her and staggered if he doesn't. However, his successes are more common than his failures, his own confidence adding to his chance of success. He is strongly masculine, supremely confident and makes a powerful impression. He is a refreshing change for women who have so often been disappointed in the lack of initiative shown by many of the men in their lives.

If approached by a Choleric man that you don't like then make your 'No' very definite. Weak opposition simply spurs him on and he is likely to take anything less than a blunt and total refusal, spoken firmly, as a challenge, secure in his conviction that he is irresistible. When immature he may even go so far as to pursue a woman simply because she does say no, allowing his determination to win at all costs, overriding the fact that he didn't want her all that strongly in the first place. The other way to really turn him off, assuming that this is your goal, is to belittle him or make fun of him in front of his friends – that he will not tolerate.

The young Choleric male may be the college stud, the football hero, or top of the class. He is unlikely to be the town's romantic symbol, the man all the women fall for; that role is reserved for the Sanguine. He is not so much good looking as ruggedly handsome. He may be the strong and silent type, he may be somewhat awe-inspiring, but being chosen by him is definitely thought of as a feather in the cap for many women.

He may pick them up, have a short fling and then drop them, moving on to conquer new territories; if so he will have told them this at the start. He won't want to be tied down, and why should he be? There are plenty of women simply waiting to fall in love with him or climb into his bed. His love of freedom and independence will assert itself and keep him on the move until such time as he chooses to be committed.

During an affair all will go well as long as he chooses the agenda and the pace. The woman who asks after each occasion 'When will I see you next?' will send him running for cover. Better to leave him unsure that you will be available later, uncertain that you want to see him again. If you are the soft and gentle type, wanting repeated assurances of love and affection, the strong silent Choleric is probably not for you — you might do better with a soulful Melancholic.

In sex there is, initially, more enthusiasm than finesse. Foreplay he thinks is a game of bridge. He is more interested in proving his virility and strength, assuming that that will impress you, than in the finer feelings a woman might have. A serious rough and tumble is more his style, possibly several of them, then up and on with life. Not for him hours languishing together listening to music and reading poetry. Leave that to the Melancholics. When he is ready for other activity he is likely to send the lady packing. If he sends you flowers his secretary probably thought of it.

Cholerics like to do all things well, and much of their knowledge comes from books. He is likely to read books on sex and to learn the ways things should and can be done. He is also interested in putting his ideas into practice and is not too shy or inhibited to explore. If he puts his mind to it, and not all of them do, he can become an imaginative and exciting lover.

Do not be the first to make suggestions of marriage, or even of living together: nothing could scare him off faster. Playing hard to get is the best way with a Choleric. If he thinks other men want you he will want you all the more, determined to beat them and end up the winner. This may be one way to get him to propose. But do not try to make him jealous – he will see through that. Let him draw his own conclusions from your absences and the fact that you seem to manage as well without him as with him.

When he does marry it will be for status as much as for love. Confident in himself he is sure he can mould the woman to his way of life. He is also sure that, should he fall for an entirely unsuitable woman, he can ignore the social rules, marry her and convert her to his way of life quite successfully. More often, however, he will choose someone who is quite suitable and who will blend in with the life he has established. Again it is his own standards that must be met, rather than those of society.

In general, his choice is a statement to the world of these standards, and he needs his wife more to show to the world as a reflection of his status than for emotional support and companionship. He wants an appropriate partner, a hostess, someone who can provide the right background for his life. She may be surprised that, after marriage, he continues to live his life as before, expecting her to adapt, and to accept that he still socialises with his friends and pursues his bachelor hobbies. He will, particularly if Stage I, still go to the pub with the lads, still go to the rugby matches or the races, still be involved with his club. Her role is to provide the home for him that he expects and to be there when he wants her. But the woman who becomes the slave or the dish-rag will infuriate him. She must be strong and have opinions and strengths of her own – as long as they fit in with his and do not disrupt his lifestyle.

Since the Choleric likes to look good, wants to respect his partner and wants his choice to add to his status, he will usually choose either a stunning-looking Sanguine or another Choleric. Since he wants a wife who looks truly feminine and is the envy of other men his choice will probably veer slightly more towards the Sanguine. If he does choose a Choleric then watch out, the fur could fly when each is at their most choleric.

The Stage I Choleric man is likely to think of his wife as a possession, one to be won, to show off, to buy expensive presents for, to dress and house and present to the world. He will see his wife as a status symbol and she must behave as such and behave correctly. They will also insist on being boss in their own home and expect things to be done their way and in their time. Remember not to expect the Stage I Choleric to be totally faithful. They will not be as flirtatious as the Sanguine man, but they do claim the king's title to other women who cross their path, should an appropriate relationship develop. It's all part of the role of the conquering hero. But at least you can rest easy in the knowledge that they are unlikely to boast of this relationship, tell their friends, or in any other way risk letting their wife know. This is less a desire for subterfuge than their preference to keep their relationships private.

Stage II Cholerics are likely to be less egotistical and more willing to be part of a couple, both contributing to the experience. He also becomes more willing to mould his life with hers and consider her needs, at least in so far as they are greatly in conflict with his own.

Stage III Cholerics will be the true patriarchs, ruling the roost but with a lenient hand and taking care of all within their orbit. A young Stage III Choleric is strong and powerful in the relationship but is also involved with his wife and has respect for her. He becomes interested in her way of doing things and recognises other values and standards beside his own. Marriage to a Stage III Choleric man can be a wonderful, deep, exciting and rich experience.

Even in marriage the young Choleric is usually less than subtle in bed. The conquering hero is again active. But now he is sure of you, now he owns you and has less to prove, and whatever imagination and trouble there was before may have gone the way of the single life. Many women have been surprised at the change that comes over the relationship once the marriage takes place. The Choleric husband is even more likely to lack finesse, going for what he wants with little thought for the needs of his partner and often unaware that those needs may not have been met. If you want finesse and romance, and particularly if you want this to continue after marriage, then choose the Sanguine lover. The Choleric takes command, dictates the speed and, once gratified, is inclined to roll over and go to sleep.

He may be considered violent by some women and, while he can be, it is more likely that this is where his lack of awareness of his own strength is at play. He would be shocked to find that a woman was frightened of him, for two reasons. First, he didn't realise he was being particularly strong and second, he doesn't want a wimp for a wife. Do not try to manipulate a Choleric with tears and pleas.

A lot depends on the way the woman handles him. If she is an imaginative Sanguine, her smiling admiration, her deft compliments and her use of endearments and caresses can make him dependent on her, while still thinking that he is the boss. With time and subtlety she can mould him into the lover she wants.

In general, for peace and quiet in their lives, she will do things his way. If she wants her own way she will still have to let him think it is his way. While the clever Sanguine can manage him, the confrontation of a Choleric wife is likely to lead to conflagration. No Stage I Choleric could stand the thought of being ruled by his wife, even in the little things.

The Choleric who chooses to develop sexual finesse, however, will be a wonderful lover. For them, the sharing of ideas is as important as the physical and when this is blended, when the two are together mentally and emotionally as well as physically, the sexual act can be true communion. Melancholics want a spiritual union; Cholerics are more interested in an intellectual union.

It goes without saying that the Choleric head of the house provides a security that other homes may lack. Many of them tend to be conservative, want to look good and be admired. They may often be the centre of their social circle, the house that people come to. He is dependable, strong and confident and can provide a stable home for the family over which he rules. You could do a lot worse.

Women

Life can be tough for the female Choleric. So many of the Choleric traits are usually thought of as masculine that when she behaves naturally she is likely to be thought of as unfeminine. The lack of outward displays of emotion that are acceptable in a Choleric man are less acceptable in the woman. The strength and independence that Cholerics display are not usually considered feminine traits.

It is also difficult for her to find a suitable partner, one who she feels is worthy of her. She will want someone who is as strong as she is and someone she can admire and respect. She will see through the Don Juan Sanguine with his tendency to superficiality. She will be bored with the reliable and predictable Phlegmatic who lets her take charge, and impatient with the Melancholic's need for attention and the long hours he spends mooning, as she sees it, over the relationship. That leaves her with a Choleric husband, yet in this partnership there are bound to be clashes as each vies for dominance.

Cholerics are generous and have much to give. This is true of both sexes. The female Choleric will give a great deal and in this way may often make her partner feel emasculated or belittled. She may be earning more than he, and may also have greater strengths in running her life. Either he has to learn to cope and deal with this or she has to learn to hide her strengths.

A further possibility is role reversal. In the past, when women could only act through their husbands, the Choleric woman might well marry a weaker man and then rule through him, being the typical power behind the scenes. He, in turn, respecting, even fearing, her strengths and her need and drive to have her own way, would be satisfied, secure in the knowledge that she would use her skills to prop him up and make him look good, not to compete with him, certainly not in public. He would be content with this, provided that she made it look as if he was indeed the master of the house. Many times he would give in for the sake of peace and quiet.

This has carried through in many marriages up to the present time. Now, however, with the equalising of the role of men and women in many aspects of marriage, many Choleric women are taking over the so-called male role. They may be the dominant breadwinners, they may have the more powerful career. They may be the ones who dictate what is done at home. This in turn frees the men of other temperaments and allows them to relax, to stop feeling they have to strive so hard to play the traditional role. Some of the husbands even stay at home and run the house. The Melancholic husband can write his novel, or pursue his art. The Sanguine can socialise, pursue his varied interests or even, heaven forbid, play the field. The Phlegmatic can organise the smooth running of his routine job, working nine to five and coming home in time to meet the needs of the children or prepare a meal, content to let his Choleric wife pursue her long-houred and demanding career, make the big decisions and take the major share of the family's responsibilities.

But it is still tough for the Choleric woman. No matter what arrangement or compromise she makes, no matter how well she adapts to the role she chooses, at heart there are often unfulfilled needs. She may continue to yearn for the strong Sir Galahad, the man she can truly respect and love who will also give her the freedom she craves to be herself. She herself is intelligent and assured, unimpressed by mere virility or bombast, but looking for the substance and wanting, deep down, someone who is her equal or more. She will want a man with whom she can be herself, not pretending and sublimating her strengths and abilities. Such a man is not easy to find.

Like her male counterpart, the Choleric woman is more likely to have a sequence of relationships, prior to marriage, rather than be promiscuous. Once married she is more likely than the male to be faithful, considering extra-marital affairs to be unworthy of her. She may also believe they cast doubt on her choice of husband, and she does not like that. Also like her male counterpart, she is unlikely to boast of her relationships or discuss the details.

A Stage I choleric woman is likely to adapt poorly to her role in any partnership. There may be frequent quarrels and arguments as each of them strives to fill the role they feel should be theirs, whatever temperament the man is. Because she is capable and self-assured, men may call her intolerant or arrogant. Because she is strong and impatient with signs of weakness in others she may be called cold and heartless. She is none of these things. She is strong and passionate but he must be able to live up to her and match her.

She longs for someone she can admire and respect. She is disinclined, in the twentieth century, to feed the male ego or to grant a man status simply because he has been born male.

Sexually the Choleric woman may fail to achieve orgasm. She may be ruled more by her head than her heart and have her mind on other matters during the sexual act. Much will depend on early encounters; if these are unsatisfactory she may find it increasingly difficult to participate fully. Many Choleric women feel that during sex they are submitting to the male and allowing him to dominate, and this they may be unwilling to do. She will respond best to the mature man who has a strong intellectual relationship with her and who understands her need to admire her partner at all levels and at the same time have his love and respect. Above all, for her to fully enjoy the experience he must have her respect and be at least her intellectual equal. Given the nature and intelligence of the Choleric woman this is not easy to achieve.

As with the man, if the Choleric female has decided to be proficient in sexual matters she can be a highly imaginative and exciting lover. If the relationship is between two strong Stage III Cholerics the result can be dynamite. If she has a less strong partner she is likely to take the dominant role. Many men will be willing to let her take the lead and thus satisfy her needs, giving her the combination of power and proficiency that allows her to be fully involved and satisfied. If he is willing she will either be the active partner, physically, or will be active mentally, telling him just what she wants him to do. If he is not willing to let her be the leader, and if he demands, even in bed, that she, knowing herself to be the stronger of the two, should still massage his ego and make him feel good she is unlikely to enjoy the event or wish to participate frequently. She may even come to despise herself for submitting and him for being a weakling, and in time may refuse to participate at all.

With maturity and development the Choleric woman learns to adapt to her role in the partnership and thus to enrich it. Her best hope is that she matures fast, to Stage III, and develops a wider understanding of the values and views of other people's temperaments and natures. In this way she can enjoy the fun and excitement of the Sanguine without being irritated by his weaker qualities or she can learn to work with rather than in conflict with a Choleric partner. The Stage III Choleric woman has learnt to handle the situations that develop. She no longer needs to be seen as the strong one. She is content with herself and within herself. She has nothing to prove.

The Choleric at Home

Cholerics are the most independent of the temperaments, sure of themselves and content to rely on themselves. For this reason they may, while single, live alone. However, they do enjoy company; after all, the king or queen needs their subjects and so may choose to share accommodation. If they do it is probably they who sign the lease and are in control, and they who decide who will share with them rather than the other way around.

The Choleric bachelor needs his pad for his conquests, a place where he can stamp his authority. The Choleric female, too, is likely to prefer to socialise round her own home than around the home of others. For these reasons, too, they tend to live alone.

Cholerics do not like to live in a mess, although they are more likely to have someone clean it for them than to do it themselves. Choleric males are very reluctant housekeepers. Choleric females will do it if necessary but are more likely to have a job or a career and pay a housekeeper. They like the home to be an organised and a proper background for themselves. But their idea of tidying is to fling clothes in the cupboard or in the washing machine and slam the doors. Dust can go under the carpet; the plates get hidden in the dishwasher. They are unlikely, even if they do look after their own place, to spend time on the finer details.

Their home is not likely to be as brightly coloured or as elegant as that of the Sanguine, or as neatly organised as that of the Phlegmatic, although they do like a measure of organisation. It won't be fussy, but some thought will have gone into creating an appropriate backdrop, something that will impress not in the Sanguine's showy way, but that will demonstrate the Choleric's substance. The Choleric male may go in for white furniture and black sheets, or a house full of chrome and glass. They may also go for the traditional look with lots of heavy masculine furniture and dark greens and crimson. The Choleric woman may have an elegant home, uncluttered and in flat colours or bold patterns. Broad sweeps rather than fussy detail will be the order of the day.

Cholerics are generally intelligent and well read. They look to the written word for information and acquire books almost without trying and then treasure them. You are likely to see shelves and walls of books in several rooms: they will keep all the books they have bought and refer to them frequently. The books bear witness to the

Choleric's many and varied interests. It must have been the Cholerics of olden times who set up the family library, large or small, maintained it and added to it. Mind you, the occasional Melancholic or Phlegmatic was needed to organise and catalogue it.

Cholerics are gregarious and like to entertain, rather in the manner of the king handing out largesse. They will have large parties or exciting dinners of eight to a dozen. They will dispense the food and the wine with a flourish but, if they can afford it, it is probably ordered in rather than cooked lovingly at home. Their wine cellar is usually good.

On the other hand they do not want over-frequent socialising or disruptions to their life. They do not want people dropping in at all hours and disrupting what they are doing. Not for them the nurturing open house of the Melancholic, nor do they want to accept whoever chooses to call; they would rather be in control and issue the invitations to the people they select. Besides, casual guests may not be convenient. The Choleric may be entertaining the partner of the moment, with bed being firmly on the agenda.

There is much to do in their lives and they want to get on with things. Once married they are likely to turn their focus more firmly on their career, hobbies or whatever else is important to them. The partner of the married Choleric may initiate much of their social life, especially if they are Sanguine. Do not expect Cholerics to remember important dates and anniversaries – and do not be sad when they don't. Such dates mean little to them and the forgetting of them is of little consequence to the Choleric and tells you little about the way they feel.

The introverted Choleric, left to their own devices, may get lost in their books and ideas, or in their current project, and need to be reminded to eat or come up for air. When they do they may be faced with an empty fridge, the Choleric having their mind on grander things than the plans for the next meals.

When they do shop it is likely to be a case of buying a variety of foods that they like on the assumption that when they want a meal they will have sufficient ingredients to hand to make one. Not for them the Phlegmatic's method of planning the next three days' meals in detail and then going out and buying precisely the right ingredients.

The ornaments round the house are likely to be bold and striking rather than pretty, the colours strong rather than delicate pastels. The grounds and garden will also reflect the grandeur and substance that the Choleric feels is their right.

The Choleric Parent

The Choleric parent likes to rule. When this desire to be in control focuses on the family they take parenthood seriously and are conscious of creating and training the next generation. They can be dedicated, devoted and single-minded and the children may well be a major focus of their life. They may work long hours to provide for their family, but when at home they spend time with their children, who in turn realise that they are important to the parent.

Choleric women can make wonderful mothers so long as they find sufficient outlets for their talents and do not feel trapped at home. If they do they are likely to feel frustrated and irritable and take this out on the children. Immature Cholerics can be intolerant of their children, expecting more of them than they can accomplish. Mature Cholerics make wonderful parents.

Cholerics are not always verbally fluent and may have trouble expressing their emotions clearly in words, yet they express them in the secure environment they provide for their children and the caring authority with which they rule it. To compensate for their lack of verbal endearments they may be physically demonstrative, dispensing hugs and playing games.

Firm discipline is provided for the children, who had better listen well the first time. The Choleric parent does not like to be disregarded or to have to repeat instructions. Discipline is usually orderly and consistent if the parent has matured, but may be erratic if they themselves have not grown up.

They make sure that a good education is provided and want their children to both have and be the best. They will applaud all achievements and signs of courage and striving. The mature Choleric will handle the less capable child with encouragement and support, but the less mature Choleric will be dismayed to find that a child of theirs is weak, timid or in the lower half of the class. They may try to assist but their impatience is likely to show through, and the more timid and nervous the child the more impatient the immature Choleric parent is likely to be. They may chivvy the child along, telling it to go ahead and get on with things, rather than show understanding and work gently to bring out the best in the child.

Father will enjoy and applaud the son who wants to go out and play football and climb trees. He will have less sympathy for the son who likes to stay home and paint pictures. He will applaud the girl who is not afraid of heights or who will say what's on her mind, and have difficulty coping with the daughter who is shy and timid.

Choleric parents will either give the children the freedom they demanded for themselves and let them develop in their own chosen direction, offering advice, guidance or support along the way, or they will have very firm ideas as to what children should be like and what they should do as they grow up. There may be a strong expectation that they will follow in the Choleric parent's footsteps.

Cholerics who focus on their careers and their own lives take less interest in the children, feeling they have done what was required of them by providing the home and the income. They may work long hours and then, when they do come home, spend much of their free time on their own hobbies, not wishing to be encumbered by the children. These Cholerics will leave the children largely to their partner, expecting things to be taken care of for them on the home front.

The career-oriented Choleric mother has a tough time. Her maternal instincts will battle with her desire for a career and she may be so torn between the two that she feels she never accomplishes either side of her life satisfactorily. She may take the children to school herself, then rush off to her demanding job, make ample provision for after-school care and then race home, hopefully in time to have the evening meal with the children and spend the evening with them. She will endeavour to take charge in both areas and, because she is strong, may manage it, but it is a heavy demand. If she is fortunate she will either have a husband who pitches in and shares the joint load so they can have the best of both worlds, or she will have a husband who puts the children ahead of his career.

Like the Choleric father, the Choleric mother will expect instant obedience from the children and help around the house. Each child is likely to be given tasks and expected to do them.

In general, both parents provide a stable and secure home for their children with well defined rules, encouragement to accomplish and develop in life, and a freedom to expand and explore and develop courage. The child of Choleric parents will not hear the constant cry of 'Don't do so and so, you might get hurt.' The Choleric parent is more likely to encourage their children to take the initiative and to learn to cope with what life offers them.

If you are a strong and successful child you will enjoy your Choleric parents. If you are weak, timid, unsure of yourself and in the bottom half of the class, you may find them overwhelming and hard to live up to.

The Choleric parents who focus on the home and family are likely to devise exciting outings for the children, to take them sailing, climbing or skiing. They will expect the girls to keep up with the boys in many of these activities, and will have little time for timidity. They will encourage sports and the development of leadership.

The Choleric parents who focus their attention on their careers or their own social life are likely to be seen as distant authorities and held in some awe by the children, who will look to the other parent for gentle love and nurture.

The Choleric in Old Age

For people of all the temperaments, the way they are in old age depends on how much they have matured. This is particularly true for the Choleric, who is one of the more difficult to live with if they remain in Stage I and the most delightful if they have matured to Stage III.

Cholerics are unlikely to retire willingly or early and settle into quiet old age with little to do. If forced to retire by their employer they are likely to find some other activity. They may become consultants or company directors, passing on their years of experience, especially if they have matured, or they may find a retirement job or a small business they can buy, and get involved in that. If they work for themselves they are likely to continue working well past the conventional retiring age. They may even do this, if still in Stage I, to the detriment of the company they run, preferring to stay at the top and let it deteriorate rather than hand over the reins and feel sidelined.

If, however, they have some hobbies or interests outside their work about which they feel passionate, they may retire early and become fully involved in these. This is particularly so if they are not in a job that holds their attention or provides significant goals or a feeling of achievement.

A Stage I Choleric, in old age, is a sorry sight. They are probably bad tempered and angry. They may have few friends, having driven most of them away. They didn't mean to and they would have loved it if people had stood up to them and been their equal. However, if they have not learnt respect for others, if they have not learnt to acknowledge the beauty and wisdom of other people and other ways than their own of doing things, they may well be left on their own.

The angry spinster who frightens the children if their ball runs into her garden is almost a caricature. Yet she exists and is probably lonely and sad, though she would die rather than admit it, even to herself. She will insist she is fine, and the world is full of fools who are not worth her time. She may have searched all her life for a man she felt was worthy to be her husband. She may have driven many away by her strength and intolerance. She may have had a career, risen to the top and lost friends along the way, as her seniority and superiority increased.

Socially she may have made other women, content with their domestic lives and living within the domain of their husbands and families, feel inferior and nervous. She may frighten some of the men, who feel that she is looking down on them knowing she could have done their job better than they did. Her brusqueness and impatience with shop assistants and tradespeople who do not perform quickly and efficiently further alienates her.

Yet she has a big heart. She has much to give, if only someone would come along whom she can trust and respect and who can deserve it. The friends she does have are probably from many years earlier when she was, relatively, softer and more open-hearted. If you can see beneath her bite to the warm heart you could make a good friend. She does not mean to hurt: it is simply that she still hasn't learnt her own strength. If she is fortunate she will have nephews and nieces and a large family who will understand her.

The Stage I Choleric widow or married woman may be in a somewhat similar situation but softened or modified by the presence of her husband and/or children. Even so, she may be thought of as somewhat bad-tempered and irascible. The world is not, in general, tolerant of Stage I elderly Cholerics, especially the women.

The Stage I Choleric bachelor has a slightly better time of it. There are women around who are willing to brave his bark. There are also more single women around (widows, divorcees or spinsters) than single men, so he can play the field. He may still be in demand for dinner parties and still have friends, particularly men friends with whom he has worked or associated over the years.

The Stage I Choleric man who is married may also be lonely. He may have driven his children away, either on his own initiative because they have not conformed to his desires for them, or on theirs, when they could take his temper and his tongue-lashing no more. His wife may have been suitably cowed and have learnt to live with him, or she may have stood up to him, in which case the relationship is likely to be stormy.

Stage I Cholerics do not give in gracefully to old age. They are more likely to confront it and fight it than adapt to it. They may not live to a ripe old age. The demands they have put on themselves, however strong they are, may have taken their toll. Their tempers may have raised their blood pressure and their hearts may not take the strain. Many, however, in spite of this, have the strength of constitution to outlive some of their more relaxed counterparts.

If both members of a couple are Choleric and remain at Stage I they have probably been divorced for some time. If they are still together life is more likely to be marked by fights and arguments than by the harmony of peaceful companionship. It is also possible that they have come to take a perverse pleasure in these fights.

Stage II Cholerics present a happier picture. They will have mellowed somewhat, and will still be the focal point of their circle of friends. If single, they will fill their life with activities and have a variety of interests.

The fully matured Stage III Choleric is a delight. At work they are the guiding stars of the company and the younger employees. If at university, they will strive to gain grants for their research students, rather than monopolising the department. They, by their own choice, gradually take a back seat and encourage others to take over, taking delight in seeing their charges develop. They will leave their positions of authority, not because they have to but because they choose to, and because other interests are calling. These are the Cholerics who may be called on to consult or be directors: they are likely to have other interests to pursue. They have much to offer and have mellowed to the point where other people are comfortable with them.

In a family they may be the grandparents to whom the younger members come for advice and comfort. They will be the focal point of the extended family, the ones who have the Christmas gatherings to which all the other family members come. They will be providing support for divorced children and insecure grandchildren.

A few Cholerics, about one in five, are relatively introverted. In Stage III these may well have chosen to be and live on their own, or circumstances, such as the death of their partner, may have created this situation. They may be working for themselves or working on their own as a lone leader at the top of a well-run organisation. They will have given their children a freedom and independence that allows for good relationships but not necessarily close living conditions. They are self-sufficient, active and happy. They generally find themselves good company, have lots of interests and hobbies and are just as content on their own as in a crowd. Having nothing to prove any more, they may set out to explore new horizons, ones of their own choosing and often invisible to other people. Whereas in Stages I and II their success in the public eye had at least some importance, now it is their own approbation that matters. They are in clear distinction to elderly Stage I Cholerics who are alone because of their irascibility.

If both members of a couple are Stage III Choleric and have survived this far, they will almost certainly have a strong and rich relationship together.

Health and the Choleric

Cholerics are generally robust and healthy. They also assume that they will stay that way. They have a solid chunky body with strong joints and dense bones. They expect much of their body and, in general, their body doesn't let them down.

Broken bones will occur because of the risks they take and the challenges they face. They will dare to climb the highest tree or scale the steepest precipice. They play contact sports and are daredevils. If injured they will still endeavour to be mobile. They will see no reason to stay at home and take time off. If necessary they will devise ingenious ways of getting around and will demand that the cast comes off sooner rather than later.

If they get sick they are surprised and impatient: surprised that their body has let them down and impatient at the disruption to their lives. When pains or symptoms start they will be ignored. Cholerics struggle on at work even if they do have a cold or get the flu. A sore throat and lost voice doesn't stop them: they simply write notes, and when they feel strongly they write in large letters and thrust them in your face.

When they are eventually forced to go to a doctor they will expect to be treated and the problem solved in one visit and with one quick remedy so they can put the affair behind them and get on with life.

If they get a dithering old doctor who wants to do a whole series of tests they will grow impatient and find a modern young one who can give them the desired quick fix. If they find a doctor who is sympathetic and gentle and advises them to take time off they will find one who is more dynamic, understands time is important and can ensure an instant cure.

On the whole, and in Stage I, they are likely to be impatient if told to change their lifestyle, slow down, give up junk food, cut down on sugars and fats or drink less coffee or alcohol. Just as they expect their body to stay healthy they expect it to be able to deal with their chosen lifestyle. If this includes business lunches, whisky-drinking board meetings, long hours and jet travel they expect to be able to take this in their stride. As they head towards Stage III they are more likely to see the wisdom of treating their body with consideration and modifying their lifestyle, thus prolonging their life.

They should pay particular attention to their heart and circulation. They can live at high levels of anger and tension, of aggression and striving, blood pressure can rise and the heart can suffer. The old stereotype of the red-faced bucolic, portly and well-fed businessman or family head is close to the mark, certainly at Stage I before they have developed a less irascible approach to life.

They can be the fast, go-go, type A person who develops ulcers as well as being at risk of heart attack. But if the Choleric does get an ulcer it will have more to do with anger, temper, impatience and frustration than with fear or gnawing worries. Maturing to Stage III fast can have a very beneficial effect on their physical health.

The Choleric When Things Go Wrong

Cholerics are normally in power, in control of their life. They are self-confident and independent. They are the leaders, the successful people who have their life in order. As they mature they mellow, learn respect for others and tolerance, and learn to channel their energies into constructive ends. When things go wrong this process can go into reverse.

The biggest problem for Cholerics who deteriorate is their temper and their certainty in themselves, which can turn into arrogance and bullying.

The young executive on the way up may make a mistake and be reprimanded. They may then walk out of the office fuming, claiming they have been insulted and that their brilliant work is being misunderstood or stolen. They will then storm into their own office and abuse their staff, blaming them for the problem. In the process they may do serious and permanent damage to relationships.

When a Choleric is trapped in a situation from which they cannot escape they can become like a caged tiger. The Choleric wife who suddenly has to give up her career and the daily contact with adult minds that she desires, for whatever reasons – pregnancy, family responsibilities, the demands of her husband – is likely to lash out in frustration at anyone who is near. She must learn to sublimate or find new outlets for her abilities and independence or she will hurt the people around her and may drive them away.

Choleric parents, when thwarted, frustrated or irritated by their children, can lose their temper once too often, and say things they will later regret. It is probably a Choleric parent who shows a disobedient child the door and tells them they are not welcome in the house again. It is usually done on the spur of the moment but it is nearly impossible for the immature or deteriorating Choleric to apologise for this behaviour or ask the child to come back.

When things go badly wrong Cholerics can become tyrants. The men can beat their wives and bully their staff or employees. They can become thugs and criminals. They may even come to enjoy violence, fighting and beating the other person. Women can also follow this pattern, though usually without the same level of physical violence.

Both sexes can become emotional and verbal tyrants, little Hitlers and Napoleons, lashing out with their fists and with their tongues. They can terrorise their families and the neighbourhood. They may get jobs where they can use their violence and give it free rein, jobs in which they are given power over others who cannot or are not allowed to defend themselves. If they are mentally stable, the decisions they make will be conscious and they will glory in the results.

If life gets too much for the Choleric, if they lose control of themselves physically and mentally and follow this direction to its conclusion they can become violent criminals, killing for the sake of killing, raping for the sake of raping. They can glory in their violence and the power it gives them. They can become sadists, enjoying the pain of others, violent pain that they have inflicted. In this way, if in no other, they can gain the authority they crave, unleash the temper they can no longer control.

If they become totally insane they are likely to be violent, verbally, emotionally and physically, and may have to be restrained for their own and others' good.

What the Choleric Can Teach Us

Many of our stable values have been eroded in the modern world. No longer is there an established way of doing things. No longer are there the social structures by which we used to live and which provided security. In past centuries, even a few decades ago, if you were unsure of what to do, what to say or how to behave, you went to your parents, your church or your elders for advice and guidance. You could rely on social structures and doing things in the right way, the way they had always been done.

You might not have had to choose a career: family tradition did that for you. You might not have had to make moral decisions about the way you lead your life: social traditions did that for you. If the established society in which you lived dictated that women stayed at home, then women did stay at home. You did not have to make the choice between motherhood and a career, between fighting or avoiding the draft, between marrying your pregnant girlfriend or not: society made the decision for you. You may not have liked it, but you could follow the rules, knowing that society would approve. If you were unsure you could turn to established procedures for guidance.

Today, people have to rely on themselves. They have to make their own decisions, either actively or by default. The buck stops here. While for many this concept of self-responsibility is exciting and liberating, for others it is frightening. People will go a long way to find others to lean on, to ask for advice, to find out what they should do. When things go wrong these same people look for others to blame for their faults, their problems and the decisions that turned out badly. The problem is, 'other people' often have their own uncertainties and insecurities.

This is where Cholerics come in. Cholerics, especially mature ones, can provide the rock that others are looking for. Cholerics are wonderfully strong leaders, they are independent, daring and courageous. They rely on themselves: they will go out on a limb, knowing that somehow, whatever happens and if things do not work out, they will manage, in some way, to get back to safety.

Mature Cholerics are not only willing to have other people lean on them, they are worthy of others' trust. While I am not advocating that you find someone to depend on rather than taking responsibility for your own life, if you do need such a person at the present stage of your development, and if you truly want wise counsel, support and development rather than weak-kneed dependency, then a mature Choleric is the person you should seek.

Mature Cholerics are capable of providing the environment in which other people can take their first steps to independence. They will teach the child to swim, standing back and letting them try on their own while at the same time letting the child know that they are there, should things go seriously wrong. They will provide the business opportunity for the budding entrepreneur, guiding if necessary but not interfering.

By their own example Cholerics are the stuff of heroes. They display courage and bravery, initiative and independence, strength and tenacity as a model for others to aim at. They show the rest of the world that it can be done, that it is worth striving for and that individuals can be strong and successful. They demonstrate leadership and show others what it can mean.

By the act of maturing, themselves, they show that self-development and growth are not only possible but rewarding and worth the effort. Maturing from Stage I to Stage III is a big effort for Cholerics, but the rewards are great. They are also visible to others and are respected and applauded.

Cholerics demonstrate great intelligence; they push out the known barriers of our world. It is the Cholerics who will launch us into space. They have the knowledge, they have the desire and they have the courage. If space is not your goal, these same characteristics can be applied to other areas of life.

These are dominantly male characteristics and life is, in general, easier for the Choleric male than the Choleric female, even in the twentieth century, though things are changing. For the female Choleric to mature from Stage I to Stage III and to do it successfully within the female framework is a great achievement. These women can show other women how to take their place in a society that is at last coming to realise that each sex constitutes about 50 per cent of the human race. Mature Choleric women can be a great inspiration to the rest of their sex as they strive to find their own identity as independent people and their place in the emerging social structures where women are entering all areas of life.

CHAPTER 11

The Melancholic Temperament

Like each of the other temperaments, the Melancholic has unique characteristics which are modified as the individual moves through the three stages. There is a very great difference between a Stage I Melancholic and a Stage III Melancholic.

Main Characteristics

In general, Melancholics are sensitive, deep, understanding and caring. People and relationships are very important to them. They are idealistic with a clear set of values and a drive to make the world a better place. They like peace and quiet, they are artistic and creative. They may also be pessimistic. They have many wonderful qualities, as we shall see in later chapters, and the rest of us are the richer for having them around. It is important to keep this in mind as we go through their growth stages as Melancholics can, on the face of it, and if you focus on the name, seem to be dreary and depressing people. This is far from the truth.

Melancholics are also difficult to understand. The other three temperaments can generally understand each other, even if they don't feel the same way themselves, but the Melancholic is a mystery. In turn, Melancholics fail to see the importance of the achievement, fun or duty that matter to the Cholerics, Sanguines and Phlegmatics respectively. Melancholics are deep thinkers, searching for the meaning of life and for their true inner selves. This may lead them into deep meditation, to spiritual paths or a religious life. It may lead them to shun material values. It certainly leads to the high level of importance they place on people and relationships and their meanings.

Life Path

A Stage I Melancholic is a pessimistic introvert deeply involved in the past and in their own inner feelings, their problems and all the dreadful things that have happened, are happening and could happen, both to them and those around them. A Stage III Melancholic is a quiet caring person who shows concern for other people, who is perceptive of the needs of others, is understanding and compassionate. They have changed from focusing on themselves, being selfish and drowning in their problems, to focusing on others and being caring and understanding. They have grown from a restless search for meaning to quiet inner peace.

This is how the progression occurs.

Stage I

Stage I Melancholics know the world is a difficult place with huge problems to be solved. They are unhappy at all times, for two reasons that between them cover all the possibilities. On the one hand, if things in their lives, are going badly they feel bad. On the other hand, if things are going well they live in constant expectation that the good times cannot last and that something dreadful is about to happen. If the good times do last they will search and probe until eventually and unwittingly they create a problem.

There is no joyous bouncing out of bed in the morning for this Melancholic. Instead they are more likely to wake up searching for the meaning of life and wondering if it is worth living, if there is anything really worth getting up for, and if anything good could possibly happen in the day ahead, which already looks drab and grey. They carry the cares of the world, especially of themselves and their own world, on their shoulders.

In direct contrast to the Sanguine, Melancholics always notice that the glass is half empty rather than half full. They will hear only the bad news and not the good, they will read the horror headlines and miss the positive announcements, they consider the person killed in an accident and not the miracle that the other three are alive. To the Melancholic the pain is more obvious than the pleasure, the fear is stronger than the hope, the failures are more glaring than the successes.

Beauty is in the eye of the beholder and the eyes, ears and emotions of the Stage I Melancholic are all tuned to the same wavelength, that of the negative, bad, depressing and hopeless. This makes them very depressing people to be around but it can lead to wonderful results when they mature.

The Stage I Melancholic is the typical wet blanket. You hear them saying 'I'd be better off dead', 'You'd be better off without me', 'No one loves or appreciates me' and 'I'm no use to anyone'. What they want, of course, is reassurance that this is not so, yet there is little you can say to convince them for, deep down, they know, they absolutely know, that this is the truth.

When you ask a Stage I Melancholic how they are, they will tell you – in detail. They like to have your full attention and one way to get it is to keep talking. Since they are self-involved they will tell you about themselves. Since they are pessimistic they will tell you about their problems and particularly about their health – their bad health, of course. They will tell you about their headache, their back pain, their insomnia, the stress that's stirring up their ulcer and about a variety of things they are afraid are about to happen to them. It is very easy for a Melancholic to be a hypochondriac. The smallest pain is, they know, an indication of some serious ailment. Woe betide the doctor who tries to assure them that it's just a mild virus. The Melancholic knows better, knows that it really is serious but that the doctor does not want to frighten them by explaining. The Melancholic always has 'dreadful insomnia' and 'never sleeps a wink', even though their partner may complain of their snores. The Melancholic is in constant pain, even if they forget which leg to limp on.

The Melancholic also focuses on the past and dwells a lot on what has happened to them as well as what is currently happening. Not that things happen to this Melancholic, who does not initiate events but is the passive receiver of whatever fate has in store.

If you are so foolish as to greet a Stage I adult Melancholic with such a seemingly innocuous opening as 'Hello, lovely day isn't it? How are you?' you will find you have opened a veritable Pandora's box, and a negative one at that. If you comment that it's a lovely day, the Melancholic will list all the things that are or could be wrong. If you are not careful you will find yourself pinned to the ground, metaphorically at least, and anchored for half an hour.

Mary's neighbour, Geoff was like that. He was a morose old bachelor in his sixties and retired. Mary, a gregarious soul, would make a point of talking to him each morning as she left for work and each evening as she came home, since he was frequently in his garden, almost as if waiting for her. When she first started this practice the conversations would go something like this:

'Good morning Geoff, how are you? Lovely day, isn't it?'

'No good. With all this sun the paint on my roof is peeling. The garden is so dry I'll have to spend ages today watering it, and I've got to go to the supermarket and the car gets so hot in the car park. It's no good, you just get hot and sticky.'

Mary did her best to cheer Geoff, but to no avail.

The next day was overcast so Mary thought she was on safe ground.

'Good morning Geoff,' she called as she walked down to her car.

'What's good about it?' he wanted to know, as he gazed dolefully at her from the kitchen window. 'All this rain will make the drive muddy, I cleaned the car yesterday and now it'll get dirty when I go into town – and I won't be able to mow the lawn and it badly needs it.'

Thinking to cheer him up and remind him of the previous day's conversation, Mary was foolish enough to comment that with all the rain at least he wouldn't have to water the garden.

'That's all very well, but this sort of rain washes the topsoil off the rockery,' was his parting comment as she drove off.

It is easy to fall into the trap of thinking that Melancholics want to be cheered up, consoled, encouraged to feel that life is not all bad or assured that good times are just around the corner. Nothing could be further from the truth. The last thing a Stage I Melancholic wants is to be made happy. They do want to be understood and commiserated with and they do want to be the focus of other people's care and concern. But rather than be cheered up they want you to realise how bad, sad and difficult everything is and to join them in their state of melancholia.

Eventually Mary learnt how to deal with her Melancholic neighbour. Now their morning conversation goes something like this:

'Morning Geoff, dreadful morning isn't it?'

'Yes, it's so hot the paint is peeling on the house.'

'I know, and you'll have to water the garden and that'll take ages.'

After a few more such complaints and commiserations Geoff finally gets the feeling that Mary really does recognise what an uncomfortable day it is and what a difficult time he's going to have. He is then able to say something like, 'Well at least I can dry the washing out.'

Once he knows that there is general agreement about the bad things, he can finally begin to contemplate, however tentatively, some of the more positive aspects and to feel slightly less sad. This is the way you can bring a Melancholic out of their melancholia, for a while at least, and permit them to be comfortable in the experience of a mild degree of optimism.

Keep in mind the double-bind in which Stage I Melancholics find themselves. They are unhappy when things are going badly or when those around them are sad, and this, rightly, seems to them to be totally appropriate. When times are tough you feel down and depressed. So far so good. But they are also unhappy when surrounded by people who are happy or when things are going well. This is not because they want other people to be unhappy but because they know the world is tough and that something bad is certain to happen soon. The thought hangs over their mind like the sword of Damocles and they wish the bad and dreadful things that they anticipate would happen and be done with it.

Donald was a Melancholic, his wife Sarah an extrovert Choleric. She regularly worked four nights a week. Then, on the evening they usually went out, Sarah was persuaded that a late business meeting was very important for her and that she should go. Donald gave his consent, content to suffer, and not mentioning there was something else he also wanted to do. It turned out to be a thoroughly boring evening for her and a total waste of time, run by a man who, in Sarah's opinion, was an idiot and pathetic, assessments an irritated and impatient Choleric will make rapidly. By the time she was able to leave and drive home she was in a filthy temper. When she got home an unsuspecting Donald asked, 'How was it dear?'

Well, she told him, she really let rip.

'He was an idiot. It was a total waste of time. He's a jumped-up squirt. He told us things that are so obvious you can take them for granted and he thought they were a big deal – bloody idiot. And then all he could do was tell us how good he was and read us testimonials to his achievements . . .'

There was more in this vein but in time Sarah ran out of breath and began to relax a bit, enough to say, 'The worst thing of all is that right now I'm in such a filthy mood I'm spoiling the little bit of time we have together.'

'That's all right,' said Donald, 'I was feeling dreadful before you came.' [when things seemed to be going well] 'I'm feeling better now' [because I am right in my assumption that things usually go wrong].

The answer, typical of a Melancholic, first floored Sarah, then allowed her to relax and stop feeling guilty for her bad mood and the ruined evening. She could even draw comfort from the fact that in some oblique way Donald was happier than if she had come in having had a wonderful time.

Is there anything that the Melancholic does enjoy? Yes, there are many things as we shall see, but it can also be said that the Melancholic does enjoy suffering. If you have ever been through a bad experience and felt dreadful, yet at some moment during that time become aware with even a small part of yourself that there is a certain pleasure or satisfaction in feeling depressed, you are experiencing the Melancholic aspect of your nature.

Melancholics take a perverse pleasure from things that go wrong. One neighbour would come visiting two or three times a week, popping in with the latest news from the village. If he arrived with a smile we would know there was something really bad to report. This was not because he liked people to suffer, but because the world was living up to his expectations and he could enjoy the drama of the event and the drama involved in imparting the news.

Melancholics enjoy sympathy. Sometimes it's as if they don't have much confidence that you will like or love them but they do feel they can rely on getting your sympathy. This is true of the full, 100 per cent Melancholic in Stage I. It is also true of everyone when they are expressing the Melancholic side of their nature. Think of the times you and people you know have used hard-luck stories as a way of getting attention or breaking the ice in social situations.

When a Melancholic is suffering they may well expect you to suffer with them. If they have to go on a diet they want you to be on it too, whether it is to lose weight, because they have allergies or because of their bad digestion. If they have to stay at home they want you to do the same: why should you have a good time when they can't? Besides, they need your care and attention.

Not inclined to keep their troubles to themselves, Melancholics, oblivious to the feelings of others, will pour out their woes to anyone who will listen. This is not so much extroversion as the outward expression of their inward involvement and their desire for you to become involved in their problems.

There is no point in trying to chivvy them out of their negative moods, being cross with them when they fail at something you feel they should have accomplished, or being critical of their character traits. They will simply agree with you. You cannot challenge them out of their depression.

If the Melancholic husband comes home having lost a client or failed to get a promotion, there is no point in your becoming impatient or challenging him by telling him he is inadequate: he will simply agree and say you should divorce him, you would be better off without him. If the Melancholic wife is too depressed to keep the house clean and her husband complains, she too is likely to break down and cry, saying he'd be better off without her, he should never have married her, he'd be happier if she was dead.

Many parents have trouble dealing with the Melancholic child. What do you do when, each time they are taken to task for not doing well at school or for a misbehaviour, they say they knew all along that no one loved them, that they were no good, that they were a burden to their family? Criticism confirms them in their negative beliefs. However, for many Melancholics this is a useful, if unconscious, tactic for getting their needs meet.

They will use this tactic to get the praise, compliments or reassurances they need. They will say 'I'm no good', 'You don't really want me on your team', 'I'll never get the job' or some other such negative statement, fishing all the time for reassurances to the contrary. However, since they continue to believe the worst, they may have to repeat this many times and eventually other people get bored. When others stop paying the compliments, the Melancholic is free to assume that their responses weren't really true and that the Melancholic's negative view is indeed the right one.

They also find it hard to receive compliments. Whereas the Sanguine will revel in a remark such as 'What a beautiful dress, how pretty you look', the Melancholic will brush it off with 'Oh, it's just some old thing I've had for ages.'

If you *can* divert the Melancholic's attention from the past to the future you will find they anticipate the worst. If it's to be an outdoor event they are sure it is going to rain. If they have bought shares in a company – an unlikely thing for a Melancholic to do since they prefer to put their money safely in the bank – they are immediately convinced the price will fall. If they plan to have visitors they become convinced that everything will be a disaster: the house will be found wanting, the meal won't be a success, the guests won't like each other. When they buy tickets for a play, book a holiday or order some goods, they start to fret that the outcome will be less than satisfactory.

Many Melancholics actually relish having bad, unfortunate or sad things happen to them. They then rehearse in their minds the tale with which they will regale people. This they enjoy; they also enjoy the anticipation of the sympathy the story will arouse. Further, they then enjoy the actual telling of the tale to anyone who will listen and the sympathy they do receive. As a result they spend much of their time hoping something bad will happen. If nothing bad does happen they may even, by small, even unconscious, words or deeds, precipitate such a situation.

> Belinda had promised Sue, a Melancholic, that she would help with the preparations for a dinner party. Sue suspected that Belinda was most likely to be free in the late afternoon, yet she worked flat out all morning getting ready, muttering to herself about Belinda's unreliability when she didn't turn up before lunch, and then she just 'had' to go to the shops in the late afternoon. Later, when Belinda phoned to say she had called round but there was no one at home, Sue said that she had been in all morning hoping for help. That night at the party she was able to be the martyr to Belinda and to complain to her husband of all she had had to do, and without any help.

The Stage I Melancholic has little time for other Melancholics – certainly not for another Stage I Melancholic, since both would want to talk about themselves and neither would be interested in listening to or sympathising with the other.

All this may sound somewhat extreme, but remember that we are describing the 100 per cent Melancholic, untempered with the Choleric drive, the Sanguine gaiety or the Phlegmatic calm. We are also considering the Stage I Melancholic who has failed to mature to the next stage.

Melancholics may consider suicide. They may or may not do it, but they will give it much thought. As a part of their search for the meaning of life they often contemplate the end of their life. If they can find no answer in this search for meaning they may begin to wonder whether or not life *is* worth living. They wonder what it would be like to die. They may consider possible ways they could kill themselves or they may imagine something happening to them – an incurable illness, an accident – that would bring about their end. They may consider what the people around them would feel like, but if they do it will be in the light of having made other people, by their death, realise how unhappy they had been in life, to make other people feel sorry they hadn't been more understanding of the Melancholic's problems.

One client, Marguerite, was about to go overseas on holiday with her girl friend. She had often considered suicide and was afraid that at any time, on the spur of the moment and given the right opportunity, such as an open window, a cliff face, or heavy traffic in a crowded street, she might kill herself. She did worry about her friend, explaining to me that her friend was very dependent and would be unable to cope if left alone in a foreign country. I chose a rather unusual option. I said that if she promised not to commit suicide while they were away I would help her when she got back. She looked surprised that I wasn't immediately commiserating with her and trying to persuade her not to commit suicide at all, but she did agree. When she returned she had clearly given the matter a lot of thought and explained that she wasn't absolutely sure she wanted to do it after all; instead she felt she should focus on what she really wanted to accomplish instead of trying to fit in with everyone else.

When another client told me she was considering suicide, I asked her how she wanted to do it and who she wanted to find the body. This startled her, as did my next question: whether or not she had made a will and who she wanted to have her possessions. As in Marguerite's case, this shook her out of her self-absorption and made her realise that life would still go on without her. Not getting the response from me that she had expected, in time she came to realise that what she really wanted was other people's care and attention.

George sat across the desk from me on his fourth visit looking as doleful as on his first visit. We had already established that the health problems he'd had when he first came had been resolved, so I asked him if there was anything that was still troubling him.

'Oh no,' he said, 'just life in general, but no one can do anything about that.'

'What's the problem?'

I was curious because I knew he had a good job in his chosen profession, sufficient money for his lifestyle and desires, and was content in his marriage.

'Oh, well,' he said, and sighed, something Melancholics do a lot, 'there really isn't much point in it, is there? There's nothing to look forward to each day, is there?'

I looked at the case history questionnaire he had filled in on his first visit and noticed that he had put a tick against 'Suicidal feelings'.

'Do you often consider suicide?' I asked

'Oh, every day, doesn't everyone? But there doesn't seem much point in doing it.'

Keep in mind, as we said earlier, that this description, as that for all the temperaments, is given as if you or the person concerned are wholly and totally one temperament, untempered by any of the other three, and stuck in Stage I. This is rarely the case; other factors commonly affect this somewhat sombre picture.

Maturing

The Melancholic longs for understanding, for recognition of their problems, for love and affection. They are self-absorbed and consequently selfish, but they would be amazed if you told them so. They are lonely and yet they are unhappy when they are with happy people and, in Stage I, not interested in other people's problems; they want to talk about themselves. They would also like to be taken out of themselves. It's almost as if they would like permission to be happy but that they know, deep down, they dare not be and that if they are, and if they allow themselves to be positive, they will be deluding themselves and be living in a fools' paradise.

Trying to cheer them up is definitely not the way to help a Melancholic. Instead, sympathise with them and acknowledge the troublesome things that could happen. Then, and only then, will they feel confident that you understand the problems that exist. Then they can relax a little and, if not fully convinced that everything will turn out for the best, they can at least begin to realise that they'll be able to cope with what happens and that they have your understanding and support. They need this deeper understanding of their true nature rather than the cheer of an unthinking optimist.

Another beneficial way to lead a Stage I Melancholic into Stage II is to arouse their sympathy. Give them someone worse off than they are and ask them to care for the sufferer. Tell them you know they can help and will be able to look after them.

The wise teacher will give the new girl at school, crying on the edge of the playground, to the Melancholic child saying something like, 'Here you are, Dorothy. Jennifer is new and frightened – remember how dreadful you felt on your first day? I'm sure you can help her, so will you be her special friend and look after her?'

Dorothy will either profess herself too miserable to help anyone else or will be ready to develop a little and will agree to befriend the lonely new girl.

The wise hostess will find the gloomy guest out on the balcony and ask him to come in and help with a dreadful situation that she feels is about to arise between two guests. The Melancholic who is ready to move to Stage II will help out, provided that the need is genuine. A fake call for help is easily spotted and drives them further into themselves.

When you are trying to help a Melancholic to mature do not let them take charge. Do as Mary did with Geoff: sympathise with each problem but move them swiftly on to the next one, until they have run out of problems about which to complain or feel anxious. If you let them take over and dwell on each negative issue they can all too easily remain in or revert to Stage I. They will abuse the sympathy and friendship you are offering and, quite possibly, grind you down into melancholia with them. Keep the conversation moving.

Another way you can assist is to ask them to make a sacrifice. Ask them to put themselves out for you: run an errand, water your garden when you're away, visit a sick friend, do some task for you, or give up something they enjoy. They will complain but, at the same time, be secretly pleased that something has been asked of them; they are comfortable as martyrs although they will never tell you this. Do not, however, take their deeds for granted. Thank them well. Show them that you appreciate what they have done and that you realise how big a demand you have made, how much you have asked of them.

You can build on this process. Ask them again, even when they've told you how difficult it will be. Subconsciously they know that life is best when they are doing things for others, yet they are not yet ready to do this voluntarily: the inflicted inconvenience is part of what makes them feel good. They may even feel dissatisfied with you if you don't make sufficient demands on them.

Ask the Melancholic secretary to stay behind in the office after the others leave, explaining that there is still urgent work that needs to be done. They will mutter about the, possibly imaginary, event they are missing but they will feel valued and appreciated. Ask a Melancholic friend to make a fourth at bridge and let them know that you're aware they'd rather be watching television but that you need them or the evening will be ruined. They will value this as an expression of friendship. Then be sure to show your appreciation for what they've done and your awareness of how you've imposed on them.

A would-be cheerful comment such as, 'There you are, you see Tom, that was pretty good wasn't it, much better than watching television yet again?' will drive him back into himself. Whereas a comment such as 'Thank you so much Tom, I know you'd have had a better evening watching television but the three of us really appreciate you giving that up so we could have a fourth' will make him feel good and even leave him hoping you'll need him again – though he'll never ask to join in. That would suggest he was enjoying himself and would deprive him of the good feeling of being asked to make a sacrifice.

If you are a Melancholic, one way to help in your own development is to discipline yourself. Make the effort to focus on the positive rather than on the negative, to focus on the good things that happen rather than on the bad. Promise yourself you will not say a word to other people about anything negative that has happened to you. The degree to which you find this difficult will be some measure of your degree of Stage I melancholia. At first you will find this reduces your conversation dramatically. But as you are forced to talk about positive things, you will also find that, although initially this makes you feel uncomfortable, as you get used to it a more positive attitude develops within you.

Stage II

As the Melancholic moves into Stage II they develop sensitivity and empathy for others, especially those who are in pain, distress or need. They come out of themselves long enough to take an interest in the problems of others and to make an effort to help them. They have an intuitive capacity, when they stop being absorbed with themselves, to be aware of the emotions, needs, motivations and feelings of other people. Their idealism can also come to life and their desire to help, to give in such a way that suffering is eased, can also be given expression and develop.

As they become more sensitive to the needs of others they are likely to adapt to suit the other person. Many Melancholics have the ability to be all things to all people. Depending on the blending of the other temperaments, they respond to the needs and preferences of the other person by being more outgoing or more quiet, more sensual or more withdrawn, more the soulful listener or more the active provider. Your Melancholic friend may not believe in astrology but, if you do, they will discuss it with you endlessly. You may never even know they are a non-believer.

Their own thoughts about the idea that life is not worth living, and that there is little that they can enjoy or to which they can look forward, metamorphose into a search for their sense of self, for the meaning of their life, the true nature of reality. They want fully to *be* in every situation, to fully live in and experience the now in its subtlest depths. They are searching for the unknown outcome towards which they should strive. The Melancholic may also ponder for hours on what is beyond time, beyond this universe, beyond eternity, searching for their own significance in the vastness of reality. These aims are often misunderstood by the other temperaments, who fail to see the need for and the depth of the searching involved in this quest, nor do they recognise the goal.

The Melancholic can never succeed in achieving this goal of total understanding since, in a sense, they are trying to discover what the goal is. In my last book* I described clients who were depressed and who, when asked to define their goals, could find none. They included people who were unhappy with their job but couldn't think of a different one they would rather have, people who were bored but couldn't think of a hobby that would interest them, who had few friends but couldn't think of the type of person they would like to meet, who didn't like their house but didn't know what sort of house they would like or that would be worth the move. This is typical of

---

Beating the Blues, Heinemann, 1995.

the Melancholic searching for something yet not knowing what it is they are searching for.

The other temperaments may become impatient with the Melancholic's search for self, for their need for self-actualisation, for the hours they spend meditating on their inner nature and their spiritual depths. Whoever said 'Sometimes I sits and thinks, and other times I simply sits' was probably a Melancholic. Yet this search, as Hamlet knew well, is essential for the Melancholic: 'To be or not to be. . .'. Melancholics may spend hours and days in encounter groups, in group therapy, doing seminars, working on themselves, all in an effort to get to the core of their being.

They need and value time they can spend in quiet meditation. This is part of their growth and development. They are not being lazy: they need this time for inner contemplation. It may be painful for them to do without it. They may subscribe to a conventional religion, but only if they truly feel it can offer them the spiritual core for which they are searching, unlike the Phlegmatic who goes to church for the ritual, the stability and the traditional values it offers. With the many Eastern religions, philosophies and gurus now popular, Melancholics may well turn to one of these for the answers they seek.

By Stage II Melancholics begin to turn outwards. They pay attention to the needs of others and contribute more to their relationships with people. If they are considering a career they are likely to choose something they feel will make a worthwhile contribution in preference to something that will bring them joy and happiness. They do not look for pleasure or profit so much as for the chance to feel comfortable and to contribute and achieve something useful. They do not value material rewards; they do want to make a difference. They will look for work or a career that is significant rather than one that provides financial rewards or power.

They have to feel they have done something that counts at some deeper level. This may be large, as in saving lives on the world stage, or small, as in making someone feel good about some aspect of themselves. They may save a rain forest or refuse to put weedkiller on their tiny garden. They may adopt or foster a child, or simply comfort someone in distress. They may take up a cause, join a lobby or protest group, or spend time in voluntary service or community work. No matter the size of the task, they have to feel good about what they have done. At first this comes from the feeling of having made a sacrifice, being put upon or made use of. In time this develops to the point, as they move into Stage III, where they are content to feel good within themselves about the contribution they have made. I have a Melancholic friend who says he calls a day a good day only if he has done a favour for someone or helped someone.

As they mature, Melancholics become progressively more intuitive and aware of the feelings of other people, and this enables them to do well in the caring professions. But they may also, from time to time, lapse into self-involvement. Much as they want to contribute and give, they still want others to make demands of them and they still want the sacrifices they are making to be recognised.

As they mature and turn outwards they also develop their other interests: in the arts, in beauty and movement, in sights and sounds, in writing and in poetry. They are good communicators and good with language. They are also intellectual and scholarly, organised and conscious of details. Cholerics are precise communicators, scientifically accurate with words and shades of meaning and may write about factual and technical matters. Melancholics write soul-searching novels and beautiful poetry, rich in creative imagery and deep meaning. They write the books characterised by sensitive understanding of other people, both fiction and biographical and historical works. They create the characters in depth. Cholerics create more action. Sanguines, if they can sit still enough to write more than a short note, will write imaginative and creative fantasies, and Phlegmatics write reports, edit minutes and keep the records.

Melancholics tend to be perfectionists in the sense of wanting to do, to feel and to experience everything to the limit: they want to get to the full (perfect) meaning of their emotions and relationships and have a general need, as purists, to have everything just right. To the extent that Phlegmatics want to be perfect, it is because they want to do what's right, Cholerics because they want to be in control and dislike criticism, and Sanguines don't care too much as long as they get the compliments they love.

In Stage I, many Melancholics' desire for perfection can lead them into depression every time they find a fault in anything. They may take so long in the planning stage that the project is never completed. They may insist in doing it all themselves, sure that no-one else will take the same amount of care. As they mature into Stage II they learn to relax somewhat in this. They still strive for perfection but have learnt to do the best that is possible and then relax, enjoying what has been achieved instead of bemoaning what hasn't.

Maturing

Again, it is useful to have help in reaching the next stage of development, though in many ways the worst is over once the Melancholic has been brought out of Stage I. For many Melancholics this next move comes through the work they are already doing. The more they work with and help other people, the more they grow and develop. Appreciation and understanding are also important. You should still keep in mind that the way to lead a Melancholic forward is through understanding and empathy and not by trying to infuse laughter into their life.

If you want them to work on a project with you, remember to focus on the good they will be doing, and not on the personal gains they will make. It is now time for them to become more willing to enjoy themselves and comfortable with doing this. A blending of fun with the projects that interest them can lead them forward.

Stage III

By Stage III the Melancholic's interest has turned further outwards and is now directed at others. In fact, their interest in other people is often greater now than their self-interest, although they still need time for quiet contemplation. Much of this development will have come about through their own pain and suffering, through dealing with their own hardships and misfortunes, whether real or imagined. As a result of their introspective soul-searching they have begun to have a sense of who they are, of the meaning of life for them, and to have formulated, recognised and tested their spiritual or religious beliefs. Their development also comes through learning to help others and to contribute to society and the world around them. They have developed great compassion and can show true understanding of other people's problems, and they have learnt to give without it being asked of them.

They have not only developed but have harnessed and discovered how to fulfil their idealistic and noble goals, in so far as they have learnt how to define them. They continue to want to contribute, to make a difference, to add value, and by this stage they know how. They have become the carers and nurturers of the world. They may be in a caring profession such as nursing or counselling, or they may simply be the local listening post, the person other people feel they can turn to when in trouble.

If they reach Stage III when young, they may do some voluntary work rather than sow their wild oats before settling down.

In their middle years a Stage III Melancholic, struggling to make ends meet financially, will still adopt another child who is in need, foster a child that no-one else wants, or take on the care of an elderly relative. Once their own immediate responsibilities have been met, such as seeing their children through university, they may give up a well-paid job to work for the poor or to do other voluntary work.

The Stage III Melancholic may be the aunt or uncle that all the family goes to when the going gets tough, or the person in the office that the others take their problems to, not for the solution of the problem so much as for the care and understanding that is offered. They may be the old family doctor who is never too rushed to ask after your family, or the clergyman with time to hear your problems no matter how long his day has been. Whatever else they are, they are very different, at this stage, from the way they were in Stage I.

One thing is essential for the Melancholic: the cause they serve must be real and the results effective. You may see the Sanguine at charity dinners that are designed to raise money but also provide the stage for extrovert fun and show, but not the Melancholic, who will be behind the scenes doing what they feel really counts. The moment a charity or cause loses touch with its heart, Melancholics will move on to find a cause more worthy of their input and, more importantly, more satisfying to their inner need to give, be effective and make a significant difference.

Melancholics and Their Appearance

From Melancholics' appearance it is easy to determine their temperament. Most express sadness, the less pessimistic express resignation and all their movements seem to be downwards.

Just looking at a Melancholic can make you think of heaviness. In fact, the Melancholic is not as large as a Phlegmatic, and may not even be much larger than the Choleric; they may also be slim, but because everything is down, from their eyes and mouths to the hang of their arms and the bend of the back, they give an impression of weight. Unlike the larger Phlegmatic who is all soft flesh, in the heaviness of the Melancholic the bones are more clearly emphasised.

Typically they have dark hair, a pale complexion and a long pointed nose. Their eyes show deep sadness: there are the telltale vertical creases between their eyebrows and frown lines across the forehead. The eyes themselves may turn down, the mouth almost certainly does and there may be deep creases on either side of the mouth, from nose to jaw.

Depending on their type and stage of development, the expression may vary from sorrow or bitter discontent to quiet and sympathetic understanding. Deep seriousness is likely to be their most cheerful expression, and when trying to be cheerful they are apt to sigh.

Their voice is husky and gives the impression it could break at any moment as sympathy or sorrow overcomes them. It tends to be toneless with little, if any, lightness of expression.

Melancholics' clothes are unlikely to be highly fashionable or brightly coloured. They tend to wear pale and muted colours and soft fabrics with a feel that appeals to them. In their search for their identity they will create their own style and combine colours in interesting ways. They keep old clothes, particularly those that have become a form of self-expression. If negative, they may choose clothes that hang on them and hide their body rather than enhance it.

Movements also express their mood. In the strong Choleric you are dominantly aware of upward and outward movements, the Sanguine gesticulates gracefully in all directions, the Phlegmatic shows very little activity and in the Melancholic the emphasis is on downward movements. Furthermore, the movements are slow and heavy, like a combined sigh and slow shrug.

In the way they walk the Melancholic expresses sorrow. The arms hang down, the shoulders bend over and the head faces towards the ground. They 'droop' along rather than walk. If they fail to avoid someone in their path it is likely to be because they are lost in inner contemplation. They may be slim and gangling, the artistic droop evident as they let the furniture support them, or they may be heavier.

In general, Melancholics look older than their years. The 100 per cent Melancholic is easy to spot.

The Melancholic Child

Melancholic babies are usually quiet and tranquil. They want to be touched, to be held and to have other physical expressions of love and affection, but they prefer quiet, prolonged and gentle contact to boisterous hugs and kisses. For much of the time they are peaceful and content to be left alone, as if already lost in their own inner world of thought and experience. You may recognise greater depths in their eyes than in those of babies of the other temperaments. They are also keen to observe the world around them and will stare solemnly at whatever is going on, internalising and digesting its significance. Do not expect smiles and chuckles; you are more likely to get a quiet and thoughtful stare.

The desire they express later on for peace and tranquillity is seen at this stage in their obvious distress when there is noise or confusion around them. They like to stay in one place and have a fixed routine so they can know what to expect. They are unlikely to respond well if their parents insist on carrying them to dinner parties, taking them to the office, leaving them at the homes of friends or relatives for babysitting or back-packing them on country walks.

They are sensitive and can be upset easily when tension or arguing is going on around them. In general, they are more intuitive than other babies and will more readily detect these uncomfortable vibes. They respond to the people around them intuitively in other ways and seem to have an automatic knowledge of how to relate to others, so many people find them very appealing babies.

As children, Melancholics are mentally alert, preferring speech to action, are usually quick to talk and have a facility for picking up words faster than many other toddlers. As soon as they become conscious of the sounds they are making they start to experiment. They may hold lengthy conversations with you and with themselves long before they can form actual words. Once the words start it may seem as if they talk non-stop. If they are born into a family or are exposed to an environment where more than one language is spoken they will readily become fluent in both or all of them. As they grow up this matures into a flair for language in general and the ability to communicate clearly.

From an early age they love and respond to fairy stories and fantasy characters. They will want you to read them stories and to make stories up for them. The best ones will have a high moral tone with the goodies always winning out over the baddies and fading off into the sunset for a happy-ever-after ending. They respond to stories of gentle chivalry rather than violence and the slaying of dragons. They prefer the beautiful to the dangerous, the gentle to the violent. Do not be surprised if your Melancholic child suddenly informs you that they are Sir Galahad, or Snow White. They identify easily with the characters in the stories and often take on their roles, possibly for days at a time.

Like the Sanguine child they may sometimes exaggerate to the point of seeming to tell lies. In the Sanguine the cause is their desire to have experienced something bigger than life, to be important and to have a good story to tell, to make an impression. In the Melancholic child it has more to do with imagination and inner experience. They create the story out of their mind and then, when it comes time to tell it, they have trouble distinguishing between what is real and what they have created. In the same way they can take on the feelings and personality of their friends and then have trouble disengaging and recognising their own self.

Most children create invisible playmates, and this is particularly true of the Melancholic child with its active imagination. These imaginary playmates are very important to them: any slight to them will be taken personally and felt deeply.

The Melancholic child still wants to be held and touched as expressions of love and affection and also of security. They may be content simply to hold your hand, or to be in physical contact with some part of you. They may want you to hold them.

Melancholics generally have a keen sense of the pain that is experienced by others, and this is true of the children as well as of the adults. Watch a Melancholic child when another child has been made to look silly, has made a fool of themselves, or is being rejected or punished. If the other child is a strong Choleric or a confident Sanguine, the Melancholic observer may even experience the greater amount of pain as they empathise with the feelings they assume the other child is experiencing.

As adults they will be more inclined to work with people than with objects and technology. This pattern starts in childhood, when they prefer to play with dolls and animals rather than with bricks and Meccano. They prefer toys with which they can have a personal relationship, rather than ones they can manipulate as objects. The loss of such a toy, or of a pet if they have one, can be devastating to the Melancholic child.

As adults, Melancholics show skill in handling and analysing large amounts of information and coming up with constructive solutions. As children this shows up in their choice of toys that pose problems that have to be solved. They are not interested in the cannons and guns of the Choleric, the fun and games of the Sanguine or the steady routine of the Phlegmatic.

Keep them out of school for as long as possible and let them learn through the games they play and the opportunities they have for exploring their world practically. They learn well through interaction with others and better that way than when they have to sit still in class and be fed information.

The Melancholic child who is in Stage I may complain a lot and tell you what is making them unhappy. If this happens, deal with it by the methods described in the general section on the Melancholic temperament. Give them someone to look after who is less well off than themselves. Lead them on, verbally, from one problem to the next until they realise that you recognise the difficulties they face and they run out of problems to share with you. The Stage II child will take care of younger siblings or playmates.

As we saw earlier, the adult Melancholic is idealistic and is searching for self, for their true inner nature and the meaning of life and their place in it. In a similar way the child struggles to establish its place in the family. This can be particularly difficult for them when a subsequent sibling is born or, if they are the youngest of an older family, when the grandchildren are born. It can also create difficulties when they face the upheaval of going to school and the need to establish their place in that system. It is likely that they will be unhappy and homesick and they should be supported, rather than laughed at for their timidity by a Sanguine mum who insists that school will be fun, or jollied along by a Choleric father who tells them to be brave. They respond to praise and are very keen to gain this. They like to be approved of, and in this way they can be helped.

School

Melancholics are perfectionists and make serious students, especially if they are given hands-on and practical classes and not simply lists of dry information. They want to experience, to feel as much as to know. They may well spend far more time on a project than is warranted in their desire to turn in the best work of which they are capable. They enjoy doing such projects and prefer to work at them on their own. They are good at languages, may be good at maths with its broad conceptual thinking, but are unlikely to enjoy confining their mind to the practicalities of science and technology. If they do, they are more likely to enjoy the beauty of botany and the individuality of animals, to which they can relate, than the hard sciences of chemistry and physics.

If they have trouble with their homework, rather than trying to explain, yet again, what the teacher was saying, give them a chance to make a game of the work, to make it practical, to discuss it with you in such a way that they have to teach you or some other child.

They respect their teachers, particularly those that are well organised and logical, and look for praise from them. They endeavour to live up to the teacher's expectations of them and will be deeply hurt by criticism or by being ignored. As in other things, criticism or rejection from their teachers, peers and parents is painful to them, no matter how slight, especially if done in public. The Melancholic child who is repeatedly subjected to such unthinking remarks as 'Be quiet, I'm busy', 'Not so loud, you're disturbing the baby', 'Don't touch', 'Don't do that' and more, can be deeply hurt. In this they experience much pain since, statistically, the average child receives 10 per cent praise and 90 per cent criticism. To the other temperaments much of this can run off; for the Melancholic the pain is internalised and absorbed.

In addition to responding to praise and high expectations they also like to make sacrifices and be asked to help. Ask them to do things even if this inconveniences them, and then give them the recognition due for what they have done.

They will not do well in a school in which violence is the norm, where there is tension and where discipline is lax. They like a calm and peaceful atmosphere where they are free to pursue their own development and learning, and their relationships to other students and adults. They want orderly classes, they want to know what to expect and what work to prepare. They will then work hard to achieve the desired results and so gain the approval they want from parents and teachers. A chaotic classroom and a casual 'well done' for whatever work they turn in will not satisfy them. They only respond to praise and encouragement that are genuine.

If your child is Choleric you will have noticed that it is unwise to threaten them: this will simply get their back up and cause them to dig their feet in, refusing to surrender or let you get the better of them. Similarly it is unwise to set the Melancholic child in competition with another child and encourage them to win. The Melancholic is likely either to help the other child who is less successful or to spend more time agonising over the pain of the loser than enjoying their own gain, should they win. Since they are perfectionists you can safely ask them to do better than they did last time, to pit them against their own previous record, and know that this will do the trick.

As they mature as students, their studies and academic capabilities improve. Once they have a chosen career and goals to achieve, they demonstrate greater application as they strive to become qualified.

Keep in mind that they need help in moving through the stages. It may be wise to emphasise the value of the support and comfort they can offer to other, less fortunate or less happy children. They might support a child in a less well-off country, save some of their pocket money for a charity or sponsor a new child at school. They will also relate well to penfriends. This will all help to bring them out of themselves and develop the nurturing side of their nature.

Do not worry if your Melancholic child rarely smiles or laughs. They will always be more quiet and serious than the others. Their goal is not to be happy, it is to be fulfilled.

The Melancholic Adult

Mature adult Melancholics are warm, caring, feeling people. And the search for meaning, in life and in relationships, goes on. They will do a lot and put up with a lot to get close to people in need, to help others and to live in peace and harmony, yet they continue to fear or expect the worst and often have an eye over their shoulder in search of the shadows. Since they expect the worst they may create it, like picking at a scab until it falls off and the wound reopens. When things are not absolutely perfect, and that, of course, is most of the time, they can become discontented and blame themselves. They are still idealists and will be searching for their own identity but, to the extent that they have matured, they will be thinking of others too.

Many Melancholics will go on to higher education when they leave school, probably focusing on people-related professions such as health care and the social sciences or the environment. Alternatively they may enter the arts, particularly the interpretative arts, via either structured training or practical application.

They like lists and plans. They like to work out the details of a project before they start. All this may mean they take some time to decide on their career and life path. They may fill in with voluntary work or with low-paid assistant jobs, locally or in poorer communities and worthwhile situations, until they make their final decision – and even then they will have to think about it.

Melancholics put people and relationships first, ahead of objects, money, power or career. In the way they relate to themselves, to the relationships they have with other people and to the other people themselves, you can observe how far they have progressed through the three stages. To recap, they develop through them in the following progression. In Stage I they expect other people to be fully involved with them and their problems. In Stage II they may be excessively focused on delving into the nature of their relationships with people, at least by the standards of the other temperaments. They may even become so involved that they start to feel personally responsible for the feelings and emotions of others, a situation that is rarely beneficial to either party. By Stage III they are willing to become fully involved in the lives of other people, yet without swamping them. Their attention moves from themselves in Stage I to the relationship in Stage II and to the other person in Stage III.

In general, the more extroverted Melancholics will focus on other people as well as themselves, placing emphasis on their relationship with each person they meet and putting a lot of energy into sensing and fleshing out this relationship. Their intuition is good, and they would be wise to rely on it. When they start to make logical assessments of the people and the relationships involved, they tend to take the most negative view and often see problems where none exist. They may look for secret agendas and hidden motives, sure, in their Melancholy way, especially in Stages I and II, that there are problems lying buried and just waiting to surface. Something, says the Stage I Melancholic, is bound to go wrong. When they rely on their intuition and their feelings things will go much more smoothly.

The more introverted Melancholics can be so sensitive to the emotions of others they may seem to be psychic, second-guessing the moods and needs of others even before the individual knows them themselves, and knowing what someone is about to say before they say it. They also understand the needs and goals of other people and can use this to motivate them when appropriate. Their keen intuition can lead them to have premonitions which will often turn out to be true, provided they don't allow logic to intrude and cloud their judgement.

Their psychic, intuitive and emotional nature can lead them into religious and spiritual circles and activities. They will enjoy the calm, the deep emotion and the music of High Church and the Catholic Mass rather than bible-thumping religions with promises of hellfire and brimstone. Spiritually they will be in tune with long periods of silence and meditation as they strive to unite with the higher powers.

This sensitivity to the feelings of others and their tendency to internalise and personalise much of what they experience can mean they are frequently hurt, certainly by criticism but often even when no overt criticism was made and none was intended. You may only discover, days or years after the event, if at all, the ways in which you have hurt such a sensitive soul.

In Stage II they demonstrate their Melancholic pessimism and the Melancholic's ability to take on and experience the pain of others. They may find they are so aware of and open to the problems of others that they cannot step back and get a wider perspective on situations. Eventually they feel guilty because they cannot solve the other person's problems. They may even take on the problems not only of people who are close to them, but of people in general, and this can become emotionally exhausting.

Just as you may have felt overwhelmed by the demands of a Stage I Melancholic, you may find at this stage that the importance they attach to your relationship with them, its subtleties, and to the deep and meaningful communication for which they are searching, is overpowering.

Full maturity in Stage III allows them to empathise and help without becoming overwhelmed themselves or overwhelming the other person. They value the relationship, are tolerant of others and able to give them space while at the same time offering care and concern.

Communication is never complete and rarely accurate. All too often you may say or do something and find that the meaning the other person received was very different to the one you intended. This happens less often with the Melancholic than with the other temperaments as they communicate well and are articulate in both large and small gatherings, but, if and when it does occur, they are first surprised and then hurt. How could you have failed to understand them when their meaning was so clear? When things do not go as planned the Melancholic will blame themselves for such a breakdown in communications, and revert to melancholia.

They continue, in adult life, to value praise, real and sincere praise, for themselves, and respond well to it. They continue to see through false praise and sometimes assume it is false even when it is genuine, such is their pessimism. They like to please other people and make them happy. As children they did this by pleasing their parents and teachers and by looking after their peers. In adult life they expand this desire to people in general, and use praise as one way of pleasing them. They comment frequently on the achievements of others, no matter how small, as a way of encouraging them, particularly if the other person is in pain or distress or is feeling inadequate. The smallest gain will be recognised and nurtured.

The more introverted Melancholic is hard to get to know and often seems shy and withdrawn. They are very private people: their introversion, combined with the typical Melancholic's introspection, results in someone who shares little. They focus on their inner life and can be too absorbed in it to be willing to spend time sharing themselves with others. Over the years you may get to know them one step at a time; even decades after meeting them you may find you are still learning new things about them.

Melancholics are often dreamers, preferring to ponder, to wonder and to theorise, than to go out and do. They may get lost in the 'what if?' and fail to be actively practical.

Melancholics generally focus on their feelings, their values and their intuition, rather than on logic or intellect, and they should do the same when making decisions. Intuitive decision-making works well for them since they have generally absorbed, unconsciously, much of the input they need and are sure of their values and standards: of what they like and what they don't, what is important to them and what isn't. Mature Melancholics find this type of intuitive decision-making relatively easy, although problems can occur in their more negative moods, especially if they revert to Stage I, in which case they assume the worst.

When they start to analyse and intellectualise, their decision-making is much more likely to be faulty and to create problems. Intellectually they assume that if anything can go wrong it will go wrong and their analytical thinking will lead them into convictions of failure and descriptions of the worst possible outcome, untempered by their more accurate intuitions and feelings. They then find themselves trying to make decisions on the basis of negative and often unwarranted assumptions, while at the same time letting their desire for perfection delay the process in case they are making a wrong decision.

Although in general we think of Cholerics as the leaders, some Melancholics can also be good leaders. This comes about not so much because of their strength and independence but because they are intuitive, sensitive to the needs of others and care about people. They are able to communicate this to people, who then choose to follow their lead, confident that their own needs will be taken care of. While the Choleric leads from the front, the Melancholic is more likely to co-operate with others, expect their co-operation in return and thus lead from within the group. This leadership role comes less from a desire to lead than from concern for the welfare of others. Since it is a role assigned to them rather than a self-chosen role the Melancholic can, at times, become stressed and anxious as a result of the expectations others have of them. Keep in mind, however, that the Melancholic does like to be asked to make sacrifices and to suffer, and prefers this to finding that no one asks for the help they would like to offer.

When there are battles to be won you can expect to see the Choleric leader taking over. When there are problems to be solved in the community, school or home, when there is a distressing emergency, you can expect to see the Melancholic style of leadership emerging. The more introverted type of Melancholic, particularly the male, may seem to be too gentle, too lacking in backbone for this role. This will change if you push them too far, if you violate their values and reach the point where their strength shows up and they do indeed put up a fight.

Melancholics may often seem to be soft and gentle, but push them hard and you may find they are stubborn, especially in anything that affects their ideals. It's as if they will put up with a lot for the sake of peace, but there is a limit. When that limit is reached you can push them no further. The gentle and undemonstrative Melancholic mother will turn and attack if her children are threatened. Since they expect problems rather than happiness, threats have relatively little effect: they are already anticipating the worst.

In spite of the Melancholic's idealism, their search for what is good, honourable, admirable and beautiful in the world, the people they champion and the causes they espouse, it can happen that in their concern to find what is good they can still come back to focusing on the negative. They fear and even search out what is bad or unpleasant, as if they feel that knowing about it will in some way help them to protect what is good. They can be like the person in pain after an accident who keeps pressing the wound to feel how much it hurts, the clergyman who fears and yet checks out pornographic literature, or the alcoholic who has a fascination with pubs.

Of all the temperaments Melancholics have the least expectation of being happy. Nor do they put much value on achieving happiness. They are more concerned with caring and giving than with being happy, so are willing to suffer and make personal sacrifices for causes in which they believe, or for people they care about.

Friends

Melancholics usually have a small circle of very good friends with whom they have developed a close relationship of sensitive understanding. Commonly, these will be enduring relationships, lasting over many years.

The Melancholic at Work

The choice of a career for a Melancholic depends not so much on what they are good at or what they will enjoy as on what will be worthwhile. The Melancholic's need to contribute, to add value and to fulfil their goals and ideals contributes strongly to their choice of profession.

The other temperaments may consider what subject they are best at and focus on it. They may consider what they most enjoy doing and will have the most fun at. They may consider where the most money is to be made and endeavour to train and then work in that field. They may follow in the family tradition and enter the expected career or business. They may look for a job that provides the lifestyle they want, such as travel, variable hours, status or prestige. Not so the Melancholic.

The Melancholic will, of course, want to enjoy what they are doing, but for them this does not mean having fun. It means doing a job that helps them in their search for meaning, that satisfies their urge to make a difference, to make sense of their life by doing something that they feel is of value to others. This value must be fundamental: not valuable in the sense of helping the boss to have a more successful business, the company to expand more rapidly, or an individual to become wealthier – unless, of course, that individual is in need. Rather than material gain they need emotional rewards.

They may enter the caring professions such as nursing, midwifery, medicine, natural therapies, counselling or psychiatry. They may be involved in geriatric care or caring for the mentally or emotionally disturbed. Even within these professions they are likely to choose the more 'melancholic' type of activity. Rather than the drama of the casualty wing they will choose to work with the long-term chronically ill, those who are enduring long-term suffering and pain, and those least likely to recover. The extreme Melancholics may want to help the sick and the dying.

Whereas Choleric doctors would be brisk and effective, taking pleasure in high-technology procedures, their ability to achieve results and urging their patients on to recovery, Melancholic doctors will be quiet, sympathetic, understanding and patient. They will probably work more gently with the patient, do more to avoid pain and radical procedures, and place emphasis on their ability to minimise discomfort and help the patients to endure what they are unable to cure.

Typically, one might not expect to find a Choleric in the medical profession; yet in the twentieth century the profession has much that the Choleric desires. It has status, power, authority and offers a good income. Melancholics, on the other hand, are more likely to enter the profession with a true desire simply to help people. They are the ones with the good bedside manner. You are more likely to find the Melancholic, rather than the Choleric, doctor working long and irregular hours and doing the difficult and time-consuming house calls. Unfortunately, in countries where entering medical school is limited to those with the highest intelligence and where becoming a doctor is something of a status symbol, it may happen that many Melancholics who would like to enter the profession, and who would be extremely good at it, do not manage to qualify for the training.

Melancholics like to bring out the best in people. For this reason you may find them in hairdressing salons, beauty parlours, fashion houses or grooming schools. This is not for the glamour, as it would be for a Sanguine, but for the inner benefit the Melancholic can bring to the client as they improve their sense of self-confidence and worth. Melancholics are also artists, whose work will have a lot to do with their desire to create a beautiful and pleasing result. They will experience this as interpreting the individual and showing them off.

In general, teachers are either Melancholic or Phlegmatic. The Phlegmatics are somewhat more likely to teach the senior classes and the standard students. The Melancholics are more likely to be working with the young, the slow learners, or handicapped children. If you find Cholerics or Sanguines in the teaching profession they are more likely to be lecturing or performing than teaching with empathy and care for the student, and more interested in the bright than in the average student.

In the arts, Melancholics will be more involved in the interpretative than in the creative areas. The Sanguine will play the stage and dominate the role: you will always be aware of the person playing the part. When the play is over you will find them holding court in their dressing room, delighting in the glamour and the spotlights. The Melancholic will sink into their role, losing themselves in the part they are playing. You may be totally moved by the character yet forget the name of the actor or actress. After the play they will leave quietly, finding it difficult to come out of the character and the emotions. They may even take on the character of the part for the entire run of a play or the duration of a film.

Melancholics can steep themselves in music, get lost in poetry and drown in the depths of a painting. Here again their love of what is beautiful and good and their empathy with the unhappy win out, and they will choose either the beautiful or the deeply emotional and sad rather than the violent or brutal forms of art. They will look for subtleties rather than overt brilliance.

They want to communicate. They may be writers using this medium to pass on meanings. You will learn from their message rather than be entertained by them. To this end they will write poetry or plays, short stories or novels. Their writing may be difficult to read and understand – you will certainly not be reading for escapism or superficial pleasure. It will be romantic, elegant and stylish, full of metaphors and similes, imagery and colourful poetic language.

Their search for the spiritual may take them into communes or into established religions. They may become deeply involved in the spiritual side of life, though this may owe more to their search for meaning than to a true conviction or belief, as they can also be sceptics. They may teach meditation or yoga, relaxation or stress management. They may become involved in the work and running of communes as well as in the spiritual side. Any aspect of work within the established religions could appeal to them, provided of course that they are either deeply committed to the religion itself or have respect for the potential of its fundamental values. They would want no part of an order that was lenient or that used its power, and the role of people within it, to gain personal or group benefit. They may also be actively interested in psychic phenomena. Because they are intuitive they may become astrologers, mediums or clairvoyants, often demonstrating what seems to be extra-sensory perception, and many people will think of them as mystical, spiritual and possibly somewhat unworldly.

They are more likely to choose social studies and the arts than the sciences. If they do have a scientific bent it is likely to take them into conservation rather than exploitation, to basic research rather than into ideas with commercial applications. They may become involved in the Green movement, in saving whales and dolphins, preserving rain forests and understanding the deeper aspects of nature. In all this they will remain aware of the effect on humanity of what they are doing. The relationships between their work and people remain important.

The more extrovert Melancholics may enter politics, in which case they are likely to take up specific ideas, usually of their own choosing, and convert them into causes and crusades. If you want them to support your cause or idea you will first have to convince them of its merits and the high ideals involved and then let them take it over as their own.

Whatever they do, they are likely to be more involved with people than with objects or technology. When it comes to making decisions and assessments they put caring for people, empathy and their relationships above sticking to the rules and being right and logical. When logic gets in the way they will dispense with it. At times this may get them into trouble as they find it difficult to discipline or punish people when this *is* necessary. They work best in one-to-one communication and where this is important to their job. For this reason, though they are not dynamic extroverts, they can make good salespeople. They will also focus on the possibilities inherent in people rather than in objects, technology or commerce. They are also able to bring out the best in people since they understand what motivates them and recognise the value of praise and appreciation.

Melancholics are usually well organised. They may keep lists of what needs to be done, of what they have done and of what they want to do, and of what other people have done. They may draw graphs, plot results and chart the progress of the enterprises in which they are involved. While the Choleric leads, the Sanguine paints the pictures and dazzles and the Phlegmatic obediently carries out orders and does the routine work, it is probably the Melancholic who organises things, makes sure they get done and takes care of the details. They may do this slowly and thoughtfully, to the frustration of the Sanguine who has rushed on to the next idea, but it will be done – which is more than you can always say of the other temperaments.

While many of the above professions mean that Melancholics may be self-employed, they are not natural entrepreneurs or dynamic businesspeople. If they are in private practice they probably work long hours caring for patients and spend little time keeping up with the bills. The more introverted Melancholics can work well within organisations and structures, adapting to the other people and the greater good of the whole since they like peace and harmony and are not interested in politics and intrigue. The latter can cause them to lose confidence and send them back to Stage I. They do want and respond to praise and to recognition of their input and the sacrifices they may be making for the good of the whole, and their boss would do well to recognise and respond to this. Much will depend on which stage they have reached. The more extroverted Melancholics will have slightly more difficulty working in an organisation and sticking to the rules, especially in Stage I when they will want a lot of attention to be focused on them and their needs.

The Melancholic and Money

Melancholics, of course, value people and relationships more than money or possessions. They prefer tranquillity to competitive striving for material gain. They are idealistic rather than acquisitive. Thus they are relatively uninterested in money, at least for its own sake. As idealists they will be more interested in discovering the meaning of life rather than acquiring wealth.

There is little point in expecting a Melancholic to be moved by the idea of keeping up with the Joneses. If a Melancholic wants something for its own sake – a holiday abroad, say – they will work hard to achieve it. But if they are content to go camping in the next county, no matter what exotic places their friends are going to, they will be totally unconcerned if they cannot afford to go too. They are uninterested in status symbols. They would think it absurd to strive after possessions or lifestyle simply for the sake of being in fashion. They would laugh at you if you suggested they should feel deprived or concerned because they didn't have money to splash around or spend on luxuries. A greater pain to them would be to fail to live up to their ideals, and not to have the time to ponder and theorise, to live in the present and wonder about the world in which they live.

They may want money for a cause or a charity. They may want money so they can help people in need. They may want money for some fundamental and important research or so that they can have the time to devote to their art. In that case they will do what they can to raise it, though in this they are not always successful. They will also use their own money for the causes they believe in, sometimes assuming, possibly wrongly, that when they are in need the process will be reversed. When they are very idealistic they may lend money unwisely, not realising the risks they are running, and they may be surprised when the borrower lets them down.

They are unlikely to be willing to choose an activity or career simply for its financial rewards. Equally they are not careless with money: they do not splash it around. Their attention to detail will generally lead them to keep track of their bank balances and have some sort of a budget.

They will be wealthy – but it will be a wealth of the soul and the spirit, not of the hip pocket or bank balance. To some they may seem to be impractical in this, but the Melancholic knows that money is a distraction. Some, though not all, even seem to be unaware that it exists, so little does it enter into their thinking, but they all know that the real business of life is in their relationships, both with the world around them and with their inner life.

The Melancholic and Time

Melancholics like to have their time organised in so far as they like to know what to expect. It is not that they want the relatively mindless routine of the Phlegmatic, but that they want time to sink into and experience the present fully, so they do not want to be rushed or harried by any sudden changes. If they are going to do something they like to make the decision in advance and to be organised and prepared for it. They can then experience the lead-up as well as the event.

This applies both to their work and to their personal life. They like an orderly work environment with plenty of warning if the plans are to be changed. This is more because they want to have time to get in tune with what is happening or about to happen than because they watch the clock. They are slow and thoughtful in what they do rather than fast, and can rarely be hurried.

The Melancholic breadwinner does not like to come home to a wife who springs a social engagement on him. It's as if he feels he is missing out by not having had the time to anticipate the event as well as to experience it. He may also feel the loss of the evening he had planned and prepared for emotionally; he may have to change his mood, from one of quiet anticipation of reading a book or playing a Brahms symphony, to one more appropriate for visiting friends or going to a film. Equally, the husband should not come home to his Melancholic wife and spring a surprise outing on her. She will have prepared the evening meal with feeling and may have created a specific mood: she does not wish this to be spoilt by a sudden change of plan.

Melancholics are not ruled by the clock; in fact they may often be unconscious of it or unaware of it. Some people have a clear idea of time. They make a commitment to be at a certain place at a certain time and they keep the appointment. They expect the appointment to last for a given length of time, and towards the end of that time they make it clear that they must be going. You may, for instance, invite a friend to your home for lunch. They will arrive on time, stay till an appropriate point in the afternoon and then, at about the time you both expect, show they are ready to leave. Not so the Melancholic.

They tend to live in the present and savour the moment with little thought for the amount of time that has elapsed. The Melancholic may be late arriving but will be surprised if you are annoyed by this. They are here now, is their attitude, so why be cross? Let's focus on the present and enjoy it. Once they are with you they will have all the time for you that you want. Long after the time they were due to be somewhere else, they may still be with you, fully involved in you and what you are both doing.

I have known a Melancholic arrive for a lunch party at four in the afternoon. He was full of stories of the amazing time he had had since he got up and quite unperturbed by the thought that the hostess, to whom he was recounting his wonderful experience, could be annoyed or put out that he had not bothered to stop what he was doing and turn up for the lunch to which he had been invited. Furthermore, he was so indifferent to time that he showed every sign of settling down to a long stay and was, in his turn, somewhat dismayed when she indicated that she had plans for the evening and he would have to go.

I know a wonderful Melancholic hairdresser who is unperturbed if his clients arrive late; he is simply pleased to see them. But they should not plan to leave the salon on time either. They may well be in for a four-hour session for a simple cut and blow-dry as he perfects his creation. The present experience and the creation of something beautiful are far more important to him than sticking to any sort of time schedule.

If a Melancholic phones you for a chat you had better have something handy to do. You could get a lot of tapestry done by the time they are ready to terminate the call. If you have other things to do, keep asking them questions and leading them on from subject to subject until they run out of news.

All this may make it difficult to plan timetables with a Melancholic, but when you are with them you will have their full attention. Since they do things slowly, you may be impatient to move on long before they have finished – but at least you can be sure they will not be getting restless to leave you before you have completed what you want to do with them.

The Melancholic in Love

Melancholics in love are the soulful romantic types. They want deep and meaningful relationships, a true spiritual communion that transcends the physical and lifts the couple above worldly considerations. People and relationships are very important to them, possibly to such an extent that it can overwhelm their partner. At their best they raise the love relationship to an art form; at their most melancholic they prefer it to fail and for them and their chosen one to suffer in the romantic style of true and unrequited love.

If they are Stage I Melancholics they will almost *prefer* this unrequited love to a happy outcome. After all, if everything is going well they will be constantly worried about how the relationship could fail. In every slight and every frown they will find evidence that the object of their affections does not return their feelings. Every broken or changed arrangement they will interpret as a sign that the other person is losing interest.

When things are going smoothly they may even find ways, consciously or unconsciously, of sabotaging the relationship in such a way that they bring about the result they fear. They may push the other person too far with repeated demands such as 'Do you love me?' 'Are you sure you love me?' 'Did you love so-and-so more?' They may claim frequently that they are not good enough for the other person, that the other person could do better, could be happier, have more fun or be better off with someone else. They are, of course, fishing for compliments and looking for reassurance and repeated statements of affection, but the end result is often to drive the other person away. The Melancholic will then be in despair yet, at some level, be reassured that the world is as they expect it to be. They now have something to complain about and to use to get other people's attention and sympathy. They can also, in their own way, enjoy their suffering.

A love affair where the Melancholic is truly loved but where a happy outcome is impossible, for whatever reason, is meat and drink to this Melancholic. The Romeo and Juliet situation is ideal – better by far to die for love than to live on in pain without it. More than any other temperament the Melancholic is likely to do just that: to die for love, or for the loss of the loved one. If the loved one is of a different religion, married, from the wrong social, financial or national background or for some other reason unable to enter into a full relationship with the Melancholic, this suits their temperament well. They will not, of course, say they are happy with the situation. But this does allow them to love and be loved without testing the relationship against the harsh realities of daily life.

The Stage II or Stage III Melancholic is a more positive lover. Provided you are willing to give them the time, they will create great romantic moments, but do not expect them to rush or be impetuous. Their understanding and empathy can be wonderfully soothing and nurturing to their partner. Their willingness to become involved in your problems can be very supportive. However, if they take this too far they can be pushed around relatively easily by a stronger or more demanding mate.

Lovers

Above all others, the mature Melancholic believes in and desires a happy-ever-after ending in true storybook fashion. The fact that this rarely occurs simply serves to give him or her something else about which to be melancholic. They are looking for a true soulmate and a spiritual partnership, often, and usually unsuccessfully, aiming to be the perfect partner in return for the object of their love.

The Melancholic lover is more likely to send you love letters, read you poetry and sing a ballad under your window than to whisk you off for an exciting weekend on an exotic island. If you want action find a Choleric, if you want fun choose a Sanguine, and if you want a placid, comfortable relationship choose a Phlegmatic. But if you are the romantic willing to be the object of someone's spaniel-eyed attention from afar, choose a Melancholic. It is wonderful for the ego. They may worship you, yet never say a word, convinced that the affair hasn't a chance right from the start.

Melancholics generally have a facility with language and will express themselves clearly, articulately and endlessly. A Melancholic couple is likely, particularly during courtship, to spend long hours discussing the subtleties of their feelings for each other. They will express sympathy for, and show a caring interest in, the other person's past, their feelings in the present and their hopes and plans for the future. They will be aware of and fascinated by the smallest nuances of emotion.

Many a Choleric or Sanguine has been loved by a Melancholic at a distance and, receiving the most wonderful letters, felt inclined to reciprocate, only to find that when they get together the Melancholic is far too dull and slow for their dynamic way of life. An active Choleric or Sanguine has little patience with sitting around and discussing their feelings. They are inclined to accuse the Melancholic of mooning away the time and being a romantic drip or wimp. This is untrue and they are missing out on much that is wonderful in the Melancholic, yet they may never value what the Melancholic has to offer, nor be able to be the soulmate the Melancholic requires. Equally, the Melancholic cannot be the fun companion the more dynamic temperaments require.

In past centuries the spurned lover, after his proposal had been rejected, would leave the country, commit suicide or disappear from society. It was clearly too painful for him to see again the object of his affections, knowing she would never be his. The woman, unloved by the man of her dreams, would retire to a convent or become the unhappy spinster whom the family felt obliged to support out of pity. If either of them were beyond Stage I and taking an interest in serving others, they might have given up any thoughts of marriage and thrown themselves into their career, or focused on charity work or some form of service to others.

Such grand sentiment is no longer possible or appropriate today, when unrequited love or a refused proposal is not the end of the world. Today, Melancholics have to make do with letting people know how much they have suffered in whatever way they can.

Melancholics fall in love first; sex comes later. Not for them carnal lust followed by the deepening of the relationship, nor are they much interested in sex for its own sake. To go after sex would be to go in search of fun, and Melancholics are more likely to suffer than to do this. Love comes first, or what they think is love. Often they will feel affection for someone and then build this up until they tell themselves it is love. In their mind they may well build a gentle affection into a consuming love, particularly if their affections are not returned or if the person is unavailable for some other reason. Each time they do this it will be the perfect love, for they seek perfection and are, at least initially, blind to the faults of the one they love.

We have seen that the way to develop a Melancholic from Stage I to Stage III is to give them people worse off than themselves to take care of. When the Melancholic falls in love they will want to take care of the other person, who in turn will feel much loved and cherished by this. They will feel that they are truly special to the Melancholic and that they can bare their souls in the assumption that they will be understood, and that their feelings will be respected. In time, the Melancholic's need for introspection and their self-absorption will take over, and their attention turn back to themselves. The loved one may then feel suddenly abandoned. Ultimately, the Stage I Melancholic becomes restless when other people depend on them too much. It is all very well to help in times of need, but the immature Melancholic wants to be able to unburden himself on others, too, and have other people pay attention to him. It all depends on what stage he has reached.

Like most people, Melancholics would be horrified if told they were selfish. Yet we have already seen that, all too often, in emotional matters, they are. Much as they care for others, if their own emotional needs are not being met, and often they aren't, then they find it difficult to give prolonged emotional support to others. Ultimately, they have a high degree of self-absorption.

There is another danger. Since the Melancholic offers a feeling of caring to everyone, the special person may feel a lot less special as they realise that the Melancholic feels this way about a lot of people.

Sex

The step is from love to sex with a Melancholic, rather than the other way around, and it does not always happen, especially if the Melancholic is in the mood for unrequited love. The sexual act, when it occurs, is often disappointing. The Melancholic feels that the physical expression of their feelings should be natural and spontaneous; it should also be preserved for people they truly love and not entered into casually. For this reason they rarely read books or learn about the possibilities from other outside sources, nor do they have much personal experience. When the big relationship occurs there is likely to be a degree of naive fumbling and the reality often falls far below the sublime expectations.

This is painful for the male Melancholic; less so for the female. The male is determined to be all things to his female soulmate, and this includes being the perfect lover. To let her and himself down by performing less than well physically is upsetting to him. She, on the other hand, is less bothered by the possible absence of orgasm, or by unsatisfactory physical pleasures for herself. Her concern is to give pleasure to her partner even at the expense of pain to herself, and as long as she perceives she has done this she can be satisfied. She is willing to sacrifice her own pleasure, in true Melancholic fashion, to please the one she cares for. In fact, she may not even expect a great deal of pleasure for herself.

In many ways it is hard for the woman to achieve this goal, as the Melancholic man expects much. He will want her to be all things to him: the unattainable and sublime love goddess, the practical wife, the nurturing mother to replace his own mother, the exciting lover and mistress, and in many ways a small child to him – not an easy role combination for one woman to fill.

When final consummation of their love is less than perfect some of the gloss wears off the relationship. Then the faults, previously hidden by the willingly blind eyes, become apparent. Since little thought was given, at the start, to what this happy-ever-after ending would be or how it would be achieved, reality, once the honeymoon is over, is often something like a dash of cold water.

Do not expect an active, dynamic and exciting time sexually, with the Melancholic. Whatever happens you are more likely to get sonnets, soulful eyes and a lengthy discussion about whether or not you are having a good time, and 'Is this what you want, do you like this?' At first, depending on your past experience, you may be delighted by what you take as the Melancholic's consideration and desire to please. In time, however, the other aspects of their temperament may show through and you will have to deal with them. If you are tired and want to go to sleep you may wish you had a more speedy lover.

Marriage

Sexually you should not expect too much on a long-term basis, particularly with a Stage I Melancholic who has something about which to be depressed. When a Melancholic is deeply depressed they can lose all interest in sex. The woman will demand of her husband, 'How can you think of sex at a time like this?' The husband may show so little interest that his more enthusiastic wife will begin to wonder if he is having an affair, or if, at the very least, he is losing interest in her and beginning to cast around elsewhere.

In general the Melancholic woman, once the gloss has worn off, may a lose a lot of interest in sex. She will then start to say no, even when at heart she still means yes, especially if she is in Stage I. To say yes would mean she wanted to have something that could be had simply for the asking and that she would be expected, both during and afterwards, to have enjoyed. There is no pain in that. As we have already seen the Melancholic likes to be asked to make sacrifices. She would rather say no, be persuaded, and take part on the understanding that she is doing this to please him. Afterwards, she will be able to lie back in the glow of knowing that not only has she suffered for his sake, but he knows it and, in some cases, even owes her some gratitude.

The Stage I Melancholic wife may even lose all interest in sex soon after her marriage. She will then come up with the usual headaches, time of the month or not in the mood, or complain that she is too tired, that she has been working all day and evening with the children and that all he wants is first a housewife and then sex. If she says no but means yes and her husband insists, she may call him a brute, lacking in understanding, and selfish. If he takes her no at face value, rolls over and goes to sleep, she will be even more miserable. She may lie awake feeling sorry for herself, either because she has an inconsiderate husband or because she believes he can't care for her any more, arguing to herself that if he truly did he would have insisted. Furthermore, she has now been deprived of the chance to suffer for him and thereby have him be grateful to her. She would have liked to give, if only he had insisted and she could have had the chance to give in and agree. What should the man do, assuming they do still love and care for each other? He should persist, gently but firmly, and let her know that he does care, he does love her. This should not, of course, extend to excessive persuasion.

The Stage I Melancholic husband will only rarely initiate sex. Once the gloss has worn off and reality has stepped in he may look elsewhere for his love goddess. Without ever leaving the marriage he may, unconsciously at least, search for the distant object of his undying and unrequited passion. Since sex is not essential for this he may well remain faithful and in a deeply caring relationship with his wife. At this point his natural passivity may come to the fore and he will be content to let the woman take the dominant role. In this it is more difficult for him to achieve his emotional needs, as he can hardly be said to be suffering, either way. If he wants sex then he can initiate it, in which case he will probably get what he wants and so cannot be depressed. If he doesn't want it then it is unlikely to be forced on him and he will be left in peace. Again, it is hard for him to be justified in feeling depressed. Yet he has this subconscious need to suffer. If it is understood that he is making a sacrifice he can then engage in sex and, in his own way, get what he needs out of it.

A strong woman is ideal in this situation. A woman who will take control, who will initiate sex, who will chivvy him along and be an active leader in what they do will help draw the Stage I Melancholic man out of himself and give him the opportunities he needs. This may even seem like the classic case of the henpecked husband, ruled by a dominant woman. Don't feel sorry for him. This role suits him perfectly, only he'll never admit it, of course, certainly not to you or to her and probably not even to himself.

As they enter Stages II and III these patterns continue, but in a less intense way. The woman begins to be able to enjoy the sex act herself, not simply for what she is doing for his sake. The man begins to take a more active role and to be able to acknowledge that he is enjoying himself and not doing it only to please her.

Melancholics experience and share strong emotions and are capable of deep and affectionate attachment. They will often build a relationship of greater worth than one based on passionate love and sex, and one that will stand the test of time. In a good marriage they care for each other and will be understanding rather than critical, especially in public when the other is in trouble.

Melancholics are good at remembering birthdays and other anniversaries. They are also likely to be hurt if you forget theirs. Long after most couples have forgotten, the Melancholic couple will still be celebrating the anniversary of their first date, their first kiss, his proposal, and any other events that are meaningful to them.

As in all the temperaments, there is much that is wonderful in the Melancholic. Enjoy their sensitivity, their willingness to make sacrifices and to please, their deep involvement in the emotional side of the relationship, their caring – and do all you can to take them to Stage III so that you can enjoy the best of them.

The Melancholic at Home

Melancholics have a strong desire for a safe and secure nest. They will work hard to achieve this. If they are the breadwinner they will do all they can to provide well financially, providing not only the physical home but the wherewithal to live comfortably in it. They rarely put the same effort into striving for luxuries, which are less important to them. The homemaker will create a place of love and comfort, where the people in it are more important than the possessions. They will both endeavour to make the home a place of peace and happiness, where the family can develop freely and where friends drop in for pleasure and those in need drop in for help.

However well they do provide for their family, because of the way they idealise their relationships and because reality rarely lives up to their expectations, Melancholics will often have a sense of dissatisfaction, and this confirms them in their underlying Melancholic view of the world.

If, however, they are following some idealistic cause, where there is little income, they will expect their family to understand the importance of what they are doing and be prepared to live in poverty if that is necessary. The missionary may let her own family go hungry as she endeavours to feed the poor. The charity worker may expect his family to live in rented quarters since he cannot save enough on his income to buy his own home.

The Melancholic's home is important emotionally. It is the people in and around the home who are important, and what the home can do and provide for them, what it can mean. The home gives the Melancholic a place where they can care for their family emotionally, where they can build relationships, where they can nurture their friends. It provides a safe haven in which they can spend time in introspective thought, contemplating the universe and their own inner world, where they can meditate on what is possible, dream their dreams and give rein to their imagination.

Their desire for peace and harmony come to the fore when they are at home. Here, above all places, they desire this tranquillity and they will often work excessively hard to achieve it. They may insist that there be no fighting in the house, that people should not argue there but should agree, for, after all, aren't they one big happy family? Yet their tendency to expect the worst may again lead them to search out tensions that barely exist and make an issue of eliminating them.

If the home is not running smoothly and the way the Melancholic wants it, they may show their stubborn streak and insist that things be done their way. The Melancholic parent may demand that the children do not fight, a difficult goal to achieve, and that if they do they be punished. In this way their desire for peace may simply lead to further tension and disharmony. The Melancholic child, growing into adulthood, may insist they will leave home and find their own peaceful dwelling rather than stay in a house where there are arguments. They would do better to work on their own development, moving from expecting the worst in Stage I to becoming less involved, and no less caring but able and willing to give other people – who may, after all, not be Melancholics and thus may have different goals – the space to develop their own natures.

For the Stage I Melancholic home is the place to which they can withdraw and where they can concentrate on their problems. If they become seriously depressed they will let it deteriorate, become messy, untidy and dirty. They will try to draw you in there to give them solace and understanding. You can help them better by drawing them out of it and moving them around, as you do the conversation when you are trying to help them.

For the mature Melancholic, home is the place from which they can provide the care and nurture they seek to give others, and you may well find tangible evidence of this. There may be children they have adopted, fostered or agreed to babysit. They may hold an open house, particularly for people in need or who are lonely. Their home is the place where friends know they can go when they want a sympathetic ear, so when you arrive do not be surprised if someone else is there sharing a tale of woe or receiving comfort and sympathy. Their home may be also be a focal point for other people to drop in for a social chat and where people will not be too busy to stop what they are doing and talk to them. You may find charity boxes, plans for the latest crusade, or the equipment for the next protest rally, and you may even be roped in to help in the latest project.

Melancholics are not all melancholic, far from it, and their home will also be a place for fun and pleasure. Their vivid imagination will allow the Melancholic to create games and pleasures for the children. Their concern that guests enjoy themselves also means they provide interest and entertainment for visitors. It is more important that people are nurtured or that they have a good time than that the place is neat, tidy and run to schedule.

While Melancholics like to think and ponder they also search out ideas, and there will be lots of books they have used for research and reference. They are hoarders and keep many things that 'might come in useful some time'. At first glance the place may seem to be neat and organised, but if you look carefully you will see evidence of many half-completed projects, or even of proposed projects that have not yet been started but will be 'one day'. They will cut out articles that interest them and you may see piles of papers and information that has caught their attention, or lists of things to do pinned up in unexpected places. Since their interests are broad, the lists will tend to grow rather than diminish. In Stage I they will see this as failure, berate themselves for not completing the projects, and become depressed. By Stage III they will have grown tolerant of themselves and have come to recognise at least some of the lists as evidence of their deep interest in the world in which they live.

This range of interests is not the dilettante darting from one thing to another of the Sanguine, but a desire to delve deeply and experience as much as they can. The Sanguine's walls will not be lined with books, but the Melancholic's will.

The melancholic's schedule may become somewhat erratic as it is altered to meet the needs of people present. If a child is upset and needs support, this will not be delayed until after dinner. The child's emotional needs and family relationships are more important than the fact that the meal will get cold. If a guest wants to talk, other activities can wait.

When guests are expected, as opposed to having dropped in casually, things may change. The Melancholic sees it as a manifestation of their care for their guest that they provide a tidy environment and meals served when the guests expect them. However, should an important discussion with the guest be under way, the meal will give way to the relationship. In this their involvement with present time, as opposed to what has to be done next, is obvious, as well as their caring nature and the importance they place on relationships.

The Melancholic Parent

While Melancholics in Stages II and III make wonderfully nurturing parents, in Stage I they can be too self-absorbed to focus fully on their children and take care of their needs. They still have overwhelming needs of their own. The young and immature Melancholic mother may find the demands made on her too much. She may suffer from depression both during and after the pregnancy, and feel that all the attention that used to be focused on her, first by her parents and then by her husband, has now been transferred to the baby, to her own loss and disadvantage.

The young and immature Melancholic father may feel the burden of having another mouth to feed, another person to provide for. This is worsened if he has to get a second job to augment the income, or suffers because of the baby's broken sleep patterns. If he has been used to getting his wife's undivided attention and she now lavishes this on the baby he may feel abandoned, misunderstood and unloved.

For mature Melancholics the story is different. They make good and understanding parents and have the time to spend with the baby. After the birth the Melancholic mother will devote most of her attention to the baby. She will spend much quiet time loving it, observing it and building up the relationship. The time she put into her love relationship is now transferred to this new life. Her quiet introversion and introspection may now include the baby as she holds it, watches it and plays with it for hours. Feeding time is particularly important: mother and baby then make eye contact and she often has a psychic, intuitive and especially close communication with her child. The same can be true of the father, who will share many quiet moments with the baby. The more introspective mothers may even seem to remain connected to the child by an emotional umbilical cord.

The home may be less tidy and clean than before, but that is simply because the mother is putting her relationship with the baby above practical considerations.

Melancholic parents are gentle with their children and relate well to them as friends rather than playing an authoritarian role. They take the responsibilities of parenthood seriously and are conscious of the task of nurturing and developing this new soul so it can reach its full potential.

Once stories are in order, the imagination of the Melancholic parent can be given full rein. The stories will never be the same from one telling to the next: they may develop into continuing serials and sagas. They can amuse their children for hours, thinking up endless games, ideas and adventures at the drop of a hat. Games will be invented, simple at first, and then more challenging as the child grows. Almost on demand they tell stories, create fantasies and keep the children spellbound. They are rarely too busy to spend time with their children, considering this to be one of the most important aspects of their life.

It is the Melancholic parent that you will see, at a party, crawling round on the floor with the children, entering into their games and keeping them amused. The Sanguine parent will do much the same but will expect to be the performer with the children as audience, whereas the Melancholic will be joining in and sharing the activity with them. The Phlegmatic, who also relates well to children, is more likely to be making sure things are done properly. The Choleric will be sending them off on an adventure or, if they do become involved, leading it.

Melancholic parents consider the emotional bonding with their children to be extremely important and will spend hours developing this. They will make time for the children at the expense of the housekeeping, mowing the lawn and other chores. They will bring friends into the orbit of their family and will take even the youngest children with them on outings and excursions, even if they are aimed for adults only. The family unit and the inter-relationships are of paramount importance to the Melancholic.

Again, however, the Melancholic should guard against expecting the worst and looking for trouble where none exists, lest by this very searching they create unease and uncertainty in their children. Frequent questions for reassurance that they are loved by their children and that the children are feeling happy and fulfilled may raise doubts where none should or need exist, thus creating the situation the Melancholic is seeking to avoid.

The home and family life of most mature Melancholics is likely to be characterised by quiet fun and laughter, games and imagination, sharing and caring. The more introverted Melancholics are more gentle and withdrawn. They care but can be so undemonstrative that, although they are always present in times of need, the child may not feel fully loved and treasured and may miss, and suffer from the lack of, overt expressions of affection.

The children, if they are of other temperaments, may become impatient with their Melancholic parents: the father may seem too soft to the Choleric child in search of adventure or the Sanguine looking for a glittering skylark. Yet they will all benefit from the nurturing that is provided.

Melancholics take their responsibilities seriously and do all they can to provide both a good education for their children, and correct moral upbringing, endeavouring to instil sound values and principles. Yet the mature parent will also give the children considerable latitude to develop in the way of their choice. It is unlikely to be a Melancholic parent who demands that the child follow a career or life path chosen for them by others in the family, or follow in the expected family footsteps or tradition. Rather, they will look for promising signs and encourage the child to build on these.

If the child's behaviour goes too far and offends against a strong value or the deepest standards of the Melancholic parent, the child may be surprised to find suddenly that their easygoing father is now adamant: they must not behave in this way. Parental stubbornness sets in and the child is balked. Some Melancholic parents will let a child experiment with drugs, social or serious, feeling that this is the way they will learn. For others even alcohol may be considered a forbidden substance, and the parent may dig their heels in and become inflexible.

In the immature parent this characteristic of giving freedom to the child may go to such an extreme that the child feels a lack of care in the lack of boundaries and secure rules by which to live. Freedom is accompanied by the need for self-responsibility and a lack of security. Being told what to do provides structure and security. The Melancholic parent needs to achieve an appropriate balance so that the child can feel secure enough to venture into the freedom they are given and can stretch their wings in relative safety.

In general, mature Melancholic parents are quick to praise their children and encourage each development and achievement. The exception is the more introverted parent who has trouble expressing and showing their feelings and isn't quite sure what to say. More than many other parents the Melancholic father or mother is likely to remain friends with their children, even through some of the more difficult growing-up years. They do this by using their intuition and focusing on understanding and developing the relationship. (Sanguine parents may also stay friends with their children, by staying young at heart).

Since Melancholic parents are likely to hold 'open house', their children will rarely be alone. Other children in the neighbourhood, as well as adults, will be encouraged to drop in and they will be made welcome when they do. Other children will want to come for the warm welcome they receive, the quiet fun and games provided and to enjoy playing with a grown-up who has time for them and will listen in a way their own parents may not have time, patience or understanding for. If the Melancholic parent is not careful, this may go so far that the children of the house feel less than special as they are swamped by the neighbours. Some may even feel embarrassed at the way their parents play with and respond to other children, and others may become jealous of the attention being lavished elsewhere.

In general, though, Melancholics are good parents and provide the important basics of nurture, standards and the freedom to develop, thus giving their children a good start in life.

The Melancholic in Old Age

Melancholics tend to age early and to look older than their years, possibly as a reflection of the burdens they feel they have carried through life.

As in all temperaments, with age should come maturity. If it does not and the elderly Melancholic is still in Stage I, it is probable that they will be unhappy, self-absorbed and an emotional burden to others. They will complain to the friends they do have and soon all but their immediate family will tend to avoid them for they can become emotional tyrants, demanding time, attention and help in the quest for an impossible happiness. If they haven't matured by now it is unlikely that they will change at this age.

If they have reached Stage II they will still be taking on the burden of others and feel they have a responsibility to cope with the problems. As they age and their energy diminishes they are less able to do this, yet none the less feel they ought to continue in their role. If they cannot they may feel guilty, unwilling to blame the natural pattern of ageing or to make allowances for the fact that they can now do less than they once used to.

When fully mature, in Stage III, and able both to provide a nurturing environment and to step back and allow others to develop on their own within that sphere, the home of the elderly Melancholic can become a place of peace and tranquillity where more troubled souls can come for relaxation and restoration, nurture and care. The quietness and relative passivity of the mature elderly Melancholic can be a sufficient gift to people in need.

Melancholics who can let go at this time of their self-imposed burden of caring for others may find it a relief, particularly if they have the perspective to realise that other people's problems really are their own and not the responsibility of the Melancholic, and that there is no need to feel guilty or inadequate. They can then enjoy their new freedom. This may lead them into more social activities and a greater willingness to have fun themselves.

Melancholic grandparents get on well with their grandchildren. Some will say they have entered a second childhood and become playmates with them. The Melancholic grandfather will go off with the grandson and get into the same muddy scrapes as they fall in the river or fish in the rain. Both will share the anticipation of being scolded when they get home. Melancholic grandparents will tell the fairy stories parents of other temperaments are too busy to provide, and their imagination and empathy will allow them to share the imaginary playmates of their grandchildren.

Melancholics are keen observers of other people and in the quietness of retirement enjoy the time to indulge this inclination. You may well be surprised at their observations and comments when you had thought they were asleep or dozing and not alert to all that was going on around them. This is enhanced by their ability to understand the motives of others and to be intuitive as to what is happening. They may be more aware of family dynamics than ever before.

For some, retirement is seen as a desirable goal, a time to open the Pandora's box of projects they have started and half completed, all the ideas they wanted to follow up yet didn't have the time for and all the interesting books and articles they have hoarded but not had time to read. They may start a hobby they have been wanting to do for years, they may travel now they are free of parenting responsibilities. They may even take up other causes they have wished to espouse but have not had the time for in the past.

Health and the Melancholic

It is easy for Melancholics to take a deep interest in their own health: you could even say that their health fascinates them. They are sensitive to and aware of every little pain they experience anywhere in their body and they are quick to assume that it heralds some serious problems. It is easy for them to be hypochondriacs. Headaches can become brain tumours, a cough can become lung cancer and that slight pain in the upper half of their body must surely mean a heart attack is imminent.

They will look for a practitioner who is willing to spend time with them and who understands the seriousness of their problems, not one who is cheerful and optimistic, assuring them that all is well before they have given the matter their most serious consideration.

They would rather go regularly for checks-ups than have to wait to make an appointment when something serious happens. They prefer to have tests done to check for possibilities rather than assume everything is all right, a difficult assumption for a Melancholic to make. Regular check-ups offer frequent opportunities to discuss themselves and the way they are feeling with someone who gives them their full attention. Only when all the tests have been done and found to be negative, when all possibilities have been considered and discarded, can the true Melancholic feel that the occasional twinge really is something so minor it need be no cause for further concern.

The time between doing a test and getting the results can be a nightmare for the Stage I Melancholic. They will assume the worst and will have created in their mind scenarios where all the most tragic scenes are played out. When the results come through and are not as bad as they had expected, or are even totally clear, it will be at best an anticlimax, for now they have nothing to worry about. If there is a problem but it is minor they will probe and question, thinking that perhaps the doctor is keeping something from them, not wanting to worry them. If the result is bad it will merely fulfil their expectations.

The way Melancholics describe their symptoms is indicative of their attitude. They never have a 'slight pain', always a 'dreadful pain'. They never get 'a touch of indigestion': always it's this 'awful and painful' indigestion. Even when they have provided sufficient symptoms for the practitioner to have made a confident diagnosis the Melancholic will continue to list further details. The wise practitioner will let them do this even if it adds no useful information, otherwise the Melancholic will lose confidence in them and the extent to which they are willing to give the matter sufficient importance. They may even go in search of another, more Melancholic and sensitive, practitioner.

They can become tense and anxious. While this starts at the emotional level it soon extends into their muscles, and cramps and muscle tension are common. They enjoy and will make time for regular massages from which they will benefit not only physically but also emotionally. They will use the time for deep pondering and introspection, for 'listening to the silence'. This, too, is therapeutic and healing for the Melancholic.

Stress can affect their digestive system and they may develop problems that result from insufficient stomach acid or digestive enzymes and so lead to inadequate breakdown of food. They may think of themselves as having a delicate digestive system. Symptoms include wind, bloating and flatulence, a feeling that food has not been digested properly. There may also be colitis and constipation alternating with diarrhoea.

In addition they should take care of their lungs and should definitely not smoke.

The Melancholic When Things Go Wrong

If the Melancholic does not develop and mature, worse still, if they take the downhill path and follow all that is worst in their natures, they can be a sorry sight. They can become emotional tyrants, totally self-absorbed and selfish, demanding love, care, time, attention and sympathy; above all, sympathy.

When you ask how they are they will nail you to the ground and fill your ears with a litany of complaints and stories of their sufferings. They will ear-bash you until you have nothing more to give, and will still continue. The more introverted ones will withdraw into themselves, experiencing real and imaginary hurts. They may develop a desire, sometimes conscious, more often unconscious, to torture themselves, to be suffering victims, to be martyrs.

They may also become sadists and develop a desire to hurt others. This will not be through physical harm or abuse, or even overt verbal abuse. It is more likely that they will think of ways of creating suffering for others so that they can experience the pain the Melancholic is going through. Why should others be happy? this Melancholic argues when they are in pain. If other people truly cared, the Melancholic assumes, even demands, they would ease the Melancholic's distress. If they are unable or unwilling to do that then they too must suffer.

Even those who try to help this Melancholic may not get off lightly. They may do all they can to cheer the Melancholic up, or to understand them and lead them out of their distress. Yet in some perverse way a time comes when the Melancholic will refuse to speak with them any more. It's as if they sense that the other person's efforts may produce results and the Melancholic, afraid of the consequences, would rather continue to suffer. Some would say they are cutting off their nose to spite their face, yet for the disintegrating Melancholic this is preferable to being willing to take responsibility for their own emotions and develop positively. They cannot achieve this without help, and if they refuse all help they will indeed sink into deep and continuing melancholia.

When they disintegrate into really serious depression they stop looking after themselves. They become indifferent to their appearance, won't wash or dress properly and won't care for their home. They will insist it doesn't matter, that no one cares anyway, no one visits them, so what's the point? You will hear them repeating that they are a burden to other people (true) and that they would be better off dead. In extreme cases they will commit suicide; at other times talk of suicide is a ploy to get your continuing attention focused on them and their problems.

There is little you can do at this stage. Certainly trying to cheer them up won't help. Listing their blessings and telling them all the things they have to be grateful for will do no good. The method remains the same. Try to lead them out of this state by the methods described for helping the Melancholic to mature from Stage I to Stage II.

What the Melancholic Can Teach Us

Melancholics are the most spiritually aware of the temperaments. At times they may seem to have extra-sensory perception: they often seem to be psychic. At their best their greatest gift to the rest of humanity is their ability to empathise with others, to get inside their skins so to speak, and to demonstrate understanding, care and concern for their welfare. They are gentle, kind and imaginative. They are idealistic and are likely to champion causes and contribute in ways that benefit people who are suffering or in need.

They are organised and take care of the many details necessary to convert the imaginative ideas of the Sanguine and the leadership and determination of the Choleric into reality. Do not mistake this attention to detail for the Phlegmatic's willingness to do the routine work, though both are needed for the world to run smoothly.

In spite of their name they are not always melancholic and depressed. Although in general they do have a tendency to see the negative side of life, many are positive and happy and can be a pleasure to be with.

Some of the world's greatest art, of all types, was created by Melancholics. Without them we would be without many wonderful pictures and sculptures, symphonies and pop songs, plays and films, prose and poetry. They have also interpreted the art of others and played, sung, danced and acted to convey to the audience the creations of the original composers and writers.

CHAPTER 12

The Phlegmatic Temperament

Main Characteristics

Phlegmatics are the stable pillars of society, the backbone of any community. They are traditionalists, honouring the hierarchies and knowing their place in them, serving the community and doing their duty. They are conservationists, in all areas of life; change, if it must come, should come about gradually and only after the changes have proven their value. They consider it important to be prepared, to be reliable and to make a contribution.

In general, Phlegmatics are quiet, slow, self-contained and relatively introverted. Unlike Melancholics, however, they are not unduly pessimistic. Instead they are slow and steady, and may even seem sluggish to the point where other people may think them stupid. They are not stupid, they just take time to think things over, time to decide what they will do and then time to do it. Phlegmatics can be average to bright, although in general you will find the quickest brains and the greatest intelligence and learning skills among Cholerics and Melancholics. Phlegmatics often have a lot of common sense, placing value on things that have practical use and application, and are less inclined to ponder on depth and meaning. They also like peace and quiet and will do a great deal to achieve it.

As traditionalists, change disturbs them, since they can never be sure that it is a change for the better. Nor do they like having to learn new ways. They like the familiar. They even prefer doing a routine and monotonous job to one with variety, a situation that would be intolerable for a Sanguine. Variety, after all, means dealing with the unexpected, and this they do not like. If they do have to learn new ways it takes them a long time and they are only happy again when the new has become familiar and routine.

They are often called prejudiced and old-fashioned. To the extent that they like what they already know and do not like to be presented with new ideas, new types of people or new activities, they can indeed be considered to be prejudiced; but this arises rather from a preference for the familiar than from a specific dislike of or for the thing or person that is new. These same characteristics can make them both stubborn and persevering.

It is easy to think that the Phlegmatic is lazy. This is not necessarily true, and indeed they are willing to work long hours when it is asked of them, but they do do things slowly. Since they are also somewhat slow to formulate their ideas and then speak, they may seem uncommunicative and non-responsive. Give them time. They have much to share that is of value, but if you continue to chatter at them they won't bother to make the effort. This result is reinforced by their lack of self-confidence, their feeling that anything they have to offer, to say or do, is probably not worth doing or has already been done or thought of. At times you may feel their silence is due to anger or irritation, but it is more likely that they do not want to make the effort to communicate or that they have some thinking to do.

In all that they do they are meticulous and thorough. They take great care over the tasks they have been given, often more care than is necessary. This can slow down a project and irritate the faster Cholerics and Sanguines who may be involved. However, they are persistent and see things through to completion, so you can safely give them a task and know that it will be completed. But they can take this too far and, once given a task, they may continue to do it even to the point of absurdity, preferring to complete a project rather than leave any loose threads.

> Robin had been asked to list all the firm's clients alphabetically by name and give each one a number. When her boss later said not to worry, they weren't going to use the numbers system after all, she still completed the list, staying late to do so, since it disturbed her to leave the job half done.

Phlegmatics lack self-confidence. They may be good at what they do but they don't think they are and have difficulty believing in their own capabilities. They are less likely to take the lead, to take initiative or assert themselves than the other temperaments. They would much rather play a background role, preferring to be told what to do rather than having to decide for themselves.

Since they are happy to have other people make the decisions and to give the instructions, it is not surprising that they are obedient and very willing to do what they are told. When they are given a clear set of instructions, they can relax. They don't have to keep worrying about whether their present course of action is the right one or not: they can simply go ahead and perform the task, happy in the knowledge that someone else has taken responsibility for the decisions. If anything is wrong they will not get the blame, and this makes them feel safe. If everything works out right the other person will get the praise, but that does not worry the Phlegmatic, who does not seek fame or glory but wants only to serve.

Do not expect the Phlegmatic to do more than one job at a time. Asking a Phlegmatic husband to mow the lawn and then telling him in the middle that the bathroom tap is leaking and needs a new washer, and that you have just remembered there is a funny noise in the car that he should check, is likely to bring him to a halt, fretting about which job is the most important. As a result nothing gets done for a while and his Sanguine wife is screaming with frustration, internally at least, thinking he is uncaring and unhelpful.

If he is a true Phlegmatic he will eventually decide to finish the lawn first, even if it starts to rain, the bathroom floor floods and his wife can't shop for food for the rest of the weekend since the car won't start.

A Sanguine husband, if he bothered to do any of these jobs at all, would have darted in with a temporary measure on the tap, phoned someone to come and fix the car and mown the part of the lawn you can see from the house, leaving the bits that don't show until later, possibly leaving them altogether until the next mowing session. In the time left over he would then have phoned a friend for a chat. Such a whirlwind of activity exhausts and confuses the Phlegmatic, often causing them to seize up and do nothing at all.

Phlegmatics are responsible, however, and will take on any task that is asked of them. When everyone else is busy you are likely to hear someone saying, 'Leave it to Peter, he'll do it', and if he is Phlegmatic, he will. It may take time, but he will steadily work through all the tasks allotted to him.

Some temperaments are born to luxury. Sanguines love it, all the time; they lap it up and revel in it. They expect it to continue simply because they know that, inherently, they deserve it and are sure that someone will supply it for them. Cholerics create their own success and luxury, as and when they want it, knowing that they too deserve it, and that they are totally capable of creating it and maintaining it. Melancholics dislike it. They rarely experience it and if they do are convinced that it cannot last. Phlegmatics don't like it either, unless they were born to it. If it involves a significant change in lifestyle this will bother them, and they soon revert to their old ways.

If you want peace, quiet and security, then stick around a Phlegmatic. If you want excitement and activity, go elsewhere. Phlegmatics are consistently kind and helpful, if unimaginative. They are good-natured, calm and soothing to be with. They like peace and quiet and are thoughtful companions.

> Lucy, a volatile Sanguine, met up with Phlegmatic John a few days after the start of a four-week sea voyage to the Antipodes. With little to do she was frequently frustrated and bored, looking for new games to play, new books to read, new parties, new anything to help pass the time. Provided she created the ideas, John was the perfect foil. He was willing to sit and read with her as long as she wanted, then equally willing to play quoits or table tennis when she needed activity. In the evening he would fit in with her choice of film or dancing.

Never be fooled into belittling this type of willingness to adapt, and don't assume the Phlegmatic is too stupid to have ideas of their own, or that they are wimpish. It is simply that the Phlegmatic is happy to have the ideas presented by someone else and willing to fit in with others and play a background role. Enjoy them for their positive attributes.

Life Path

To develop, the Phlegmatic must learn to make decisions, grow to trust their own judgement and start to take a greater interest in other people and things. They need to learn flexibility and how to adapt.

Now let's see how the progression occurs Stage by Stage.

Stage I

Stage I Phlegmatics are modest. They may have good ideas but will usually hide them. This is partly out of a dislike of being in the limelight and partly out of a lack of confidence. They are uncertain of their own value and usually assume that whatever they think of is bound to be less good than someone else's idea. After all, they reason, if the idea was any good someone else would already have thought of it. If you persuade them to let you know what they are thinking, you may be surprised at the wealth of their insight, but you will have to drag it out of them bit by bit and be sure not to let any possible criticisms show or they will keep their ideas firmly to themselves.

If told to do something they don't want to do, Stage I Phlegmatics will not refuse, they will simply not do it. Told to do their homework or to tidy their room they will either do it or, if they don't want to, will go quietly to the appointed place and just sit. If they don't want to study they may sit at their books and let their minds go blank. They will go to their room when told to tidy it, but rather than tidying it they will read a book. They lack the courage for an all-out refusal so they achieve their ends by calm and passive refusal or avoidance.

Cholerics and Sanguines are the initiators. Phlegmatics wait for others to lead. This is particularly true in Stage I when Phlegmatics may even become a type of slave. The Phlegmatic child is the one who is ordered around, told what to do and expected to fit in with the others. And the Stage I Phlegmatic will be happy to do this and will relish the role. After all, having someone tell you what to do and being able to do it is meat and drink to the Phlegmatic: it is one way of being appreciated without having to make an effort.

A Stage I Phlegmatic is poor company, unless you want passive attention. They are poor conversationalists but are willing to listen. In fact, they are excellent listeners. It is not that they are necessarily interested in what you have to say, it is just that listening makes no demands on them. And they truly believe they have nothing to say that is of interest, so they might as well listen to someone else.

Ask 'What did you do today?' and you are likely to be told 'Nothing' by a Phlegmatic who believes that this is the truth. It is up to you to fill the gap by regaling them with your day's activities. Do not feel that you are hogging centre stage; they are happy to have it that way. The Stage I Phlegmatic will do everything possible to avoid being noticed. They like to be part of the crowd, preferably at the back. If, for some reason, attention is paid to them they try to hide. Even the person at the back may be near the light switch, or asked to close a door, so they will move into the middle. To be singled out in a crowd and asked to do something is an embarrassment.

Just as they do not feel what they do is worth recounting, and they are not particularly interested in what you did, they are also relatively uninterested in what is going on around them. Gossip does not excite them, nor does current politics or world affairs. They are most interested in their own inner world and whatever they are doing at the time.

In Stage I new ideas are usually shunned. There is no sense of adventure, no desire to explore the new. The schoolchild would rather have the same books that the previous year's class had than read anything different. They want to stay in the same house, keep going to the same school, have the same group of friends. They hold on to old clothes; buying new clothes is a torture to them – what if the colour is wrong, the style is wrong, the combination is wrong? The first time they wear the new outfit they are acutely embarrassed, and may even dirty it on purpose so that it no longer looks new. They are disturbed both by the attention they may get and the possibility that they or the parent may have made a wrong choice.

The same things hold true for the Stage I adult. Leaving home and setting up house for themselves is a major trauma. Often they are content to let someone else choose the house, the location and even the furnishings. It is so much easier to say later 'Oh, Mother chose that' or, 'That came from my mother-in-law, I had little choice.'

The unwillingness to consider new ideas or ways shows that Phlegmatics have little imagination. It is almost impossible for them to consider how to furnish a room or have any idea what the finished product will look like. They are honest simply because they don't have the imagination to concoct an alternative story. Equally, if they don't wish to answer a question they will simply not do so. They won't prevaricate, or think up something to say. They won't even refuse to answer. They will just quietly change the subject and avoid confrontation.

Don't expect a speedy decision from any Phlegmatic, and certainly not from a Stage I.

A classic example of this occurred when Phlegmatic Tom moved into Choleric Liz's house after they had decided to live together. Tom commented that her refrigerator was inadequate but, typically, he offered no solution. Liz, desiring to please, said she was happy to get a new one. Unsure, as yet, of how they were going to handle the finances on any such capital outlay she asked, 'How do you want us to buy it? Jointly or, since it's my house and furniture, do you want me to buy it?'

After a very long pause, during which Tom went on with what he was doing, she turned away, not liking to force issue.

Three days later Tom suddenly said, 'I think we should share the cost.'

'Of what?' Liz asked, having long since put the conversation behind her.

'Of the refrigerator, of course. What did you think I meant? We were just discussing it.'

'But that was three days ago. I assumed you didn't want to buy it yourself or have us buy it jointly, so I figured I would, and I haven't thought much about it since.'

'Oh, I thought you would have been hanging on for my answer,' was Tom's surprising reply.

No hurrying that Phlegmatic.

Stage I Phlegmatics need time to make decisions since they have to consider all possibilities, weigh the pros and cons and then gather their courage together. So long as the decision has not yet been made, they cannot have made the wrong one, so they are inclined to postpone the moment for as long as possible.

Phlegmatics have a strong sense of duty. Cholerics have a sense of duty too, but more as the result of their strong code of ethics and their sense of being in command and responsible for others. While the Choleric has a dashing and courageous form of duty, Phlegmatics take seriously the routine duties of life: they are the backbone of social structure and this means security. If the Phlegmatic agrees, even casually, to be home by a certain time they will be home by that time, even if they have to rush and even if it isn't important. Simply because they say they will do something they feel duty bound to do it.

Maturing

As with the other temperaments, the move to Stage II is not automatic. It may come unaided, in time, but it is best achieved with help. Phlegmatics need and benefit from guidance but they do not wish this guidance to be overt. The Sanguine wants and needs to enter into a positive relationship with their mentor. The Choleric does not need to know theirs, but will acknowledge them as someone they admire. Both Cholerics and Sanguines are happily overt in their roles. The Phlegmatic, however, does not welcome any such attention or even recognition of the fact that there is a mentor. They would rather find someone they can respect and then imitate them from afar. They will simply copy them slavishly. If they are found out in this ploy they will be extremely embarrassed.

Just as the Choleric has to learn tolerance and respect for others, a Sanguine needs to develop depth and stability and the Melancholic needs to be less absorbed in their own problems, the Phlegmatic needs to evolve. It is important for Phlegmatics to learn to come out of their shell, to develop confidence in themselves, to be willing to stand up and be counted, to develop and use their initiative and to take some more positive action.

There are many ways you can help. If a Phlegmatic friend is trying to decide which restaurant to go to and you are trying to help them make the choice, offer them a couple of names and then say something like, 'Of course Mrs James and Mr and Mrs Evans always go to Barbicans, it has such excellent food.' This will settle the decision for them, provided, of course, that the people referred to are worthy. Having said this, you should pass swiftly on to another topic.

There are several components to this guidance. First, you have named some important people whose opinion the Phlegmatic can reasonably be expected to respect and trust. Secondly you have praised the food, a sensible basis on which to choose a restaurant, rather than something less tangible. Suggesting that it was the 'in' place of the moment would carry little weight with a Phlegmatic, though it would impress a Sanguine. Thirdly, you have moved on to something else. This all means that the Phlegmatic can give it a few minutes' thought and then say casually, 'I think I'd like to go to Barbicans', making it seem as if this is entirely his or her own decision. If you ever indicate that you think they chose it because they wanted to copy Mrs James and the Evanses you will make them most uncomfortable.

Given such guidelines the Phlegmatic can gradually come to terms with decision-making and can grow in independence. In time there will be increased willingness to cope with new ideas and activities, though you should have no great expectation that they will go on to have a lively imagination of their own.

You can also help them to overcome their shyness and reserve. Take them to things. In a group situation draw them out on a topic that you know they enjoy and with which they are comfortable. In this way they can quietly show their true worth to other people without having to boast. They will be forever grateful to you for the opportunity and will remain loyal and staunch friends.

Gradually they will become more comfortable in groups until in time they feel at ease in quite large crowds, provided always, of course, that they are not expected to take a leading role. They still prefer a background role but are less likely to be embarrassed when thanked publicly for their help or contribution.

Stage II

Stage II Phlegmatics like to belong. They will join the local social club, the bowling club or the church committee. They will become members of many social, educational or religious institutions. They appreciate the structure of these, and the quiet privileges they have as a member. They will assist on any occasion at which volunteers are required, though you may have to co-opt the quieter Phlegmatics rather than waiting for them to offer. They will be glad, however, to have been asked so that they can fulfil their desire to serve. In time they may join the committee, and may even take a Phlegmatic position such as treasurer or secretary.

Maturing

Helping the Phlegmatic to move from Stage II to Stage III is much like the earlier step. Continue to draw the Phlegmatic out and give them a chance to show their worth. By now they are developing their own strength, and the process can be aided when they are given a position of authority and responsibility or when their place in society and their role in the establishment is fully acknowledged.

Stage III

By this stage, Phlegmatics, while still quiet and thoughtful, have become secure in their position and their lifestyle and comfortable with the decisions they make. They have probably reached a position of trust, at work, in the family and among their friends. Other people know they can be relied on. If Stage III Phlegmatics say they will take care of something, other people can know it is in good hands. In fact, all too often their background support role is taken so much for granted that it is only noticed by its absence when the Phlegmatic is not there.

Stage III Phlegmatics are great peacemakers. They show little or no emotion, do not take sides, do not become irritated and impatient. Both or all sides in the argument can feel that in the Stage III Phlegmatic they have a passive and unbiased mediator who is willing to listen to what they have to say and give it proper consideration. As a result they are likely to abide by the final decision.

They are soothing and relaxing people to be with and very reliable. There is no conflict in their life – it takes two to make a fight. They are not rude, do not argue, and are not difficult to please. They do not step on people's toes or make waves. In groups they will fit in with the others, agreeing to see or go to whatever film, pub or restaurant the others pick. In a group of independent Cholerics it is soothing to have a Phlegmatic around. For these reasons they have many friends.

They can deal with emergencies, being the one unruffled firm and solid rock on which others rely as they rush this way and that wondering what to do and how to cope. I have a beloved relative whose attitude in the middle of any upset is expressed in one of her favourite phrases: 'It'll all be all the same in a hundred years.' Her willingness to take what comes is reflected in another of her sayings as she locks the ducks in their shed each night: 'Good night, take care, sleep well, see you in the morning if we're all spared.'

Although shunning the limelight and a leading role, by virtue of their reliability and steady application Phlegmatics have risen in their jobs to relatively senior positions. Since they have upset none of their colleagues they may have been promoted ahead of others with more inherent merit, but also with more enemies.

Financially they will be average to comfortably off but not wealthy. They will, if possible on their income, have saved and invested wisely. They will have taken care of their pensions and be able to live comfortably, if somewhat frugally and carefully, after they retire. They will have made provision for dependants and have had a precise and detailed will drawn up, possibly several as their circumstances have changed. It is likely that they have been in the same job for years and are looking forward to a handsome retirement benefit.

They have developed from passive listeners into active listeners. Family and friends will come to them when they need a listening post and, by now, someone who will even give some advice based on their experience.

Phlegmatics and Their Appearance

Phlegmatics tend to look older than their years, just as Sanguines tend to look younger. Phlegmatics are large both in terms of being tall and in being heavy. They do not, however, have firm chunky bodies like Cholerics but tend to be flabby and with poor muscle definition. They are not necessarily fat, but do tend in that direction. They may also seem fatter than they are because of the softness of their flesh. Their heaviness, when tending to overweight, is often thought of as the type of weight gain associated with glandular problems. There are few clear-cut lines or any signs of their bones showing through.

In the early years the Phlegmatic baby is likely to be the biggest and the chubbiest. It's as if all their effort goes into growing their body. They will lie there quietly, content to watch the world go by, enjoying their food and converting all those calories into body weight rather than physical energy. This is in contrast to the Choleric, who is too busy being active to put a lot of energy into growing: they are impatient to get on with life and to bend their body to their will. Phlegmatic babies are generally somewhat clumsy and slow to learn manual dexterity, in contrast to Sanguine babies who take a delight in the movement and use of their limbs and fingers.

As with the other temperaments, character and temperament are visible in the head and face. Phlegmatics' heads are large and oblong to oval. Their hair is usually brown or mousy in colour, relatively thick but possibly limp. Their skin may be somewhat pasty and dull, and may also be freckled.

The face has few clear-cut bones or planes. It is usually still: not for them the lively mobility of expression of the Sanguine. Their eyes are dull and their expression is passive, in sharp contrast to the bold outward stare of the Choleric.

Phlegmatics have large fleshy noses and their mouths are soft with fleshy, often moist and poorly defined, lips and, because they take time to absorb information, they seem slow to respond and may look expressionless. It is not that nothing is happening inside, just that it is taking a long time.

They rarely laugh but will smile quietly, more often than not at their own thoughts rather than at a flip joke, which, in any case, they may well have missed. The jawline is poorly defined, if visible at all. You will often see Phlegmatics with cheeks that flow on into their jowls.

The Phlegmatic's walk could be described as plodding, although the stride is long. They may even appear to shamble along in a somewhat ungainly fashion. They keep going straight ahead and are unlikely to get out of your way. This is not due to lack of courtesy, simply that it is difficult for them to decide which way to move or even to change direction at all. In the time it takes the Phlegmatic to think about it, the Sanguine would have leapt sideways and be past you. Their arms hang loosely by their sides, rather than swinging like those of the Choleric, or as a quietly integrated part of the walk and general movement. All their movements are slow, both walk and gestures. They do not, however, droop as the Melancholic can.

Their legs are likely to be firm and solid rather than well shaped or graceful. Clearly they are there for the purpose of supporting the body rather than for grace and mobility. They may have thick ankles and wrists and long but solid fingers with thick ends and square palms. Although they are capable of delicate work they are more often somewhat clumsy with their fingers.

Phlegmatics are heavy-footed and plant their feet firmly on the ground with each stride. Their feet are straight as they walk, or even pointed slightly inwards, and they are likely to be hard on their shoes and wear the soles unevenly.

Phlegmatics' dislike of the limelight is reflected in their clothes. They prefer dull, quiet and unobtrusive colours to bright colours, simple designs rather than bright patterns or bold stripes, and blending tones rather than sharp contrasts. The style of their clothes is also conservative. They feel no urge to rush to keep up with, or even be ahead of, the fashion – they leave that to their Sanguine cousins.

Clothes, they feel, are there to serve a purpose: to keep the body warm and decently clad. So the Phlegmatic sees no need to buy new ones until the old are too worn to wear. When you add this to the Phlegmatic's dislike of change you will understand why they often keep old favourites for so long they look shabby. It is not that they are slovenly or messy, simply that because it looked fine last year they assume it will continue to look fine. They are, however, neat and tidy so their clothes will be well and frequently washed, tears and lost buttons will be mended and replaced at once: there will be no safety pins for the Phlegmatic. They are more likely to iron everything, down to the last teacloth and duster, than to go out in a crumpled blouse or shirt.

With age there is a certain tendency towards an even more Phlegmatic appearance. The walk becomes slower and they tend to put on more weight. Their legs and ankles get thicker and their clothes somewhat old-fashioned.

The Phlegmatic Child

Phlegmatic babies may, other things being equal, take their time to be born. Even at that stage they are probably not keen on change, and leaving the womb and going out into a totally unknown environment is the biggest change they will ever be called on to make.

In general, they will be less active than other babies, content, as long as they are well fed and comfortable, to lie quietly and drift between sleep and their own inner experience. If they are hungry or wet they will let you know, they have the voice, but otherwise you are likely to get compliments on having 'such a good baby'.

They may move later than other babies, crawling later, waving and hitting later, grasping objects later, but not because they are stupid. It is simply their natural reserve and their tendency to live within themselves. They are unlikely to show the physical dexterity and lightness of movement of the Sanguine child, and will be probably be rather clumsy. Again, these are all aspects of their temperament. If you are a busy mother with other children to look after you will be grateful for their placid nature.

They will be content to play for hours with whatever toys you give them. They will want to hear the same fairy stories over and over again: that way they can be sure of the ending rather than being uncertain of what will happen next. They are not keen on excitement and would rather play the traditional games with set rules than go off on an unknown adventure. They tend to be obedient, not so much from a desire to be good as a dislike of doing something different and risking an unknown punishment. 'What would happen if ...' is not a game a Phlegmatic child enjoys. They will sit for hours sorting coloured blocks, doing a single jigsaw puzzle, building a Meccano model from a printed plan, or arranging the doll's house to look like their own home.

You can take them anywhere. The ambitious career mother who dreams of a baby she can take to work and have in the pram beside her desk, where he or she will lie quietly between feeds, will probably only accomplish this if the baby is a Phlegmatic. The parents who like to socialise will be able to take their Phlegmatic child with them and put the child to bed in whatever home they are visiting. The Phlegmatic child can be taken out, given toys or a book or two to read and will stay quiet and keep himself amused through endless adult activities such as committee meetings, shopping excursions, visits to the dentist, or coffee mornings.

School

At school the Sanguine child may go off into a dream world of exciting fantasies, the Choleric may be planning her next role as ruler in the play break and the Melancholic worrying about what will happen when things go wrong. The Phlegmatic child will be waiting quietly until he is told what to do next.

Since change is traumatic, the first day at play school, kindergarten or senior school is likely to be difficult for the Phlegmatic child. With time and the repetition of the steady routine, however, they will settle in and relax. For as long as they stay in the one school and with the same group of children, they feel secure. The move to the next class at the beginning of each year is a mild trauma, but with other constants, such as their friends and the location of the school, they deal with it. The problem comes when they move to a new school. Parents of a different temperament may try to tempt them with the excitement of the new things they can do, but this is the wrong way to go about things. Let them know all the ways in which the new school will be like the old one, not different to it. It is not that they are afraid or cowardly, simply that change for them is very disturbing and it takes them a while to adjust.

Cholerics have trouble going from junior to senior school because they have to adjust from being king of the castle to being at the bottom of the ladder again. Sanguines love change for its own sake, Melancholics will worry anyway, but for the Phlegmatic the trauma is the mere fact of having to make a change.

They will study steadily and do their homework on time. Not for them the last-minute panic of the Sanguine. They like to have their work done with sufficient time to check it over if they feel this is necessary.

In team sports they are likely to play in defensive positions or positions where their weight, rather than strength or speed, are important. All in all, however, they will not be too keen on sports or rushing around in general. They will easily obey such admonitions from school prefects as 'Walk, don't run, down the corridors.'

They will be the steady plodders rather than the high achievers. Lacking the flamboyance or extroversion of Cholerics and Sanguines and not demanding attention as do the Melancholics, they will get on quietly with their studies, often surprising the teacher by the quality of the work they hand in or the questions they ask. Mind you, they have trouble asking and getting answers to their questions. They need time and an understanding teacher, a combination that may not happen often. Teachers are frequently all too pleased to have some students sitting quietly and thinking things over so they can handle the noisier ones, and so they ignore the quiet Phlegmatic child. This is unfortunate, as Phlegmatics have a lot to offer if they are given time and encouragement.

Phlegmatics like peace and put up with a lot to maintain it. They are often the ones who calm down a fight, simply because they remain calm and detached. They are not belligerent or aggressive by nature, nor are they easily goaded. If pushed too far, however, for example by a taunting bully, they will eventually lash out and can be surprisingly violent. This results from the fact that they can be clumsy and that they sometimes underestimate their own strength. If they fall into a bad pattern of behaviour, or get into a bad crowd, it is difficult for them to change, even when they say they want to and are encouraged to do so by parents and teachers. At this point they need understanding, encouragement and someone who will lead them gently in a new direction.

They can do well at school, though they are not, on average, as bright as the Cholerics and Melancholics. They tend to achieve by steady hard work and application rather than by flashes of brilliance and inspiration. They will pass exams and may go on to further study. They will also be comfortable choosing a steady job, straight from school, and be content to work their way up through whatever company or organisation they have joined.

If they work after school hours or in the school holidays it is more likely to be stacking shelves in a supermarket than darting around on a newspaper run. They want to be told exactly what to do, then they want to be shown what to do, then they want to be supervised until they have repeated the tasks and they have become a safe and steady habit. You can then leave them to get on with the job and rely on them to do it thoroughly every single time.

By the end of their school career they will probably be prefects. They may not be head boy or head girl, since the Cholerics will vie for that role, but they can be the pillars of their society, the reliable and stable students on whom the teachers come to depend. They will help organise the younger students into teams and into jobs on special occasions. They will see that the chores are done, the notebooks collected and the library books returned. All in all they are likely to leave with reports using words such as 'reliable', 'honest', 'works hard', 'applies himself/herself'.

If they go on to university or training college, much the same pattern will continue. The move will be stressful initially, then they will adjust and continue with their education, following their predictable behaviour patterns.

The Phlegmatic Adult

On leaving school or college Phlegmatics will follow a conventional, traditional and typical path. They will do what their friends are doing, or what their parents did, or what other people they admire have done. They will take on a regular trade or profession rather than attempt to carve out an individual niche for themselves.

When considering a job they will look for a well established company, a job with long-term prospects and a good retirement or pension plan.

> I once did a summer job from school at a place where there was a man of twenty-three. He had apprenticed there, studied in the evenings and was now a qualified analytical chemist – a good job for a Phlegmatic – but not particularly happy with his post. I asked if he was going to leave and look for another one and was amazed when he replied that he couldn't do that, he had already put five years' contributions into his superannuation which he would lose if he left. My mind boggled at the thought of the forty years ahead of him!

Phlegmatics tend to keep themselves to themselves. They are slow to respond to questions or to change their activity when asked. They prefer their own company to being in a crowd and can rarely be persuaded to adapt to what other people suggest unless they give it a considerable amount of thought and then decide they want to. For these reasons they often irritate other people, particularly the quicker Cholerics and Sanguines, who feel they make poor company. In this, however, their good qualities are being overlooked. They can make sure and loyal friends if you understand them.

Friends

They are likely to have the same friends year after year. They are loyal and faithful and like to be surrounded by people they have known for a long time. They will stay in touch with their old schoolfriends, attend reunions and may even send out a regular newsletter. The same is true of their relationship with their families. They will be the ones that keep in touch with distant cousins and organise the get-togethers at weddings, christenings, birthdays and so forth. It will be the Phlegmatic parent who drives the children to sports at the weekends, to classes after school and who picks them up after parties. They will do this not only for their own children but for others whose parents are too busy or too disorganised.

They will also do their duty, as they see it, in their community. They will be part of Neighbourhood Watch, on the parents' committee at their children's school, and attend council meetings or the meetings of their clubs or associations. If they do take a position on the committee it will be as one of the crowd, one of the helpers. If they do rise to an executive position it will be as secretary or treasurer, rarely as chairperson. They will make sure that all the correct procedures are followed and reports are sent out as they should be. They do not make good initiators, nor do they make good revolutionaries.

In religion they are likely to choose a church that has solid and traditional rituals, and will draw comfort from the security these provide. They do not like the flamboyant, and so probably prefer a church with simple procedures.

You can trust the Phlegmatic in more ways than one. Give them a job and you can trust them to do it. Get a verbal agreement from them and you know they will stand by it. They keep their word and live up to all the commitments they make. They also like the world to keep faith with them and are deeply disturbed when it doesn't.

Socially you can expect the men to enjoy male-only activities, whether at the pub or their club, at weekends away on fishing trips, or simply on a regular men's night out once a week. The women also enjoy activities in which only their sex is present. These may focus round the children, domestic matters or community events and are likely to occur regularly and follow a predictable pattern.

Phlegmatics are warm-hearted and can be hurt easily, although they may not show this. Because of their reliability and their preference for working in the background they are often taken for granted, yet they like and treasure compliments and appreciation as much as anyone. If they do not get the recognition they feel is their due they can build up an internal resentment. Don't expect them to come up on stage to receive their vote of thanks, however: they are more likely to bob up from their seat and sit down again quickly. This does not mean they are any the less appreciative, simply shy.

The Phlegmatic at Work

Phlegmatics are good steady workers. A boss or employer can rest easy once he has asked a Phlegmatic to do a task that has been specified in detail, knowing that it will be done thoroughly and completely. They are willing to do routine and repetitive jobs that would bore the other temperaments; in fact, this is the type of work they prefer. They do not want to be the boss, they do not want variety, they do not want to have to make decisions or to make frequent changes to their activities. They do not want to wake up in the morning wondering what the day will bring, they want to know exactly what they will be doing at work, to know they have done it before, done it well and that they will do so again.

They make excellent factory workers, doing repetitive jobs on production lines. They enjoy routine clerical work and do not get frustrated by filling out the same forms or filing the records over and over again. They make wonderful secretaries and assistants and take a quiet pleasure in making the boss look good. They like to serve and to support the company or organisation to which they belong.

I recall, while at school, visiting a Shipham's paste factory and watching a woman put her ten fingers into ten jars on a conveyor belt and turn them over, impaling each one on a rubber spike on a conveyor belt as she let them go. I asked her if she didn't get bored and she answered, 'Oh no, it gives me plenty of time to think.' Later I watched a man sticking the labels on the jars, jar after jar as they went past him. I didn't even ask him a similar question, he had such a look of quiet content on his face.

Phlegmatics are willing to be physically active in their work and may be found on building sites, delivering the mail or clearing the rubbish. They tend, on the whole, though by no means exclusively, to be artisans and craftsmen rather than intellectuals.

Phlegmatics are unlikely to be in business for themselves, preferring to work for someone else. This is fortunate since if they were in their own business there would be the danger that, due to their conservatism, they would fail to keep up with innovations, changes and with the needs of their customers. Working for a boss can also mean changes but someone else will be making the decisions, and if Phlegmatics are lucky they themselves will have time to adapt slowly.

An employer can be pretty sure that his Phlegmatic employees will stay put. They are unlikely to change jobs unless there is severe provocation and it is not unusual to find them in the same job for many years, if not decades. The nannies and family retainers of the old days, who stayed with the one family their whole working life, were probably Phlegmatics.

To train a new Phlegmatic employee you should demonstrate what is to be done, in small chunks, and let them get the hang of the job a bit at a time. Show them what to do, then keep an eye on them as they do it, making gentle modifications or suggestions until they get it right. Once they have mastered the task you can be sure they will do it reliably, again and again. They are bright and capable provided they have someone to copy. Do not leave them to work things out for themselves: they will then seem to be stupid when in fact they are not.

In general, Phlegmatics will become pillars of strength within the workplace. They will rise to positions of mild authority, passing on instructions from their boss to the people they have under them and reliably supervising their work. However, since they are not always comfortable being in authority they may insist they do not need staff and so become overworked. They will stay late, if necessary, to ensure the job is completed for they hate to leave work, or any task, unfinished. They will arrive on time, take no more than the prescribed time for meal breaks and apply themselves steadily, not wandering off to the cloakroom at intervals looking for a break or a diversion.

Since they are generally quiet and serious their work may go unnoticed and unappreciated. This is unfortunate: Phlegmatics respond to praise as much as anyone, even if they don't always show this.

You are likely to find them in large organisations, in business, in government departments, in administration. They like to maintain organised records and data and you will find them in stock control and in libraries. In law offices they do the searches, but do not, of course, perform in court or rely on quick thinking and repartee. Leave that to the Sanguines, but make sure the Phlegmatic feeds them the information. They will keep the books and records, and keep track of the finances. They are meticulous with figures and make good accountants. If you find them in your bank you may not get the full loan that you want, unless you can convince their cautious nature that you are a good risk. In the stereotyped female role they make excellent clerical secretaries, but unless very mature they may fail if promoted to the role of personal assistant, where initiative and quick decision-making may be required while the boss is away.

They are excellent people to have when security checks are being made, or in quality control. They will see that standards are maintained, that all the safety checks are run and that everything is as it should be. If a Phlegmatic is leading a project and says it is safe to continue, it probably is.

Phlegmatics who are more extroverted than the average can make good teachers, willing to repeat material until it is understood, and having patience with slow pupils. They enjoy teaching the young and the average students, but may leave to the Sanguines the job of teaching the bright students.

They will do a lot to make sure people around them, including their boss, are satisfied. They work well in liaison between groups, between parents and teachers, in wage setting and arbitration, keeping the peace and helping others to do the same. If a Phlegmatic is in the arbitration chair the underdog will feel they are getting a fair hearing.

Liking predictability, Phlegmatics will probably take their holidays at the same time each year: they may go to the same place, even with the same group of people, which allows others to plan around them. Their holidays are important to them – a fair reward for a fair days' work.

Overall, the heart of the Phlegmatic's life is the home and family, and this should be kept in mind by their boss. They will be loyal and reliable workers, but at heart the Phlegmatic knows they are working to have the wherewithal to provide for their partner and children. Home is the heart; the rest is the means. None the less they often have work and careers that they value and that are important to them.

The Phlegmatic and Money

Elsewhere it has already been said that Phlegmatics are not comfortable with wealth. They will comfortably accept whatever level of income and money they were used to when growing up. The way it was when they were a child is the norm: that is the way they are used to, that is the way it should be. Within a small margin, they expect to continue at the same level and will be comfortable doing so. If, when they leave home, their income diminishes this is unlikely to worry them. They may even expect it, seeing it as only natural that they have to earn their way in the world and build up gradually to their accustomed standard of living. If they are very unsure of themselves they may even doubt that this is possible.

If they win a lottery, receive an inheritance or marry money they will feel uneasy and believe that this wealth cannot last. If it does they are likely to save it, buy conservative shares with it or leave it in the bank. If a Phlegmatic's wife has won the money she will be told to keep it for herself.

In marriage the Phlegmatic is likely to let his wife keep control of the finances, handing over his salary without a murmur. If she is Phlegmatic herself she may resist this, but find there is little she can do as she does most of the shopping, and he leaves the bill paying to her. She will manage their financial affairs conservatively, apportioning parts of their income to each type of expenditure and putting some aside into a savings account if this is possible. Money will also be set aside for regular payments such as insurance, rates and mortgage. The appropriate insurance premiums will be paid, always on time, and money will be paid into a well-thought-out insurance or pension scheme, plus a little extra put aside for rainy days. In this way they will endeavour to take care of their financial future as well as the financial present. If she is not a Phlegmatic she will probably be happier to take over this role, though if she is a Melancholic she will worry over it, sure that they will not continue to make ends meet and that something disastrous will happen. If she is a Sanguine, her Phlegmatic husband should worry.

If she is the Phlegmatic and he is not, she will let her husband manage their finances, certain that he can do a better job of it than she can. This may be true if he is a Choleric, but if he is Sanguine she is almost certainly wrong in this assumption and may live to regret her decision.

Phlegmatics do not spend money carelessly. They spend it on what is utilitarian and what is sensible. They do not spend for ostentation. They spend money on such things as redecorating the house, buying new clothes or replacing the family car, not because they want a change but because it is necessary. They do not derive any particular fun from spending money or buying new things, certainly not in the way a Choleric or Sanguine does; indeed, they mourn the passing of the old items that are being replaced. However, they must, eventually, keep up with the community's standards, do the right thing and follow others' example.

When buying they must be led gently to the sale. There is no point in the salesperson trying to sell to them, trying to persuade them to make the purchase. Once again, the appropriate carrot is to tell them what some local prominent person has done and allow the Phlegmatic to follow suit.

Objects are valued for their usefulness rather than their beauty. Phlegmatics waste not and want not and when something has outlived its purpose it is given to the most deserving charity, for there is surely some life and value left in it yet for someone whose need is greater than that of the giver. If a good use cannot be found for something they may keep it, storing it and labelling it meticulously, in case, at some future time, it does turn out to have a use.

The Phlegmatic and Time

Above all temperaments the Phlegmatic is likely to be on time. They like routine, they like things to be orderly, and they like things to happen on time. They keep to their word and when they say they will be somewhere at a certain time, they will be. They will come when they say they will and they will leave when they planned to. In part this is because it is the correct thing to do, in part they may have some other appointment later on and they do not want to be late for it. They like meetings to start on time, proceed in an orderly manner and finish on time. The exception to this is when they have been given a job and asked to finish it. They may then stay at work until it is done, but they will phone home and tell their wife or husband that they will be late.

When other people do not keep appointments, do not show up on time, or outstay their welcome, the Phlegmatic's routine, their organised life, is thrown out and they are uncomfortable. It does not occur to them that the Sanguine may be so lost in what they are doing they are unaware of the passing minutes, the Melancholic so lost in themselves and the moment that time has stood still and the Choleric feels in charge of all things, including time. Phlegmatics assume that other people think as they do and so, if they are late, something could be wrong. However, Phlegmatics do not fret and flap, so if you are late they will simply wait quietly until you do turn up; they are not quite sure what else to do, so there is little point in doing anything. They also have a quiet acceptance of fate.

If they have a project to do they will plan it out carefully so there is no last-minute rush. They do not need to ask for time extensions, but are more likely to have their work finished early and suggest a review, with time to make any possible beneficial changes before the final submission. They will collect all the necessary data at the start, then settle down, sort it and come up with their final report. If it is a physical project such as building, dressmaking or cooking, they will assemble the materials and then get on with it right away, rather than putting it off.

Because they do things slowly and thoughtfully they need more time than other people to complete projects. They are not to be hurried but, like the tortoise who finally beat the hare, they do get there in the end.

The Phlegmatic in Love

Phlegmatics are neither passionate nor romantic, but they do make caring, reliable, responsible and faithful partners.

Men

The Phlegmatic man is large and appears solid and reliable. But he finds his size a disadvantage, and this applies to his love affairs as well as to the rest of his life. He feels that his size will lead women to expect a lot from him, but because of his low self-confidence and his reluctance to take the initiative, he fears he will not live up to women's expectations.

The young Phlegmatic may be the last to lose his virginity, watching from afar but afraid to take the leap, quite sure that when the time comes he will not know what to do and that he will make a fool of himself. What if he does it wrong? What if he doesn't please her? What if he can't do it? What if she laughs at him and tells her friends? These and other thoughts run through his head along with the conviction that he won't even get to first base anyway as the woman in question is unlikely to accept him. He is a lucky young man if an older and more experienced woman takes pity on him and begins to educate him in this area.

He may see a woman he likes and wishes to invite out, but be afraid to ask. She may even be aware of his interest and be keen to go out with him. Yet he still holds back. If, in the modern idiom, she is happy to issue the invitation he is likely to say no out of embarrassment, and to be confused by her forwardness. There is now a new problem. After all, that is not the way it was done in his father's time, and we know that above all he is a traditionalist. If she is clever she will engineer a situation such that little initiative is required on his part. Perhaps they are in a group which is discussing going to a movie. He would like to go and to take her with him. All she has to do is say something that will let him understand that she'd like to go and to be his partner. If they go in a group she can manage to sit next to him and to let him know, in subtle ways, that she finds his company pleasant. At the end he may have the courage to invite her out again. If, however, she says no and explains that she is busy, he is likely to assume that she is really saying she doesn't want to go out with him again and he may well not repeat the invitation. If she is interested, she must make sure she lets him know she would like a repeat invitation.

The couple may then go out together for a while. He will gather confidence but may still doubt that she cares deeply or that she would like to marry him. He may even be scared of frightening her off by asking. She, on the other hand, is likely to find the big bear appealing in many ways. He has attributes that she values and of which he himself is unaware. He is reliable, he will make a steady provider and be there when she or the family need him. He stays around whatever her mood, he will fit in with whatever she wants to do. If at times she is frustrated by his lack of imagination, at least she isn't dragged off to the races or to football matches in which she has little interest. He doesn't argue or try to dominate and control her, nor does he criticise her. He doesn't get into a flap in a crisis and in many situations he may cope better than the more active Sanguine or Choleric.

Come the time to live together or get married and she may have to make another push. There may be comments about what they could do, or the money they could save if they lived together. In the end she may even be the one who proposes. If he wants this too, he will almost certainly be relieved that she took the initiative and may even, in the end, come to believe, since it had been in his mind for such a long time, that it was his idea and his initiative. It is best that she doesn't remind him otherwise. This is often a marriage where the woman is the leader, but leads by supporting the less confident and less aggressive Phlegmatic.

He is likely to have been attracted to a small woman, someone tiny, in need of his protection but not demanding too much from him. If she is petite and shows how much she adores him, his confidence will rise. If she is witty and fun, bright as a button and amusing he will be delighted, feeling that she can bring into their home the lightness that he lacks. The delicate Sanguine suits him well initially and is often the choice he makes. But she should not assume that his achievements will be in proportion to his size.

Women

Life is easier for the Phlegmatic female. She is content to let the man make all the moves. The traditional role of the passive female, waiting for the male to act, suits her perfectly. She would be horrified if someone suggested she invite him out. If he doesn't ask, then there is nothing, in her mind, that she can do.

She is content to be the passive partner, waiting to be invited out, waiting to be proposed to, ready to fit in with whatever he wants and accepting his role as the leader and the stronger of the two. Unlike the Choleric or Sanguine woman who wants to follow their own inclinations, the Phlegmatic woman is content to adapt to her partner. This gives many men a satisfying feeling of being in control and ruling the roost.

Since she too lacks self-confidence, she will be surprised and grateful to be invited out and be the centre of someone's attention. She is likely to marry, if not the first person that asks, then nearly so, for, not being interested in the grand passion and not feeling that the world is well lost for love, she is pleased if she is content with the man and feels secure. She will then faithfully try to adapt to his needs and provide a well-run home for him, rarely looking elsewhere or being unfaithful. After all, she likes the known and is nervous of change. She is happiest if her friends and family approve of her choice and would probably not marry in the face of opposition from these quarters.

Once married, the Phlegmatic male is likely to try to change his wife if she is of a different temperament. The Sanguine vivacity and extroversion that delighted him when they first met he will find disturbing in his home. He will encourage her to settle down into his quiet routine, a difficult thing for the Sanguine to do. He would be wise to continue to value her novelty rather than try to change her.

The Phlegmatic male will do all he can to provide for his wife and family. He will help around the house, whether she goes out to work or not. He likes to get up early and, if she is lucky, may even bring her tea in bed, or coffee, but tea is more traditional. He has no aversion to sharing the cleaning, the cooking, the shopping or any of the other chores. He will also look after the garden and do repairs around the home. However, he will do them at his own speed and one at a time, completing one before starting the next. His wife should not rush him or confuse him with multiple requests. If he sets out to paint the interior she should be prepared to have patience. It could take months, if not longer, but in the end she will have a job that is done well and thoroughly. She is also likely to have to ask to have jobs done, since he is unlikely to take the initiative. If she does ask, and tells him exactly what needs to be done, he is pleased to be able to help.

The Phlegmatic man takes his duties as a home provider seriously. He is not looking for the flamboyant, but for the stable and the good. If his wife has money of her own this will make him nervous and he is likely to insist that she keep it for herself, that they can live on his salary or their joint earned incomes. Moving up into a financial bracket to which he is not used would make him nervous. He is only comfortable with wealth if he grew up with it, and even then he will use it quietly and not make a big display.

When he comes home from work he will have little to say. A Stage I Phlegmatic is so involved in what he is doing he will not have noticed much that went on at work. He will not have heard the gossip, noticed changes or been aware of what other people are doing. When he gets home and his wife asks if he had a good day he is likely to say 'yes' and leave it at that, having nothing more to say. He will be surprised if she accuses him of being taciturn, secretive or unobservant. She, on the other hand, may regale him with stories of the children's doings and events in the neighbourhood. He is content to listen, or to let her talk while his mind wanders off. If she then, in exasperation, asks if nothing at all happened in his day he is likely to repeat that, no, things were just the same as usual, and he really believes this. As he matures through to Stage III he will become more observant and have more to share.

Similarly, the Phlegmatic wife will have little to report of her day's activities. If she goes out to work she will assume that his work is much more important than hers and be content to listen to what he has to say about his day. If she stays at home this is even more true, for she doubts that domestic details can be of interest to her husband, out in the real world and living a much more varied life.

If she, being of a different temperament, wants a bright social life she will have to make the arrangements, and do so ahead of time, letting him know what she has planned. A spur of the moment suggestion from her that they go out and do something is likely to be met with Phlegmatic resistance. He is more inclined to settle down with a book or in front of the television, or turn in for an early night. He is also disinclined to let her go out and have a good time without him: he desires her quiet company.

If she gets upset and says she doesn't think he loves her any more he will look surprised and say, 'But I distinctly remember telling you so. Twice, in fact – when we got engaged and on our wedding day.' For him that is enough: he has trouble understanding that she needs repeated assurances. When he says something he means it, and when he means it, he means it for a long time. So, having told her once, she should be satisfied. Besides, he feels he is demonstrating his love for her every day by providing for her and helping her. He puts greater faith in actions than in words

For these reasons a Phlegmatic wife is suitable. The Sanguine may become frustrated at being caged up, the Choleric may storm out and the Melancholic needs all the attention the Phlegmatic is willing to give. The more mature he is, the more likely he is to take a greater interest in her wants and needs and to try to satisfy them rather than to change her.

The Phlegmatic wife will put more emphasis on creating a well-run home than on catering to her husband's sexual needs. Physical needs rank low in her priorities and she may have trouble realising how important they are to him.

Sex

Neither the male or the female Phlegmatic has much interest in sex. They marry for a secure home and children, not to satisfy a grand passion. His sex drive is low, lower than that of the other three temperaments, and if he has to make the first move he may often feel it is not worth the bother. She, provided she is not Phlegmatic, will almost certainly take the leading role at least as often as he does. She should not read this as a lack of interest on his part, or a lack of love and affection for her; it's just his nature, the same nature that makes him faithful and supportive in so many ways.

It is quite possible that the female Phlegmatic is a virgin on her wedding day and she is proud rather than embarrassed by this, no matter what age she is. If her mate is a Choleric she will be overwhelmed by his confidence and strength but will submit willingly to her wifely role. She may well be embarrassed and confused by the demands made on her by a Sanguine husband, but be content to listen patiently while her Melancholic lover extols her virtues. After all, little is required of her and she is content to let him talk; she is, after all, an excellent listener. The quiet attention she gives him may be all he needs to feel they share a common experience.

Phlegmatics are not romantic and there will have been few, if any, romantic dinners with roses and champagne before marriage, and even fewer afterwards. The Phlegmatic is also lacking in charm or finesse in bed. The Kama Sutra is not for them; the missionary position, simple and basic, is. They have little idea of subtle refinements that may please the other person and will do little or nothing that is outrageous or daring. Yet when the Phlegmatic male is with other men he may contribute his fair share of sexy or dirty jokes.

If both partners are Phlegmatic they probably have a routine sex life, with patterns and procedures they set up early in the relationship. They will probably repeat this, with little variation, throughout their married life.

Sex is something to be done quietly in the dark, in bed and after the children have gone to sleep. In extreme cases it may be on the same night each week. Phlegmatics do not have a large sexual appetite, so once a week is probably plenty, if not too often. Sex, in their mind, is primarily for the purpose of having children and not for pleasure. Sex may be used to ease tensions, to reduce the build-up of sexual pressure, or to reassure each other of their affection. She may, once the novelty has worn off, see sex as her duty rather than as a pleasure, yet she will perform this duty unfailingly and willingly as part of the marriage bargain, a bargain whereby he provides the wherewithal for their lives and she creates the creature comforts. The male may recognise this and express his gratitude afterwards for the service she has done him, and his concern for her welfare.

The idea that his wife has sexual needs rarely occurs to the Phlegmatic male, who still believes that 'nice girls don't'. This is fine if his wife is Phlegmatic, but frustrating for her if she is not. If she is Choleric or Sanguine and used to taking the initiative, at least some of the time she may be dismayed at his conservative reaction to her actions.

Sex is also something that is isolated from the rest of the marital relationship. Where the Sanguine couple may start their erotic build-up in the kitchen, kindle it over dinner, ignite it on the sofa and then, excited and naked, retire to bed for the culmination, this would never do for the Phlegmatic couple. These two go to bed first and then decide whether or not tonight is one of those nights. For this reason it is difficult for the Phlegmatic partner to believe that what happens during the day or the evening may affect their partner's mood and desire for sex. Phlegmatics, particularly the males, like to tell people the truth and reform them 'for their own good'. They can also be critical, sarcastic and have rows, though this does not happen often. No matter how bad the mood over dinner, the Phlegmatic male will be surprised if his partner is unusually uninterested in sex when they go to bed.

As the marriage continues, and if it is not a very successful one, she, being Phlegmatic, will often 'have a headache' or 'be too tired', especially in Stage I. By Stage III, or in a good marriage, she is taking sufficient interest in her partner to think more of his needs than of her own disinclination.

Two Phlegmatics are likely to spend much of their time together in quiet and companionable silence. The entire evening may go by with no more said than a discussion as to which television programme they will watch. On their anniversary they may go out to dinner and sit quietly together, saying little. The extroverts at other tables may think they are bored and wonder why they bothered to go out together at all, or even if this is the end of their relationship. To the Phlegmatic couple, however, their excursion has been an adventurous break in their daily routine and something they have shared and enjoyed quietly together. Besides, this anniversary dinner is a part of their annual ritual and they value such rituals and live by them.

Phlegmatics do give each other presents, but they tend to be useful rather than fun; necessities rather than luxuries. He is not mean, but is unlikely to appreciate her desire for new clothes while what she has is still useful. If she does want a new outfit her best strategy is to point out and criticise the most outrageous of the new fashions. Then let him see some, the ones she wanted all along, that are less outrageous. He will be so relieved at her relative conservatism that he will be happy for her to have what she has chosen, particularly if she points out that so-and-so's wife (a man he respects) has bought something similar. She will provide small presents for him, conscious that she is, in any case, spending his money and not her own. She may even put some of her own time and effort into making or modifying the gift. She, too, will make sure that it is something useful, knowing that he will not like the waste inherent in the gift of an unusual luxury.

By the time they retire into quiet old age they are both, if Phlegmatic, likely to be together and to be grateful for, all in all, a good and stable relationship, thinking in dismay of the disarray of the marriages of many of their friends.

When considering this section you will realise that for Phlegmatics it is more about life's practicalities and quiet companionship than about love, romance and sex. This is the way the Phlegmatic would have it, and demonstrates the proper and relative importance of each of these in their lives.

The Phlegmatic at Home

The home of a Phlegmatic, like the home of all temperaments, matches their nature. It will not be in the heart of the city, amid all the hustle and bustle, since they like peace and quiet. It will not be in one of the new areas since they are traditionalists, nor will it be in one of the avant-garde sections of town. At the same time they like things to be respectable so it is unlikely, unless they cannot afford anything better, to be on the seamy side of town. The Sanguine might buy a cheap house in a poor district and then do it up to make a delightful and 'amusing' home. They might even set the trend and be the start of that area's transformation. Not so the Phlegmatic.

In general, the Phlegmatic will continue to live in one place, one district or one style of area. If they grew up in a flat they are likely to continue living in a flat. If they grew up in a quiet suburban street, which is likely if they had Phlegmatic parents, then they will probably buy their own home in a similar street and district. Even if they wanted to change, which is not likely, they would be unsure what to change to. Needing to copy someone they know and respect, or people that they trust, and because these people are likely to be slightly more established versions of themselves, little change is likely.

You should not be surprised when a Phlegmatic son stays at home until he marries and then buys a house similar to that of his parents, a few streets away. The Phlegmatic daughter may also stay at home until she marries and will either do the same thing, or she will adopt her husbands' style of home, since that is what is normal for him. If she does the former she will very soon start to recreate her old home in the new setting.

If she was happy with her parents and if her mother had a certain style of furniture, she is likely to buy the same. If her mother had lace curtains on all the windows, she is likely to have them too. If, however, she was unhappy at home, or if she had a schoolfriend she admired, then she may well copy their home.

Phlegmatics are likely to buy a home that is considered 'a good buy' and a sensible purchase. They are unlikely to take risks, to speculate on a property boom in a given area, or to buy an unusual or imaginative house. They will buy it with a sensible mortgage, and since they are conservative with money they will have saved sufficient for the deposit. They will then pay it off steadily, over the next thirty years and retire, proud that, finally, they 'own their own home'. They will consider this one of their achievements and the reward for a lifetime of hard work.

Everything about the home will be conservative, neat and tidy. The lawn to the front door will be mowed regularly, the beds edged neatly and with bricks or some edging material holding back the flowerbeds. The borders themselves will be straight or circular. There will be few meandering lines in the Phlegmatic garden: they are too difficult to mow around and keep tidy. Bushes are trimmed, trees pruned and weeds removed regularly with a fine attention to detail. This is done, not out of any innate love of gardening, though that may be there, but for the purpose of keeping the garden tidy. If they do not like gardening they will organise a low-maintenance garden, with lawns from fence to fence and no flowerbeds, or with shrubs and ground-cover plants. One Phlegmatic of my acquaintance simply concreted in the whole front garden and put out half a dozen tubs with flowers, saying this was the easiest way to keep the place tidy. Another put down artificial grass. They may have a wrought-iron or timber garden table and chair set, not so much because their garden gets a lot of sun, but because it is the thing to have. Mind you, they wouldn't be tempted by colourful canvas deckchairs – too bright and too impractical.

Inside the home the layout will be sensible and conventional. Even if the best view is from the top floor, they wouldn't dream of having the bedrooms downstairs. They may have a 'public' sitting room, kept for best, and live in the kitchen. Furniture is bought because it is practical, a sensible shape and colour, rather than because it is beautiful or exciting. You will also find it's the same as the furniture of one of their friends, or of the vicar, or someone up the road. Like their clothes, the colours will be muted and sensible without strong contrasts or patterns.

Things run like clockwork. The same routine is followed daily. If the beds are made before breakfast, then they are *always* made before breakfast. Breakfast will be the same each day. At my boarding-school it was the job of the prefects to lay the table for the headmistress in her private dining room. Everything on the table had to be in *exactly* the same place every morning, not an inch either way or there was trouble. We were told it was to train us in the proper way of doing things. I used to think it was because she read as she ate and didn't want to have to look for things. In retrospect, she was a clear Phlegmatic.

As mentioned earlier, there is probably a routine menu, followed weekly. Once a sensible week's worth of menus has been worked out, why change it? Besides, it makes the shopping easier; that is then routine too. The changing seasons cause a bit of a problem, but rather than a gradual and adaptive change there is likely to be the sudden decision that it is now summer and so there will be salads, and so there will be – one a week until the menu changes back to the winter pattern. There will be little experimenting with new foods or new recipes. Instead the meals are good, plain cooking along traditional lines. Boarding-schools run like this and they are a good example of a Phlegmatic institution. Most institutions are Phlegmatic.

If the washing is always done on Mondays then woe betide the non-Phlegmatic child who fails to put her dirty clothes out on Sunday evening. There is little chance of them being washed for another week. If the Phlegmatic mother does do them on Tuesday, they will still have missed the ironing day and this is likely to cause her all sorts of bother.

The Phlegmatic housewife considers it her duty to provide a stable and secure background for her family and to do her work well and reliably. She will work hard and do things the way her mother did. There are unlikely to be many new gadgets; she may even feel that the very concept of labour-saving is wrong.

The evenings will be predictable: the meal on the table at the same time each night and the same routine followed each weekend. This means that the Sanguine spouse who brings unexpected friends home had better bring home a meal as well, rather than expect the unexpected to be whipped up at a moment's notice. It also means that the home can be relied on. Spouse and children can be sure that their clothes will be washed, mended, folded neatly and put away, the food will be prepared, the larder stocked and someone will be there to greet them. This provides great security for the other people in the life of a Phlegmatic woman.

Bedlinen will be plain – again no bright colours or matching patterns. Central heating is more likely than an open fire so that the heat is regular and predictable. Pets are probably not tolerated or, if allowed, must be kept outside.

All in all there is much quiet nurturing but little demonstrative emotion. Although there may be little in the way of excitement and adventure, there is much that is steady, reliable, safe and secure.

The Phlegmatic Parent

Phlegmatic parents provide a stable home for their children. They will rear their children as their own parents reared them and expect an ordered family life. They will probably settle for two children – after all, that is the norm – and hope that they have first a boy and then a girl.

Phlegmatic couples take it for granted that they will stay together and that they will provide a secure home for their children until the children themselves choose to venture out into the world. Phlegmatics take parenthood seriously. It involves responsibilities and duties that they take on automatically and wholeheartedly. Their desire to serve now extends to their desire to serve their children and provide a proper home life and upbringing for them.

Routines in the Phlegmatic household are not made to be broken. While the order of the home life may feel restrictive to some children, to others it will provide welcome security. As soon as the children are old enough they will be given their own duties to perform and they will be expected to keep their room tidy and put their dirty clothes in the laundry basket.

When misbehaviour occurs, due punishment will be meted out. It will be consistent and predictable and the children are likely to feel they have been treated fairly and evenly. The Sanguine child may balk at the routine, the Choleric child may rebel at the parental authority, but at least they know what to expect.

Even play and relaxation time may be scheduled. The Phlegmatic mother may have too little time to play with the children. She puts work first and must finish the ironing or mending, finish whatever job she has started – and when are *they* ever finished? Then and only then can she relax and play. She demonstrates her love for her children by the home and surroundings that she provides rather than by an abundance of loving, hugging and playing. Yet she does love to serve them and cater to the needs of the whole family. The child of a Phlegmatic mother will always have clothes neat and ready: no rush and scramble at the last minute, no tears and no safety pins. The clothes may not be smart but they will be neat and serviceable. There will be no frantic search for a football jersey, only to find it under the bed. She will have found it, washed it and got it ready for Saturday's game well ahead of time.

The Phlegmatic mother will bake cakes for family occasions, provide neatly packed school lunches, ferry the children round town and generally do all she can to make their lives comfortable. In turn they are expected to obey her rules and adapt to the family routine.

Time will be set aside for homework and parental help provided if appropriate. The Phlegmatic parent will want to know what has to be done and that it has been done. Then, and only then, is there time for play.

In all this the Phlegmatic's nature is evident. Their desire to serve is obvious, their conservative traditionalism is clear in the way they want their standards – those of their own parents – maintained. Their willingness to do their duty shows in the way they put the children and family ahead of their own personal needs. They see their children as an integral part of the family unit rather than as individuals. If the children misbehave in public the Phlegmatic parent takes it as a reflection of their own inadequate parenting. Everyone must do the right thing and be seen to have done the right thing. The reward, for the children, is the security of a well-run home and parents who, particularly if they are both Phlegmatic, probably stay together.

Outings and social events will normally involve the whole family and will be well organised beforehand. Phlegmatics prefer planned rather than impetuous or spontaneous events. When the occasion occurs both parents will be dedicated hosts, focusing on their guests and making sure everyone has everything they need. This will include the children, who frequently become the focus of attention.

Only occasionally will a babysitter be called in when the parents go out for the evening. In some ways the parents may even set their own lives aside as they serve the greater needs of family and children. Attention is paid to the extended family, and Phlegmatic parents will often have family and friends round for gatherings, reunions and special occasions. In their view this large network of people provides the stability and continuity they want for their children. They observe family and social occasions such as anniversaries, birthdays and school reunions. These are an inherent and important part of their life.

If both parents are Phlegmatic it is probable that each will have their clearly defined roles, as will the children, and the children will know where they stand.

Father will leave for work regularly each morning and be the provider. He may have to work late at times, but this will be rare. He will be an integral part of the family and let it be known that he works to provide for them rather than putting work first. Mother has her role as provider within the home. Both will be involved in family discipline and care.

The Phlegmatic in Old Age

Phlegmatics age gracefully and appropriately. In general, they settle down to their duties, focus on home and family and rearing the next generation, as well as their duties within their community. They are content to serve and take a back seat. For this reason, by their actions, they often seem to be older than their years.

Unlike Sanguines they are not in search of fun and eternal youth: they are not mortified when wrinkles appear and hair turns grey. They take the passing of the years as part of the universal pattern of things, as predictable as the sun rising and setting.

None the less, some changes can occur as they grow older. Phlegmatic parents who were serious and responsible in bringing up the children may relax into more fun-loving grandparents once they have done their duty and accomplished the task of raising their own family. When they have launched them into the world they may well relax and think a bit more about their partner. They may do a few things they haven't done to that date – not too much though, it wouldn't do to go off the rails. They might go on a trip or two. If so, they are more likely to go on a package tour than to go off on their own and be independent. That way they can be sure there will be no unexpected emergencies to deal with. They can also feel that the best route has already been chosen, the best and most appropriate hotels have been picked, and all the important sights have been seen and visited. If they go home and are asked, 'Oh, didn't you see so-and-so?' instead of feeling foolish at the omission, which they would feel if they had planned their own trip, they can respond calmly that the tour guide had made the choices and shown them what was most important. They can relax within the security of what the organisers planned.

In general, however, Phlegmatics settle down into a quiet retirement. If they have lived well by their own standards and done what they felt they had to do, they will be content. They will have their hobbies, run their home, look after the garden. They will continue, at least for a while, to be active in community affairs and are likely to be available to babysit for the grandchildren.

If they have remained in Stage I they will have turned inward and become very self-focused. If they have matured to Stage III there have been major changes. By Stage III the Phlegmatic is quiet and thoughtful. They have become trusted, liked and respected. Although still relatively introverted and reserved they have developed more awareness of other people and their needs. They have become a little more adventurous in their activities and are willing to try out some new ideas. In general, they are comfortably off, able to live nearly as well after they retire as before, largely as a result of their thrift and the careful management of their assets. A quiet and contented old age is the result.

Health and the Phlegmatic

Phlegmatics are, indeed, phlegmatic about their health. They do not worry unduly, but if they get something wrong they will make an appointment to see the appropriate person. Having made the appointment, they will put the matter out of their mind until the time comes. They do not fret and brood as would the Melancholic, they do not let their imagination run riot, as would a temporarily negative Sanguine, and come up with all manner of exotic or horrific possibilities.

When the appointed time arrives they will turn up, probably early, and wait placidly until their turn comes. The doctor or therapist may have to drag some of the details out of them as they do not like to push themselves forward or claim attention, and they would not like to feel they were making a fuss about nothing. Yet they also know that symptoms should not be ignored.

If they are told that tests have to be done they will submit to these obediently. They consider it stupid to argue with the doctor or question medical decisions. They have come to a professional, the professional knows best and so the Phlegmatic agrees with what is suggested. They then wait quietly for the results. The Melancholic would be convinced the problem was serious, more serious than they had been told. This thought does not occur to the Phlegmatic. If a test is planned or if they are waiting for the results there is nothing more the Phlegmatic can do, so again the matter is set aside. Once the results are back and the information is assessed the appropriate decisions will be made.

As soon as they feel the pain of toothache they will make an appointment to see the dentist, but will explain that there is no particular rush: other people in real pain should be seen first. They make the appointment at once not because it is an emergency but because that is the right thing to do, and they will get the hole fixed while it is small. The Sanguine, with a low threshold to the imagined pain of the drill and the needle, and a disinclination to interrupt the fun things they are doing, would delay and do nothing about it until pain becomes the driving force. The Melancholic would know it was serious and that the tooth would probably have to come out. The Choleric would make the appointment when he had time in his busy schedule and expect quick and simple treatment with little or no waiting.

On the whole, Phlegmatics will go to the professionals they went to as children. They are traditionalists, so they may still be seeing the same family doctor that they saw as children or, if that person has retired, they will be going to the same practice and seeing, somewhat reluctantly, the new man, or woman. They would go to a doctor rather than a natural therapist, since that is what most people do, unless they had been brought up in a house where herbalists and naturopaths were preferred.

Phlegmatics tend to have regular check-ups. Rather than wait until there is pain or a problem, they prefer to visit their dentist often and have regular medical check-ups. Women will have regular PAP smears and check their breasts routinely for lumps. Men, especially as they grow older, tend to have regular heart checks and have their blood cholesterol and triglyceride levels monitored at routine intervals.

They may suffer from glandular problems. If these involve the thyroid it will normally be underactive and they will tend to gain weight. They will find it difficult to lose it again, so they should endeavour to stay slim, or relatively slim, rather than let his happen.

They should also take care of their liver, which may be somewhat sluggish. They should not over-indulge in alcohol or rich and fatty foods. Not only will these stress the liver, they will increase the tendency to gain weight.

The Phlegmatic When Things Go Wrong

If Phlegmatics disintegrate and deteriorate rather than mature and develop, they can become negative and apathetic. They will retire inside themselves and become totally self-absorbed, indifferent to the moods and needs of people around them. At first they may continue to do their job and perform their duties, since this is an ingrained pattern with them. But if the declining process continues they will stop bothering to keep up standards, and will not go to work or care for people around them. They will become lethargic drop-outs.

If they are pushed too hard they can become violent. This will take the form of the classic 'bull in a china shop': their clumsiness combined with their size can cause havoc. Some of the senseless and destructive crimes are done by Phlegmatics who have been pushed too far or had more stress than they can handle. The Phlegmatic foster parent about to have the child taken from her and returned to an alcoholic mother may kill the child as the only way of protecting her. The Phlegmatic who finds his fiancée has decided to marry someone else may go off the deep end and kill her or beat her up in a fit of blind rage.

Their rage is not like that of the Choleric, controlled and powerful.

It is blind, mindless and thoughtless, in the sense that all perspective is lost.

They may become compulsive, developing repetitive behaviour, things they have to do over and over again. They may keep washing their hands, making their bed or checking to see that the windows are closed. They may become obsessed with rituals.

If they go insane they can become catatonic, sitting in a corner, lost in their own world and totally out of touch with all that is going on around them.

What the Phlegmatic Can Teach Us

Phlegmatics are reliable, more so than any of the other three temperaments. We would all be in trouble if they were not around. It is fortunate that they make up such a large proportion of society, as they provide the calm and steady background against which the other temperaments live. They preserve the traditions and values and they keep records of our history. They provide a steady and dependable haven when the Choleric is in a rage, the Sanguine is being irresponsible and mischievous and the Melancholic is in deep depression.

They complete jobs and see projects through to the end, even if it takes longer than they had planned. They will be the ones that stay back after the party and help you clear up. They do all the dull and routine jobs that no one else wants to do, but that make life run more smoothly. They will spend hours sticking on labels, sending out invitations, checking who has paid the club membership fees.

They show people how to endure, not through active strength but from a basis of quiet determination to see things through and not be beaten. In an emergency, when the first drama and crisis are over, the quiet strength of the Phlegmatics will hold the community together. They will be running the soup kitchens, delivering the blankets or quietly and steadily getting on with the job of tidying up and restoring normality.

Phlegmatics love peace. When the Choleric is insisting they should be in charge and possibly fighting other Cholerics for control, the Sanguine is trying to have a good time and be entertaining and the centre of attention and the Melancholic is looking for someone to tell their sad story to, the quiet and solid Phlegmatic is like a rock in a storm. It is comforting and helpful to have someone who will do as they are told by the Choleric, applaud the Sanguine and listen to the Melancholic.

They will do a great deal to avoid conflict, so other people can get their emotions off their chest and settle down without having to cope with the Phlegmatic's needs. Phlegmatics are wonderful people to have around when there are emergencies, when you want to let off steam, when you need a quiet haven.

Since they are also great arbitrators, they are peacemakers when warring factions are in confrontation. If everyone else could develop some of the Phlegmatic's calm and patience we would have a more peaceful world.

Phlegmatics provide a secure home from which the family can foray out into the world. In today's changing society this is especially valuable. It may not be the most exciting of homes, it may seem dull and boring at times, but it is always there, it has always been there and it will continue to be there for you whenever you need to return to it. Equally, they may not be the most exciting of people, but you will certainly appreciate them when you need their calm and their quiet strength and when you need someone to listen to you, to be there for you and to support you. This support is, of course, of the passive kind, since much of their value lies in their ability to listen quietly to you, without trying to make decisions for you or tell you what to do. They give you the sounding board you need so you can have your say and the time you need to work your problems and your ideas out for yourself. Whatever you decide at the end of the process, and whatever mood you are in, you will almost certainly find they are in agreement and are backing you up in your decision. It is in their nature to do so.

CHAPTER 13

The Sanguine Temperament

Main Characteristics

Sanguines are bright, alert, entertaining, emotional and expressive. They are optimistic and usually extroverts. They love freedom and act impulsively, for the joy of doing and the joy of the moment, rather than the achievement of where they're going. They love life and want to participate in anything that catches their attention. They want to do it *now*, and they will continue to do it at least for a while, until they get bored with it and want to move on to the next thing that attracts them. Wherever the action is, that is where you'll find them. They are generally popular and admired, and enjoy being the centre of attention. They are great storytellers, even if they do embellish a little for effect, and they have a great sense of humour.

Sanguines are usually tall, slender and extremely good-looking, often with blond hair, blue eyes, a mobile face and a ready smile. Their movements are up rather than down, as they dance and weave their way through life.

They are interested in all that is going on around them, yet whatever they are doing there is always the possibility that they might be missing something – that something even more interesting might be going on elsewhere. This means that there is a problem if you want to keep their attention focused on any one thing at a time. At a party their eyes keep darting around. When you talk to them you will see them constantly glancing over your shoulder to see who else is there and what else is happening, unless, that is, you are their passion of the moment, in which case you will have their full attention. All this changes if they are part of a circle of people and in the central role, since they love playing to an audience and will focus on that, if it is large enough. They will also play to the galleries for they are at their best with a large audience. If the audience is small they will often hold on to the listener physically, as if afraid they will run away and leave the speaker alone.

They are often the trendsetter of their group of friends. You will find them bright and entertaining to be with. They bubble with enthusiasm and have a wide-eyed, almost innocent, curiosity about the world around them. Life is more exciting when they are around: even the dullest things can suddenly come to life. They are the ones who suggest what to do next that will be fun, interesting and exciting, and the day seems brighter when they arrive.

They consider themselves to be sincere, honest and loyal, but with their enthusiasms, their great imagination and a tendency to fantasise you need to be wary of the absolute truth of what they say. They would be horrified if you told them they were untruthful, but they see no point in spoiling a good story for the sake of accuracy. With their creative imagination they may even live in a bit of a fantasy world, daydreaming the impossible and then believing in it. It is easy for the Sanguine to make others believe the stories they create. You may also consider them unfaithful or disloyal, breaking the pledges and commitments they made so easily yesterday. You must remember, though, that that was yesterday. Today is a new day and new urges are calling the Sanguine to fresh pastures.

All Sanguines dislike repetition and hate to be bored, so it is all too easy for them to become Jack or Jill of all trades and master of none and fail to gain experience. If they don't mature and learn to curtail their roving nature, physically and mentally, they can fail to gain in-depth experience or knowledge of any one thing, be it a job or career, a hobby, an interest or an emotional relationship.

Not for them the contemplative life, deep thought or quiet meditation. In fact, they find meditation extremely difficult. They do not enjoy peaceful contemplation, nor are they deeply thoughtful or introspective. They constantly need outside distractions and interests, and they also need their audience, although for the more introverted Sanguine (they do exist) this audience can be whoever will finally see the results of the current project. They project themselves into their surroundings and add to them. This is both because they have lots to give and, more sadly, because their own inner resources are often inadequate.

They do not like hard work, repetitive jobs, manual labour, or getting themselves dirty. Boredom is almost physically painful to them and they will do a great deal to avoid it, throwing parties or going in search of activities. They may do this to the point of just not being there when you expect them and giving the impression of being unreliable – as indeed they can be if their interest is not maintained.

Life Path

The Stage I Sanguine is a self-centred egotist seeking light and laughter. Life is for living and for having a good time. They crave novelty, amusement, bright colours, light and movement. But above all they want to have fun – no matter what it costs others to provide it. And since they have few inner resources, this often has to be provided from outside. For those who do this and for those who are around them they are a delight and a joy, as long as all goes well. They will captivate you with their wit, humour, lively imagination and their interest in things that you took for granted. However, they have a lot of growing up to do.

In Stage II they endeavour to mature. They will start out with the best of intentions: to study, to concentrate, to apply themselves. This may be difficult for them and there may be many failures, but they will almost certainly be forgiven for these lapses, simply because they are such good company.

They can lack strength of character and, beginning to recognise this, they may cover up their lapses with little (or large) white lies, all of which they come to believe. They are great talkers, with the gift of the gab – and what a beautiful way they do have with words. They can make the listener feel wonderful and are all too ready to promise you the world, but with limited ideas of how they will deliver – in fact that thought, absent in Stage I, is only now beginning to enter their head. It is more important to them to make a good impression and to please so they can make you feel good, which in turn reflects well on themselves. As they mature into full Stage II they settle down and learn to control their tendency to be superficial and to complete things they start.

By Stage III, all being well, they have developed into lovable and generous people. They are intuitively able to deal with all that is new and exciting, to relate to other people and to share their interests with others, so they can inspire others. With maturity comes the ability to complete projects, to develop depth and to stick a little closer to the truth.

If they do not develop and mature in this way they can either stay permanently young and immature, even in their nineties or, more sadly, can degenerate into superficial liars and cheats, spinning more and more outrageous yarns in a wasted endeavour to get and keep your attention and recapture their lost youth and popularity. They can also flit from one activity to another and be the perpetual wanderers and drifters.

So, now let's take a look at this exciting temperament in more detail and see how the progression occurs.

Stage I

In many ways, Sanguines are the typical children of the temperaments and childhood is, of course, the appropriate time for Stage I. Sanguines maintain their zest for life longer and age more slowly than the other temperaments. They love exploring the world and are disinclined, in Stage I, to settle down.

The Stage I Sanguine is as bright as a butterfly and, like a butterfly, flits from flower to flower in a way that other temperaments and more mature people may find superficial. They live life on the surface, refusing to take things seriously, flitting from one idea to another with no staying power. They act without thinking, following their inclinations wherever they lead with little thought for the consequences.

Make sure you have some Sanguines at your party and it will go with a zing. If you are new in town it is a Sanguine who will create a welcome party and introduce you around. A Sanguine is always looking for an excuse for a party.

Sanguines are full of ideas and start lots of projects but, in Stage I, give up at the first obstacle using the excuse of something new that has caught their attention. If a project is short and simple they may complete it. If, however, it turns out to be lengthy and requires serious application they are unlikely to continue once the first flush of enthusiasm has passed. They will stick at things, but only if and because they are enjoying the moment, the process. They are not goal-oriented and will not endure for the sake of the outcome. It must be enjoyable right now.

Martin had applied for a position that would have suited him admirably. It involved making new contacts, selling both products and an idea, and bringing new people into his organisation. It offered him the freedom to work his own hours, work from anywhere he chose, travel as he chose and gave him a reason to introduce himself to new people. All this is meat and drink to the Sanguine. Unfortunately, Martin was a very immature Sanguine and the project had one drawback: he would be self-employed, albeit within a larger organisation and with a supervisor who would be working with him and directing him. Whether he made the call, went to the training meetings or followed up on one of his customers was, ultimately, up to him. In a discussion the concept of the temperaments came up and he discovered that both he and his supervisor were Sanguines, at Stage I and Stage III respectively. His immediate comments were, 'Can I change? Can you help? If only I could be more stable, there is so much I want to do. What should I do?'

It was such a cry from the heart that the supervisor did all he could, but in no time Martin had changed address and moved on.

For many Stage I Sanguines there is real pain for them in their nature. They long for at least some depth, some steadiness, some inner peace. We will find out shortly how they can achieve this.

All Sanguines have trouble with the truth. Above all they want to please and entertain; they want you to like them and be impressed by them. A little exaggeration, or selective recall, if necessary, comes automatically to the Sanguine in Stage I. Who knows what the real truth is anyway? Was the glass half full or half empty? Of one thing you can be sure: the Sanguine's story will provide more fun and excitement than that of the other temperaments.

If they are children, and others are involved in telling you what happened, then you would probably be wise to temper the Sanguine's version with the more plausible information you will get from the Phlegmatic child.

Sanguines have lively imaginations, are very creative, love colour, light and movement. They have an accurate eye for colour and can carry a shade in their head and come home with the perfect match. Let them (adults as well as the children) splash around with water paints and float colours over sheets of wet paper. The movement combined with the colours and the chance to create pictures as they watch will captivate the Sanguine. The fact that the result is not enduring will in no way disconcert the Sanguine, who will have lost interest by then anyway.

Sanguines are interested, at least for a while, in almost anything that catches their attention. Thus they can have a smattering of knowledge on a wide variety of subjects and talk about all of them. Just don't, in Stage I, probe or question them too deeply or you may find that the few sentences they have given you are all they know on the subject, or even that they have made up some of the 'facts' to broaden the picture.

They can be ruthless and aggressive, but this is rarely obvious. They have such charm and desire to please that they are more likely to get their own way by spinning their web of fantasy and seducing you into doing what they want. If they do become aggressive they are likely to do it with such charm that, at least initially, others accept their behaviour without criticism.

Sanguines love movement and freedom, especially in Stage I where they do little to control these urges. They fidget, they swing on chairs or move around a room. Their restless nature may lead them to travel extensively, packing up at a moment's notice, regardless of the effect on family, lovers or friends. They may take off on spur-of-the-moment holidays with little thought. Luxury is important to them: it makes them feel good. They like to lead the glamorous life and would love to be jet-setters.

They may change jobs frequently: a job may even be jettisoned without notice as the urge to move on overwhelms them. In Stage I they may do this with little regard for normal responsibilities, either at work or to their dependants who will suffer because of the loss of income. They discard possessions as they go, convinced that they can acquire newer and better ones as they need them. In many ways they treat friends in the same way, knowing they have a great facility for meeting people and making new friends, at least superficially. They love to meet people, will talk to strangers and take an interest in all that is going on. All this can be very disturbing for their spouse, assuming they have stood still long enough to acquire one.

While they do make friends quickly and easily don't expect them to be there for ever for you or assume they will be loyal. They can use people, picking them up and dropping them as their interests change. They are flirts, love to be admired, enjoy the chase as much as the conclusion and can be promiscuous and unfaithful. They can seem to take the words out of your mouth as you laugh and joke with them. But do not look for loyalty or reliability in an immature adult Sanguine, stuck in Stage I.

They would never save for a rainy day – why should they? Rainy days don't happen in the Sanguine's charmed world. In fact, they're not even sure the future will happen. Today is all-important. Their impetuosity extends to money and possessions and they can be generous, giving things away on a whim. Rarely reliable with money, they can become positively reckless if they don't mature. Gambling adds spice to the life that, in some restless inner way, they sense is losing its meaning. The tall slim stylish man or woman you see elegantly draped over the gaming tables, probably drinking too much, certainly womanising or flirting outrageously and loudly declaring that life is wonderful, is probably an immature Sanguine in a headlong but fruitless search for that elusive state of real happiness.

Sanguines don't like to quarrel, thinking it stupid. Why argue when you could be enjoying yourself? When they do fight it is a quick flare-up, and just as quickly forgotten. They are surprised if the other person holds a grudge or even remembers what was said. The Sanguine's sunny nature has moved them on to new pastures.

When the Stage I Sanguine feels negative or bored they may refuse to get up in the morning. When they do, they can't be bothered to shave or put on make-up. Instead they drift around aimlessly and restlessly from one thing to another. They can be selfish, unjust and assume the world owes them a living.

They will cry less than the other three temperaments, and when they do it will be quickly over, as will their negative periods. When reality does not live up to their dreams, when the Sanguine finds that things are not working out quite as they had hoped, they may take stock and realise that changes are in order: that they must turn over a new leaf and make a new start. They may even tell themselves it is time to grow up.

Stage I Sanguines have very little willpower or self-discipline. To move to Stage II they have to develop this, and to develop more staying power once they have set out on a course of action.

Maturing

Like the other temperaments, Sanguines desire to mature, to develop the positive sides of their character and to transform their less desirable traits. They recognise, often unconsciously, that if they do not do this, if they do not rise above their Stage I nature, they will lose a part of themselves.

The immature Sanguine has become used to doing what they like, to being irresponsible and to following their inclinations. By the time the Sanguine begins to feel a desire for some stability and to locate a fixed centre within themselves they are ready to move on. Since they know they have less willpower than the other temperaments they worry about how this can be accomplished, just as Martin did, though as it turned out he was far from ready for the move.

Sanguines have an unrealistic outlook on life, expecting it to be wonderful at all times. To develop from Stage I to Stage II they have to become more realistic, to learn that there are highs *and* lows and that both have their value and their place – although their lows will never be as low as those of the Melancholic. They have to settle down and harness their restless energy. They need to develop depth and yet maintain their vibrancy and varied interests. They also need to have a closer association with the truth and be more accurate in their version of events while maintaining their vivid imagination and sense of fun.

An excellent way for a Sanguine to do this is to find a role model that they can look up to, admire and imitate. This role model is rarely a parent – the parent knows them too well in their immature Stage I state. It can be a friend, a teacher or a lover; it may also be their boss at work or it may be someone new who has entered the Sanguine's life at the time they are ready to mature. In this way the Sanguine can 'make a fresh start'.

The role model may, gently, let the Sanguine know they see through some of their taller stories, but they will also enter into some of the Sanguine's dreams and 'be on their side'. They will have faith in the Sanguine and be able to demonstrate this repeatedly until the Sanguine develops a trust both in the role model and in the relationship; in themselves and in their ability to mature.

It is important that this role model is consistent and secure and doesn't show weakness or uncertainty. Sanguines must realise that they can't influence their role model. The young Sanguine desperately needs the sense of security that this person can and must provide if optimum transition is to occur. Initially the Sanguine may criticise and deride the potential role model. If the latter succumbs the opportunity is lost. If, on the other hand, the role model is impervious to the attacks, they may earn the Sanguine's respect, and the opportunity for growth and development is present. The Sanguine will then strive to develop the characteristics they admire in the role model.

The mentor should also have an element of glamour to them and lead the sort of life to which the Sanguine can aspire. Thus the Sanguine can feel that in maturing they will be achieving something desirable and not just losing their irresponsible youth. The maturing Sanguine will delight in basking in the approval of this mentor and will do all they can to continue to mature and genuinely earn this approval and respect. They will endeavour to show the mentor their best side and to live up to the good image the mentor has, and must have, of them.

While it is important for the mentor to let the Sanguine know they are not fooled by their tall stories, if the Sanguine once feels that the mentor sees through them to the point that they become critical instead of supportive, the Sanguine can easily revert to Stage I fantasy behaviour in a vain endeavour to impress at the superficial level. If at first they don't succeed in this they will spin more and more extravagant tales and behave more and more outrageously.

To help the Sanguine, gentle guidance can be very beneficial when the Sanguine tendency to change direction occurs. If they have set out on a path and then show signs of abandoning it, let them do so for a while, just sufficient to take the edge off their restless urge, then guide them gently back. Do this repeatedly and you will help them to become more focused and consistent.

Timing is all-important for a Sanguine. They have an urge to do things the moment the idea occurs to them. When they are ready to move on they want help immediately, not later. If the moment is lost and the urge goes, it may never come again. 'Strike while the iron's hot' is the motto of the Sanguine: it should also be the motto of all who deal with and try to help a Sanguine.

Stage II

The development from Stage I to Stage II can take place at any age or time of life. It will also take place over time, with many oscillations to and fro. If the changes start in childhood or in the teens the Stage II Sanguine child will settle down at school and be a more consistent student, learning each subject in greater depth than previously. They will begin to have a sense of direction for their life. They will become more reliable as friends, more settled within their family. If no maturing occurs then, in the worst cases, they may be the troublesome adolescent or the teenage drop-out or drug addict, the person who lies and cheats to get his own way and lead the life he wants.

The danger is that they will try one job or career and then, when things get either difficult or boring, change to another. Or if things get too easy, predictable or monotonous they may also move on, looking for change. The Stage II Sanguine will have learnt some stability and acquired ways to cope with this restlessness. One way to do this is to find a job that, in itself, has lots of variety and excitement. Alternatively, they may find one that has several different components, so that they can move from one to the other.

When a Sanguine friend started in the natural therapies he was fascinated by every aspect of the subject and his mind would flit from herbs to nutrition, to homoeopathy to massage. My suggestion, when he asked for my guidance, was that he pick the one area that interested him the most and discipline himself to focus on and specialise in this field. I then suggested that, within this field, he allow himself to work in whatever area interested him at that moment. I also suggested that, when he graduated, he should create a life where he did more than one thing. He now sees patients, gives lectures and has developed some outside, but related, business interests. These very different components allow him to change his focus as the mood takes him, yet he still works towards a single goal. In addition he is proud of his ability to develop within the parameters of his temperament.

The Sanguine loves to travel and move house. A Stage I Sanguine may prefer to rent and move at frequent intervals. With maturity comes a willingness to buy a home and settle down, at least for a while. Don't, however, expect them to stay in the same place for the rest of their life. They will still move house, change districts, even countries, with a willingness that makes the Phlegmatic very nervous. If you are married to a Sanguine and want to stay put then make sure they have plenty of opportunity to travel during the year, and that they go on holidays to fascinating and faraway places. Even planning the holiday can settle their restlessness for a while as they scheme and fantasise their way through the travel brochures.

One answer to the Sanguine's dislike of being bored is for them to find ways of meeting people: lots of new and interesting people. For the Sanguine this is easy to accomplish as they happily talk to strangers and convert many of them into friends. Some of these will develop into genuine friendships. While the Stage I Sanguine created an expectation, based on a few quick facts, and assumed their new acquaintance would live up to it, the Stage II Sanguine is more willing to respect reality and explore the relationship, delving deep and finding out what the other person is really like. The trick for the Sanguine is to develop the desired maturity without losing the positive attributes of their nature.

Sanguines like eating out, but place more importance on the look and style of the restaurant than on the quality of the food. Not for them the cheap restaurant with minimum frills, located in a back street but serving *wonderful* food. They want style and good looks;

they also want a steady flow of interesting people and the sense that they are in the swing of things, in the front of fashion and at the centre of where it is all happening. They shun the intimate table at the back, preferring to sit centre stage where they can see and be seen. As they mature, however, they do come to value quality as well as the style.

Sanguines must feel in harmony with their surroundings: this applies to buildings and cities and also to country and rural settings. Their home is usually beautiful and full of light and colour. In Stage I this is often achieved superficially as they go more for effect than for substance. They stick coloured posters over holes in the wall and splashes of paint over the damp patches, they may cover an old box with a coloured shawl or stick patterned paper over old and rotting shelves. As they mature to Stage II, they will begin to put down roots, even if they are still more ready than other people to pull them up again. They will also take care, wanting things to be good and not simply to look good on the surface. They rarely think of saving money and would rather have their assets visible in the way they live and dress.

In the country they will love to dance and run through sunny glades, avoiding the long slog up steep hills. Instant gratification and beauty every step of the way is the Sanguine's requirement. If it is not available they will either be bored (Stage I) or find small things of beauty over which to exclaim, drawing others into the experience and discovery as they do so (Stage II). It is the Sanguine who will delight in and show you the beauty of light on a leaf, the wonder of insects, wings hovering over a rock or the detailed colouring of a bird's feather. If the going gets tough they will, initially, keep up the spirits of other people with their infectious joy and enthusiasm. But if things continue to get tough they will (Stage I) degenerate into whining complainers as they get dirty and tired and, lacking the endurance of the Choleric, the plodding stoicism of the Phlegmatic or the acceptance that things commonly do go wrong of the Melancholic, they will run out of reserves with which to deal with the situation.

By Stage II their bubbly superficiality has settled into a sunny nature that is almost always happy, rarely complaining or sad. They will occasionally flare up if things don't go their way, but this will be brief and quickly forgotten. They are quick to forgive and forget, and surprised when other people are still upset some time after the event.

With maturity, their total disregard for time, due largely to their enjoyment of the present, coupled with their desire to rush off after new interests and distractions, improves and they take a more responsible attitude to commitments and to the needs of others.

They fall in and out of love many times, quickly and totally, each time being 'the one' (Stage I), yet they have difficulty forming a deep and enduring attachment. Married or single, they are unlikely to be faithful. Certainly their thoughts will drift many times as they imagine the possibilities. The Stage I adult Sanguine may have many divorces and remarriages or many affairs that tear them apart as they try to find ways of having their cake and eating it. With maturity, the Stage II Sanguine achieves the ability to commit to a long-term relationship and then to recognise that the excitement they feel with each new possible temptation is indeed only a passing fancy. They may still indulge, but they will know in their hearts that it is a transient interlude, and will do all they can not to jeopardise their long-term position. We will look at more examples of this later.

Sanguines are good with children and, because they retain their sense of fun and laughter, they are frequently popular with them. This is heightened by their desire to please and their chameleon nature. They will care for their children and dress them to look good. In Stage I there may be a plethora of safety pins and only the bits that show may be clean. By Stage II the care goes deeper.

They like to be popular, admired and praised. In Stage I this could take the form of superficial flattery. Now, in Stage II, they try harder to earn the respect they crave and appreciate it more, particularly as they are aware of the strides they have made in maturing. However, even at Stage II they look up to and envy the Cholerics, who rarely boast but show their worth by their deeds and are automatically admired for who they are and what they do.

Maturing

Eventually they are ready to move on to Stage III. To accomplish this move the same role model can be used or a new one chosen. If it is the same role model then they, too, must have matured. There may even be several role models. It is worth keeping in mind that these three stages are intellectual concepts and that, in reality, there is a continuum of maturation; the process proceeds, if somewhat irregularly and erratically, throughout life. In certain circumstances the Sanguine, more than some other temperaments, can dart back and forward through the stages.

The progression to Stage III can occur at any age. It may occur in childhood, it may be delayed until old age, it may never occur. If it doesn't, or worse, if they remain stuck in Stage I, you may see the 'mid-life crisis' at its most disruptive. In general experience, maturity and ageing come latest to this temperament, and when they do they cause major changes and shifts.

Stage III

The Stage III Sanguine is thoroughly delightful. They have maintained their many and varied interests and enthusiasms and their ability to bring sunlight into other people's lives. But they have also settled down and become content with what they have, realising that that greener grass on the other side of the fence only looks that way and that it, too, will have the occasional weeds when closely inspected.

In social settings they recognise the areas of interests of other people. And, because of their own wide-ranging interests and the enthusiasm with which they have explored these ideas, listened and remembered, they can talk at length about the listeners' interests. Other people are likely to comment on all the mature Sanguine has done and experienced. (If the Sanguine is immature they are more likely to call them flighty and consider they have frittered their life away.)

In maturity, their imagination and creativity remain but now these can be better harnessed and channelled. Stage III Sanguines can initiate research and projects and provide ideas for others. Although their enthusiasm is more controlled and realistic, they will still feel confident that they can handle whatever will happen and that obstacles can be overcome. As a result they generate the confidence and ideas that other people can put into practice. Do not expect even a Stage III Sanguine to dot all the 'i's and cross all the 't's.

As parents and grandparents they will be favourites with the children, entering into their games and even inventing some of their own for they still, even in maturity, retain a childlike enjoyment of life.

They remain optimists but can now share that with others in a way that is realistic. They can support and sustain others when life gets tough, more successfully than they could in Stage I when more firmly grounded mortals found their enthusiasm too fantastic. They will help people around them, but still only up to a point. If their ideas are not taken and used they will, in time, move on and help or work with other people who are more receptive to their ideas. You'll never convert a Sanguine into a persistent Phlegmatic – and who would want to?

At whatever age a Sanguine matures – and remember, this maturing process is independent of years – they will stay looking and acting young for longer than any other temperament. Even a Stage III Sanguine will act young: it is part of their nature.

Sanguines and Their Appearance

Sanguines are delightful to look at. They are the light and airy dancers and butterflies and their looks betray this. They are tall, slim, graceful and beautiful with long thin bones, resulting in long slender limbs, hands and feet, and long fingers and toes. They are well proportioned and attractive. Their colouring is light, their bone structure fine and their features arresting.

In both sexes the head is well proportioned, usually with long slender bones showing through. The cheekbones, for instance, are high and clearly defined. The jawline is clearly and delicately defined, unlike the ill-defined jaw of the Phlegmatic or the square jaw of the Choleric. Their hair tends to be blond or light, fine and glowing and their eyes are usually blue.

Their complexion is good and their skin is usually clear and free from blemishes. Whereas the Choleric is often ruddy and the Phlegmatics and Melancholics often have pale, grey, pasty or dull skin, the skin of the Sanguine is invariably smooth and glowing, even translucent.

You can easily tell a Sanguine by their facial expression: it is bright and intelligent, alive and alert, reflecting what is going on around them and their interest in it. Whereas the Phlegmatic may make you think of the glandular type, the Sanguine's face expresses their nervous energy. Their eyes light up with excitement, clearly showing their moods and always moving to catch anything that might be happening elsewhere and that might provide further interest.

You can easily read a Sanguine, they live very much on the surface. If they are bored or unhappy you will be able to see it in their expression. When things become depressing, or even simply serious, they will try to change the mood or wander off to a situation that provides more fun and stimulation.

A retroussé or slender nose sits above a mobile mouth that is soft and delicately shaped. Sanguines' lips are well coloured and mobile, delicate and clearly outlined; they smile easily, showing pearly white teeth. They smile a lot: they would much rather be happy than sad and so they tend to focus on the fun rather than on the sorrows. They also like to give a good impression and this is done better by smiling than by scowling.

Their voice is light and musical, often lilting, rising and falling as they express their interest in whatever they are saying. It is a voice that is easy on the ears and a pleasure to listen to. They laugh often.

Sanguines dress with style, either in fashion or creating it, but always with a desire to please, impress and look good. Their slim figures show clothes off to advantage and they are rarely overlooked in a crowd. They like new clothes and lots of variety, preferring to throw things away and start afresh rather than spend time, wasted time in their view, caring for what they have. Disliking routine and domesticity, they are reluctant to wash and iron or mend and repair. Since this is in conflict with their desire to look good and their easy ability to convince themselves that all is well, you will often see them with a safety pin showing or an imperfection in a place they confidently assume will be invisible to others.

Sanguine men are tall and slim and wear clothes immaculately. Whether in business clothes or wearing black tie and tails they will look elegant and well dressed. Their casual clothes also look good. Even when doing a rough job they will make sure their slacks or jeans fit well and that colours are co-ordinated. When everyone else is looking grubby at the end of a messy job the Sanguine will still look good. This is partly due to a natural elegance and fastidiousness, partly to their desire to look good at all times and therefore the result of the effort they put into it, and partly because they hate to get dirty and so have left most of the hard and dirty work to others.

The women tend to be tall and willowy and they, too, usually look good. They are the women who can take old clothes and, with a few accessories and their own individual style, dress them up and look gorgeous. They show clothes off to advantage and are often models. They love new clothes and to be able to buy the latest fashions and discard them when they find even newer ones. Looks are more important to the Sanguine than to any other temperament.

They like to dress smartly and fashionably, they love novelty, bright colours, graceful clothes and looking chic. They may lack individuality as they like to be in the latest fashion, yet they also like to create an impression, so they will add their own touches.

Their movements are graceful and well controlled. They enjoy ballet and gymnastics, and like to move and dart around, much as their mind darts from subject to subject. They walk airily, as if dancing gracefully over the ground like a ballerina, and move out of other people's way on a crowded pavement, not so much out of consideration for others as for the sheer joy of ducking and weaving. They are light on their feet and light on their shoes.

They wave their hands constantly and frequently touch their face or pat their hair. They may have characteristic movements they repeat and these may annoy others, but in general their movements add another dimension to their words as they weave their stories and their fantasies, delighting their less imaginative audience.

They would rather run than walk, stand or pace than sit still. Their restlessness and grace result in many characteristic poses. They will swing their legs up on to the arm of a chair, sit with their feet propped up on the desk or curl up on the floor. They do not just stand still, they lean gracefully against the mantelpiece or drape themselves elegantly along a sofa. As you watch them sit casually on a rock, balance on the prow of a rowing boat, or climb into a small sports car you may even think their movements and their poses are practised, so graceful and easy do they seem.

The Sanguine has a fine sense of balance. If they do fall they can leap to their feet so fast they don't even touch the ground. Sitting still on a chair is not easy for them. They will lean back and balance the chair on its two back legs, to the point where it almost topples over. This is particularly true of Sanguine children when bored in class. It is almost as if they hate to be contained behind a desk, and it earns them many a reprimand from the teacher. In other situations they, particularly the men, will twirl the chair round, straddle it and sit gazing at you over the back of it.

Sanguines not only look good, they also know they look good and they enjoy the fact. Their looks are important to them and you will often see them glancing in mirrors or reflective windows, checking on their looks and admiring them.

Look for the Sanguine in a group of admiring people. They will either be the centre of attention, spinning imaginative tales, or one of the dominant and active listeners round a Choleric who is holding court. Not for them the wallflower stance of the Phlegmatic on the edge of the crowd, watching to see what is the right thing to do, or the droop of the Melancholic waiting to tell a tale of woe.

The Sanguine Child

The Sanguine baby is a delight. Blond haired and blue eyed they are commonly smiling and happy. They may be chubby initially, but are long-boned and will quickly develop the long and slender look that will be theirs as adults and that makes them a delight to dress. Their fingers and toes are also longer than those of other babies.

As babies they smile, laugh and gurgle more than the others. They will also demand to be kept amused. Do not leave them to their own devices to meditate on this new world they have entered. Keep them entertained with things to look at, preferably moving and with light and colour. Hanging chimes, the movement of trees, sounds and activities going on around them – all these will keep the Sanguine baby amused. Left to their own devices they have few resources, but they take delight in everything they see and hear. They are keenly alert, developing an interest in their surroundings faster than the other temperaments, with the possible exception of some Choleric babies. When lonely or bored they will be quick to let you know with piercing and high-pitched cries and screams. These will turn to smiles the instant you turn up to amuse them and distract their attention by showing them some novelty.

You will hear comments about how pretty or attractive they are, how happy and alert. You will not hear comments, usually reserved for the Phlegmatic baby, about how good they are and how peaceful they are when left to themselves. This is a baby you should spend time with and keep amused.

As they sit up and react to the world around them, give them new toys to play with, preferably brightly coloured, light and mobile. They may be delicate and soon get broken, but this hardly matters as the Sanguine child soon loses interest in things and wants something new to play with. They like toys that move rather than heavy objects. As they grow older they will prefer the grace of bows and arrows to the might of heavy cannons. They like pretty things they can play with rather than toys with which they can build or from which they could learn. At the same time they do enjoy toys that are tools they can use.

The Phlegmatic child will love those colouring books where each space is numbered. You put colour number 27 in area number 27, and so forth. This gives them peace and the security of knowing they are putting the right colour in the right place. This would never do for the Sanguine child. Give them a wash of water and let them float colours around. Let them paint and use coloured crayons. Give them coloured Plasticine and let them model. They have an instinctive delight in colours and textures; let them develop this. Don't worry about the shape or what things are meant to be. The Sanguine child will simply be experimenting – their imagination will fill in the rest. Encourage them in the use and development of this imagination as much as you can, since the high-tech world of twentieth-century society will do all it can to beat it out of them, and the rest of us will be the losers.

Tell them fairy stories with as much creative imagery as you can muster and with happy endings. In this way you will encourage their imagination and let them know that, at least in stories, they can satisfy their desire to believe the world is a happy place.

As young children they are probably in Stage I and will have a new hobby every few weeks, a new favourite sport every season, a new favourite food every month and new friends with startling frequency. One term they may be passionately interested in jigsaws, wanting as many as they can have so they can switch from one to the other; the next it may be cars or musical instruments. Whatever it is, while it is the interest of the moment, it is all-consuming. There is little point in you telling them you won't buy them any more just because you know they'll have lost this particular interest in a few weeks' time. They simply won't believe you. For the moment the hobby, the current passion, occupies their every spare moment; yet the passion is short-lived. If they want a doll it is better to give them a make-do doll now and help them create clothes out of whatever scraps you have than to ask them to wait until you have saved the money to buy them a good one, for by then they will have lost interest and your money will have been wasted

I recall the birthday party of a Sanguine child when one of her friends arrived with a pair of castanets. Nothing else would do – the Sanguine child had to have a pair too, and *now*. The harried mother told her not to be stupid, the shops were shut and it would have to wait. After the party a more understanding father took her along the beach until they found a pair of bivalve shells that would do duty instead. Blissfully happy, she took them to bed. Next morning broken bits of the shells littered her bed, an impatient mother berated the father for being so foolish and the daughter had clearly lost interest in the matter. Only he and his daughter appreciated the value of what he had done.

As a parent you may have to run to keep up with your Sanguine child's interests. Above all, remember that what they want, they want now – not at some future birthday or Christmas. If it is not appropriate or possible to give them that set of paints or train set now, don't buy it assuming they will still want it at some future date when a present is in order. There is bound to be something else they want by then, and they are likely to have lost interest in the paints or train.

One Sanguine child went on holiday to the seaside for the first time. Nothing would do, as he played in among the rock pools, but that he have a fishing net and a toy yacht. The parents had spent all their money on the holiday and had little extra left for spending. The Phlegmatic father saved and was able to buy the child the chosen yacht out of the following month's pay, only to learn that it was no longer wanted. The more understanding mother had spent all her energy fashioning wire into a ring and attaching an old stocking to it with a stick for a handle for a fishing net, and making a yacht out of a hollowed log and a hand-rigged sail. At the same time she went with the child to all the toy shops and they fantasised for hours as to which yacht they would buy when they had the money. Half the fun, as the child later realised, was in the dreaming. After all, once you have bought, the dreaming stops and the possibilities have become limited by your completed choice.

Sanguine children will love and hug you. They are demonstrative, share their emotions readily, and love to tell you how much they love you and that you are their special friend. Be warned though: these emotions can be turned on and off readily, as they are already in the groove of wanting to say and do what pleases you now, with little or no constancy or thought for the morrow. Stage II or III children, less common than Stage I children, will have developed greater constancy and be more steadfast and loyal to their friends.

Sanguines have a nearly insatiable desire to explore and will have few fears, not because they are brave but because they cannot conceive of coming to harm. Harm, pain and accidents are things that happen to other people. Their daring is born of the conviction that they are exempt from the rules, both of nature and the powers that be, in the form of parents or teachers. They take a delight in their body, love to climb trees, take part in gymnastics or do anything that involves them being light on their feet, quick and nimble. They may seem to be accident prone, but this is because they will rarely gauge the strength of a branch before climbing it, or check the ice before skating over it.

To the extent that they are wonderful creators and full of new ideas, they may be the ringleader of their gang. They will be quick to accept a dare. They will make plans with little or no thought for the practicalities: these they will leave to others. Cholerics will apply the strength and determination, may even take the idea over as their own, and will certainly demand to play the leading role; the Melancholic will check out the details and worry about the things that could go wrong and about the children that can't keep up. The Phlegmatics will wait to do as they are told. All of this is tedious to the Sanguine, who has eyes on the distant horizon and the next game.

> The Sanguine child will commonly have an imaginary playmate. I recall one Sanguine child, Sally, tall, slim, with long blonde hair and graceful movements. She was an only child but accompanied by Mary, her invisible playmate. Mary had to have a place laid for her at table and a meal put in front of her. Sally's understanding parents complied and, when they asked why the food was still on the plate, accepted Sally's answer that Mary wasn't hungry today. They would also accept the statement that Mary had asked Sally to eat some of the food for her. They even, occasionally, bought clothes for her too, buying two outfits at a time. Typically Sanguine, Sally was fastidious and liked her clothes to be clean, so the spare set often came in handy. It wasn't until she was nearly seven that Mary faded into oblivion.
>
> Less understanding parents might have made fun of this or considered it a dishonest way for Sally to get more for herself – more sweets, more attention, more love (she demanded two

hugs, one of which she would pass on to Mary). To Sally, however, Mary was very real and they had wonderful conversations. Mary was the audience Sally needed but would otherwise not have had, living in the country. Mary was the sympathetic ear who totally understood Sally when others didn't. Later, Sally took to writing stories and to painting and drawing as outlets for her creativity.

Truth

It will be the Sanguine child, heading the dejected group that has failed to come home on time, who spins the most fascinating reasons for what went wrong with their schedule. As you look sceptically at them, they will embellish their story more and more in an effort to convince you. Just as readily, they will have convinced themselves that their story is true, even if some of their friends are saying, 'Well, not actually *that* big a dog, and the man wasn't actually *all that* frightening'. They will be horrified when you point out their exaggerations, not to say lies. After all, they didn't mean to cheat on you, that is the way it should have been. Even while things are happening they are likely to be fantasising around the experience and embellishing it, ready for future retelling.

We have all heard the wonderful tales concocted by a Sanguine child to explain why they are late. 'Well you see, I would have been on time, but there was this traffic accident, and it was *huge*, and there was blood *everywhere* and *no one* was allowed to go by, and since I had seen it I had to stay, they said I was a star witness and very important, and ...'. Don't be silly, says his Choleric sister, it was only one person knocked over and they were hardly hurt at all. That silly old policeman was making a lot of fuss about nothing and he didn't need your statement anyway, he said so.

The unwise parent will accuse the Sanguine child of lying. This will confuse the child, for in their imagination their description of events is an accurate picture of the way it happened. If you call the child deceitful and let them know that you see through the story they are telling you, you will make them feel silly and ashamed but it will do nothing to stop them doing the same thing next time. They will simply conclude that you just don't see the world as it is (for them) and will stop trusting you.

Restlessness

The Sanguine child hates to sit still. If there is a prolonged task to do let them have frequent short breaks. Far from extending the time the task takes this will speed things up as they will apply themselves with renewed zeal each time they restart. If they have twenty sums to do, let them have a quick play in the sandpit for five minutes after they have done each block of five. Make each session fun. They enjoy the now; the goal at the other end is less important to them.

Sanguine children can seem to be precocious, imitating the adults and talking on subjects of which they have no knowledge. This is often done to impress and to be the centre of attraction, as well as because of their enjoyment in the sheer pleasure of the moment.

School

The Sanguine child will be thrilled by school and the idea of learning but may lack application. If a subject interests them they can score straight As. If the teacher fails to hold their interest in it, or the class goes too slowly for the lively Sanguine mind, the Sanguine child's attention will wander and they will cease to learn. From term to term the favourite subject, and the favourite teacher, may change.

That marvellous Miss Jones, teaching all that exciting stuff about the different countries of the world, may become boring Miss Jones when she tries to instil the details of commerce and trade of a single country in the next term. Mr Kent will be the new hero as he describes the wonders of science and draws the big picture of what science can do, but will become a monster next term when the children are expected to learn the details of an experiment or an equation. Neither Miss Jones or Mr Kent should take this change of heart personally.

As they go on through school the Sanguine child's results will be erratic. They may seem to be excellent in a subject one term and come bottom of the class the next. Either their interest has switched to another subject or the teacher has failed to maintain their enthusiasm. If something becomes difficult they would rather disclaim all interest in the subject than either work at overcoming the difficulty or admit defeat. For as long as their interest is maintained and there is a sense of achievement they will explore the subject and the ideas with enthusiasm, showing great intelligence, although this is more often a reflection of a lively and darting mind than the true or deep understanding of the subject experienced by the Choleric. It can also reflect their willingness to talk on any subject, even if they are not sure of their facts.

Their report may read 'lacks concentration', 'could do better if he would apply himself', 'troublemaker, must settle down'. In truth, the teachers would do well to understand the volatile and lively nature of the child and to work with this. Some Sanguine children may even be told they have learning difficulties, simply because they have not been given enough that interests them sufficiently for them to feel the subject is worth their prolonged attention.

If you have a new class or project or are presenting a new subject, your best course is to get the Sanguine children interested and they will then make it seem such fun that the rest of the class will want to join in. Long after the Sanguines have lost interest the rest of the class will be reaping the benefits of their lively introduction.

It may be difficult to organise, but the ideal schooling for a Sanguine child is one in which the teacher teaches whichever subject takes the child's fancy at that particular moment. If they are excited by the subject they can learn as much in a week as they would in a term of slog when their natural attention is diverted elsewhere. A week's rapid study of French might divert to ten days of passionate interest in first French and then European history, followed by a stretch of wanting to learn every aspect of the rivers and towns first of Europe and then of other continents. This might in turn lead on to a desire to explore maths or the sciences involved in sailing and flying, followed by an interest in astronomy. Perhaps the old days of flexible tutors gave Sanguines a better start in life than the rigid school system. Yet the Sanguine child does love the crowds at school, the audience and the fun and games.

As the Sanguine child matures to Stage II they learn to discipline their attention and to study even the subjects that they find boring. Some Sanguines hate their own instability, as they see it, longing for a magic wand that will stop them flitting from flower to flower and never settling. Other Sanguines relish their nature and enjoy their lively mind. A lot depends on the teacher. If the child is praised for their interest they will learn to work with all the positive aspects of their nature. If they are condemned for their lack of staying power they are likely to come to think of themselves as shallow and worthless.

Let the Sanguine child be the extrovert in class. However, gentle discipline is necessary to lead them to complete the things they have started. It is a little like catching a cricket ball with rigid hands or letting your hands give as the ball arrives. Go with the Sanguine child's sanguinity but lead them gently into the way of developing depth and perseverance.

Sanguine children are rarely intellectual. They have a broad range of interests and often have trouble deciding what they will do when they 'grow up', something a Sanguine does with difficulty.

Indeed they may well have a different answer almost every time to the 'what do you want to be when you grow up?' question, but do not laugh at them. Applaud them instead for their willingness to look at and consider lots of options. Provide, as far as you can, an education system where their options are kept open as long as possible. Eventually they will have to decide, but the more rounded their education has been the richer will be their life. They will also suffer less from the frustrations of finding they do not have the prerequisites for certain courses of action. Sanguines, more than any other temperament, hate to have to retrace their steps, or to catch up on educational steps or subjects they have missed.

Sanguines may choose to stay on at school and study for university, particularly if there is a subject in which they excel. Yet their restless desire for freedom may also draw them out into the world. If they do not mature they will almost certainly prefer the instant pleasures of a pay packet or salary and the glamour of entering the adult world, to the persistence required by the long-term goals of study and development that could lead them to a more rewarding career and future.

One reason they might go to university is because they simply don't know, yet, what they want to do or be and a stint at university will postpone the decision – if they can only decide which subjects to study or which university to go to. Or they may go to art or drama school. They are unlikely to go to a secretarial college: even the thought of the jobs that would result from that will bore them to tears.

If the Sanguine child or teenager does not mature their life is likely to be marked by a restlessness, a superficiality and tendency toward triviality that leaves them endlessly unsatisfied and searching. Other people will become less and less tolerant as they take their childish ways and their fantasies into adulthood. Whether or not they continue with their studies, if they don't mature they will flit from one subject to another as their fancy takes them, or they will swap from one job to another without building up expertise in any one area.

The Sanguine who does not mature is likely to become a drifter or get into trouble. They will try cigarettes, alcohol or drugs. All these offer new experiences, excitement and variety. They are also consistent with the Sanguine's desire to live in the present, enjoying the moment with little thought for the consequences. They contain the element of risk and dare that makes life exciting, and an implied glamour and sophistication that appeals to them. It soon becomes easy for them to lie or cheat to finance their habits and evade the authorities.

The Sanguine Adult

On leaving school and moving on to the adult stage, the Sanguine is more likely to think in terms of expressing herself and of having a good time and an exciting social life, than of making serious moves into a career. Sanguines will want to to explore, to travel, to make new friends. They may try several different jobs in an attempt to find one that appeals to them. Impatient with formal learning, they may decide to learn their trade or craft as an apprentice, particularly since they are good with their hands and enjoy practical work. In the world of fashion and beauty they will learn as they work. Study courses should be short: the thought of many years of training is enough to deter most Sanguines and stop them even before they start.

You can almost say that Sanguines never grow up. They never become true adults; more often they become grown-up children. They make a game of most things in their life, and they will find some way to make their work fun. Housework can be turned into a game with the kids, or they will fantasise that the queen is coming to visit and they are getting ready. They are unlikely to clean one room at a time. Rather they will start to clean one room, take dirty clothes to the laundry, decide to put the machine on, fail to find the washing powder and so decide to tidy the shelves, come across an old mixing bowl they thought they had lost, take this to the kitchen and decide to bake a cake. The original room is long forgotten and the Sanguine is surprised but not dismayed when they go into it later in the day and find it is still a mess. They will simply start the process over again. A mature Stage II or Stage III Sanguine will manage to get the whole house clean, but they will still use this method and have much more fun doing it than if they had stuck to a rigid plan. The Stage I Sanguine will get so sidetracked they finish up in the garden or out shopping for something they didn't plan to buy, and the entire house may never be clean at any one time.

Sanguine gardeners are similar. They walk towards the shed to get out the lawnmower, stop to pull some weeds, take the handful to the compost heap and decide it is time to turn it. Halfway through they will get bored and take some of the compost over to a flowerbed. Passing the vegetable bed on the way they realise it is time to transplant the cabbage seedlings. If the Sanguine has matured, again the whole job will eventually get done, and the doing of it will be much more fun than if they stick to one job (not a common Sanguine trait) rigidly until it is finished. By the time the first job was complete and they reached the compost they would probably have lost interest in turning it. Strike while the time is right and make each activity fun. Live in the now; the future doesn't exist anyway.

Sanguines will probably go away for lots of holidays. If time or their work schedule forbids this they will make frequent weekend excursions, either going away for the whole weekend or, if funds and family ties make this difficult, going out for picnics and day-long excursions. Staying at home weekend after weekend is not the Sanguine's idea of fun. They like things to look forward to, they like surprises and they like the unexpected.

A Sanguine couple came to see me. Their marriage was nearly on the rocks as they battled to keep their business afloat and stay in touch with each other. I suggested they set aside one night each week and, on alternate weeks, one of them was to plan a surprise outing together based on what they thought their partner would like. Next week it would be the other partner's turn. They also set aside one weekend a month as a fun and surprise weekend, no matter how much the business needed more overtime. Again they swapped roles and took it in turns to surprise the other one. Being Sanguine, of course, they also downed tools and took off from time to time as the spirit moved them, but this only occurred when they got desperate and was no real solution. Having these regular surprises to plan for and look forward to saved the day. Being Sanguine they got nearly as much pleasure planning the occasions as participating in them. Knowing that they had this one evening a week and one weekend a month when they could let off steam helped them to apply themselves the rest of the time.

In general, Sanguines are extremely social. They will have lots of friends, invite them over and hold open house where friends are welcome to drop in any time. They love to be invited out and will often suggest group activities, leaving others, of course, to arrange the details. Sanguines are disinclined to have a quiet evening at home watching television after a long day at the office, followed by a routine weekend with shopping, mowing the lawn, fixing the car and a visit to the pub on Sunday. They must have variety and will probably be the ones to create it. They will also choose to be with other people rather than on their own.

Friends

As friends you will find Sanguines delightful. They will bring sparkle to your life. You'll be delighted if they accept an invitation to your dinner party, knowing it will now be a success. If it's for a date some time in the future you might want to confirm it closer to the event, or they could, if in Stage I, have become sidetracked by another possibility or opportunity. They would not see this as letting you down but as their right to go with what interests and involves them at the moment. By Stage II they are more reliable – but check anyway.

Susan had a standing arrangement to call in on an older woman each Wednesday on her way to a meeting and spend an hour with her over a cup of coffee. Susan then fell head over heels in love (the only way Sanguines do it) with someone who went to the same meetings. They met up early each Wednesday and went to the meeting together. Some weeks later a saddened friend called Susan and wondered where she had been. Susan, clearly a Stage I Sanguine, was devastated at what she had done: she had totally forgotten about the friend as she became involved in her new passion. The friend could then do one of two things – she could either be hurt and angry and consider Susan less of a friend, or she could understand Susan's Sanguine nature and accept her impetuosity. Some people have the maturity and wisdom to take the latter action, but many stop short at feeling hurt, and some wonderful friendships are lost. The trick is in understanding the nature of the person with whom you are

dealing rather than expecting them to conform to your model
of the world and how it should be.

If you are in trouble and need help, call on a Melancholic friend to
give you heartfelt sympathy and commiseration, a Phlegmatic
friend if you need someone reliable to do as you ask, a Choleric
friend if you need someone to fight your battles with or for you. Call
on a Sanguine friend if you want to be cheered up. They will rush to
your aid, provided they are free, with bunches of flowers, witty
cards, bright ideas and lots of cheer. They will raise depression to
laughter, have you playing hockey with your crutches or draw car-
toons of the debt collector. Whatever they do they will lift your spirits. Just don't expect them to help you to put their ideas into practice.
Their rosy view of the future may be a definite possibility but they
will be short on ways to bring it about. They may start off with you
along the road to the solution but are apt to disappear at the first
obstacle that is not easy to overcome. Do not, however, feel let down.
Their job was to cheer you up, show you directions and give you
hope, not to solve your problem – that is something you have to do.
It is simply a lot easier to do it with a Sanguine cheering you on.

They make great friends, but don't expect too much of what is
outside their nature. If they do seem to let you down it is not because
they don't care, it's just that there is only so much doom and gloom
that they can handle, then they fly off to sunnier gardens.

If you are very lucky and know a Stage III Sanguine, hold on to
them. Not only will they cheer you up now, they will stay around
and cheer you through the process of getting better.

Sanguines are generous with their own emotions, time and possessions. They may be equally generous with yours, and you may
find this disconcerting. When they give they love an audience, and
the Sanguine will look forward to the act of giving and gain as much
pleasure from it as the receiver gains from the present. Set them up
to play Santa Claus and you can be sure they will be there for the
Christmas party.

The Sanguine at Work

Sanguines are graceful creatures: they are also long and slender
rather than strong and muscular and want to exercise their physical

dexterity in their work. This does not necessarily mean manual labour – something, in fact, which they usually avoid, certainly the dirty side of it – but they do delight in their control over their body and over any tools they have to use. The secretary (a dull and unwelcome job for a Sanguine) will at least enjoy the way her fingers can dance over the keys. The waitress will delight in her dexterity in handling plates and equipment. The driver will enjoy the way they can nip around traffic. All will enjoy manual and bodily dexterity in whatever they do.

You will find Sanguines in the arts, in all sorts of arts: in music and dance, as painters and sculptors, as actors and singers. You will find them in peripheral areas such as photography, athletics and crafts. They crave action and their work will involve this.

Another thing they will all demand is variety. Each day should be different and exciting or else involve their passion of the moment. Based on these considerations it is easy to look at large segments of the workplace and conclude that you will not find Sanguines there, or rarely so.

Manual labour is not for them. As we saw earlier, they hate to get dirty. If they do have to do physical labour they will clean themselves up as quickly as possible afterwards. Not for them the quick whisk with a cloth to remove grease stains from their hands, and the gradual build-up of grime under the nails.

Typically, the Sanguine builder or car mechanic will go straight to the washroom at the end of the day – and often during the day – and spend the time that is needed to eradicate all signs of dirt and grime, all signs of his daily labours. He will do this even if his workmates are laughing at him and calling him names for caring so much about the way he looks.

You will find them in the construction industry, but often creating and providing the impetus rather than involved in the hard slog. Mind you, they do get a kick out of using heavy machinery and becoming adept at manoeuvring bulldozers or high-flying cranes.

He will tidy himself up, but he will rarely do the same for his workplace. He may well leave soggy towels and discarded working clothes lying around. They are of no interest to him once they have served their purpose, and the Sanguine is not inherently tidy. Nor is he organised, so his workbench will look as if a bomb has hit it. He may make a creative tool board, with each item outlined in the most appropriate colour; he may start out by designing a space with a place for everything. That is the creative and interesting part.

However, the daily maintenance of this space and the routines required to tidy it up after each day's work are too dull and boring for the Sanguine.

A Sanguine who is a car mechanic is unlikely to be on the production line. Doing the same task repeatedly, day after day, would drive the Sanguine to drink, resignation or madness. They might be working on the creative side and might then occasionally have to get their hands dirty. They would then clean themselves up fast and move on to some other interesting task. Variety, they crave variety. You may also find them test-driving the new car, the new aeroplane, seeing how fast it can go, pushing it to the limit, simply for the fun and the excitement of the feel of it. If forced to do a routine assembly-line job they can become so restless – 'ants in their pants all over their body', as one client put it – that they get to screaming point and may well create trouble just for the sake of alleviating the monotony.

They crave people, enjoy people and want to be around people. So you are unlikely to find them in an office on their own poring over paperwork, columns of accounts or checking detailed reports.

Sanguines will work best at a job that their minds can encompass. Keep it short. The Sanguine likes to be able to finish a job within a short time span: hours, or days at the most. They do not relish the long-term project that will take three years. If this exists the wise boss will break it down into digestible chunks and feed them to the Sanguine one at a time, while still letting them know they are part of a bigger whole. The Sanguine likes the sense of completing something and moving on.

Since they enjoy their body, particularly its grace and agility, you may find them in jobs requiring these attributes, working as dancers, gymnasts and athletes. As athletes, look for them among the sprinters, not the long-distance runners. All jobs have their routine, and to be a fine gymnast you have to practise over and over and over. This is where the Sanguine can come unstuck, so their trainer should bring as much variety as possible into the training. However, if they love the activity sufficiently they may well rise above their impatience and tolerate the training for the joy of using their body. They may even be found engaged in long-term practice and training that puts the other temperaments to shame. If so, this is not done with the final goal of wining in mind; it is done because they simply love what they are doing, right now, right this minute. Their desire for fun and glamour as well as excitement may see them mounted on downhill skis, behind the wheel of fast cars, sky-diving, or surfing.

The Sanguine is a people person and likes to be part of a team. That's to say, they like to have at least one other person around them, someone who will be their audience and who will do all the routine part of looking after them, doing the dull administration and keeping track of the details. They also like to be out front, they like to be seen as the figurehead, the person with the ideas.

The Sanguines will work within a team, up to a point, but they may be troublemakers, the pea under the many mattresses of the princess. They may flout authority, seeing it as superfluous. A mature Sanguine will handle the situation but a Stage 1 Sanguine can be a cocky recruit. They can be the new boy in the team or the new girl in the office, who fails to acknowledge the full authority of the boss. If a Stage I Sanguine is foolish enough to get a secretarial job, better left to the Phlegmatic, they are the ones with nail files in the drawers where the paper clips should be and the ones who spend more time in front of the mirror than checking the filing.

They love variety, applause and the limelight. The routine of a model's life is difficult for the Sanguine but they tolerate it if the glamour and variety are sufficient. They love acting but often prefer to play in a television soap with an evolving storyline, or make a film, rather than act in the same play night after night. To do theatre they have to find some variety to maintain their interest. They may be the actor or actress who fluffs their lines and leaves everyone having to ad-lib for a page or two, just so they can bring excitement into the evening. This may drive the others mad but their sparkle and creativity more than compensate. However involved they are in the part or character they are portraying, they are also aware of themselves, unlike the Melancholic who becomes the part. With a Sanguine you will always be aware you are watching a specific actor or actress playing a role.

Extrovert Sanguines like to bring people together. They may organise negotiations, meetings and conferences. They may instigate them, inspiring first the other speakers to agree to speak and then the audience to come and listen to them. It is likely to be the Phlegmatic who does the actual organising, but the idea is the Sanguine's. They can dream up combinations of people that others might not think of, dinner parties that you'd never contemplate, yet the Sanguine is able to be creative and see how the different people can mix and match.

The arts often appeal to the Sanguines. They enjoy the colours, the sounds, the action, the expression. Just as the gymnast will practise, not because of any streak of Phlegmatic temperament, but because they love to use their body and revel in the movement, so the musician will practise. They are committed to steady preparation for the performance, and the activity of the practice, the creating of and the playing of the music, is a pleasure in itself, each time.

The slightly more introvert Sanguine will enjoy tools and the delicate use of their hands. They will value their manual dexterity and take delight in doing small and detailed work, as well as mastering difficult instruments.

You can expect the quieter Sanguine to be able to do delicate tasks with instruments, but do not expect them to keep repeating the job. Give them the unusual and complicated repair job to do. They will also love driving for the feel of the steering wheel and their ability to become part of the car. The tennis racket will become an extension of their arm. They may even, in spite of their light frame, use large and heavy equipment, yet do it with a skill and dexterity not shown by the other temperaments, as if the equipment becomes a part of them.

If this type of Sanguine goes off the rails be wary of what they can do with weapons. The professional killer for hire, who does a particularly delicate or accurate job, is likely to be a Sanguine who has failed to develop constructively.

Sanguines enjoy business rather than academic pursuits and can succeed well in selling since they are personable and popular.

Extrovert Sanguines can be very successful entrepreneurs, negotiators and diplomats. They are resourceful: they can and will take their work seriously but it can also be a game for them and they can bring that same sense of enjoyment into it for others, at least for as long as the Sanguine is there, keeping the kettle boiling. They can make even the dullest job interesting, for a while at least, until they get bored and drift or fly off to the next project.

They can rescue people and companies that are failing. It may well be this type of Sanguine who is called in to a company that is going bankrupt. They come up with the creative ideas that can turn the company around, they may know the people, skills and resources that are needed, they may bring all the necessary resources together and administer the project until the company is firmly on its way to recovery. But don't expect them to stay around once the problem is solved. The exception to this would be a very mature Stage III Sanguine.

The Sanguine is usually good at making money and is usually successful in business, but may lack staying power. This may lead them to doing well, amassing a lot of money and then taking time out to spend it. Since they often have little idea of the value of money and are impetuous they can spend it all too easily. They may even lose it in unwise investments. They then set to and amass another fortune.

They will take risks, particularly the intellectual Sanguines; risks that could leave other people nervous wrecks. They do this because they love the excitement and in the knowledge that if it goes wrong they will abandon that idea and move on to the next. The more emotional Sanguines may try to minimise the real risks, preferring to have happy times without the risk. Their love of life, extending into their work, can lead them into error because they may simply refuse to consider the darker side of situations, preferring to sweep this under the carpet. Do not trust a Sanguine to make sure your aeroplane is safe to fly, the accounts have been done properly, the legalities of the contract are sound or that you have a sensible security system installed in the factory.

Sanguines love action, physical action. You may find them as waiters darting around the tables, driving ambulances or police cars for excitement, involved in rescue squads, or as detectives with a new problem to solve each day. You may even find them doing seemingly routine jobs such as loading the shelves in a supermarket, because of the activity and the pleasure they manage to bring into the physical activity of it.

The relationship between Sanguines and their boss can help them to mature from Stage I to II. The boss can, to some extent, play the role of the hero and role model, enabling the Sanguine to stabilise their personality.

Sanguines like status and prestige in their job and a sense of their place in the hierarchy. They do not necessarily have to be the boss. In the same way that they enjoy pleasing an audience they can enjoy serving in their work, delighting in creating a beautiful effect. They are excellent in PR and in creating proposals. The Sanguine can enjoy working for someone, particularly if they admire them and if they receive praise where it is due – and occasionally even where it is not. They will then enjoy basking in this approval and work hard to earn it. Their boss should, however, know how to keep them in their place, being both authoritative and kind but keeping their distance. If they treat the Sanguine employee as an equal, even for a short time, the Sanguine's sense of security in the stability of the working relationship is lost, and so is their chance to mature. Once Sanguines have lost respect for their boss it cannot be retrieved. It is better for the Sanguine to move on and try again.

Sanguines like a uniform as well as status. They like a title and they respond to rewards and recognition. Their title does not need to be that of 'head'. A title such as stationery manager will improve the work of the Sanguine secretary in the typing pool. Just so long as they receive recognition, accolade, status and approval you can have the best from your Sanguine employee, without their faults.

In general, Sanguines are not career oriented. They will work, preferably at something they enjoy, for the sake of the rewards and what can be done with them. They will do even better if their work is a hobby or activity that they love and enjoy and at which they can earn money as a fortuitous side-benefit. To Sanguines, social life is important, as is family. They want to enjoy the evenings, go exploring at the weekends and have time to spend with their large circle of friends. Do not expect them to take paperwork home or put in long hours of voluntary overtime.

The Sanguine and Money

Sanguines love money. More specifically, they love what money can do for them. They *adore* luxury. They want to dress well, look good, be surrounded by beautiful things, to be loved and adored – and to do this in the way they want, they need money. It may only be a small amount of money, enough to buy some extra ribbons or a pretty frock, enough to go and see the latest movie, have the latest toy or go to the fair. Or they may want millions – such Sanguines would not think in terms of anything as mundane as thousands – for designer clothes, a private yacht and a castle to live in. It is all relative.

Sanguines do not like hard work and will be happiest if their wealth comes to them without too much effort. The exception is the situation where they simply delight in what is labelled by society as their 'work'; in this case their enthusiasm will generate their income. They prefer an inheritance, a wealthy marriage, a lottery win or a clever entrepreneurial success that owes more to quick thinking than to prolonged study or earning it by the sweat of their brow – and after all they hate to get dirty or to sweat. Because they use money with such flair they often do receive it. The wealthy husband enjoys seeing his beautiful Sanguine wife decked in wonderful clothes which she wears to advantage, and loves being able to show her off in elegant surroundings. The elegant Sanguine male is a welcome guest at any party and will be showered with invitations and opportunities. Most gigolos are surely Sanguine. Many opportunities open up for these people who add value, cachet, glamour and an exciting image to any venture.

Since Sanguines live for the pleasures of today they see little point in saving and, in fact, will often overspend. They will buy the best wines for a dinner party, the best food. They want to have the best, show they have it and share it around. They love to splash out on clothes, cars and possessions that add to their glamour and allure. They will spend more than is necessary on their friends, for they love to please.

As entrepreneurs they commonly have an unstructured income. You may find them in jobs where they can do overtime as they need it, get tips or take a percentage. They may have a second job they can do when funds run low or some highly individual and innovative way by which they can earn or generate extra income as they need it.

If they remain in Stage I they may go into debt, being over-confident that 'something will happen' to pull them out. If it doesn't, and if they degenerate further, they may take to gambling, to investing in risky ventures or even outright stealing. Their quick and nimble fingers serve them well in this, and if they degenerate they can become skilled card-sharps. They can also use their wits and charm to come up with imaginative, and often successful, ways of tricking people out of their money. Their total self-confidence leaves no room for worries about getting caught. If they are, they are equally sure that their ready charm and quick tongue will get them out of trouble.

Stage II or III Sanguines are often successful entrepreneurs or are self-employed and have more legitimate ways of increasing their income. With their happy optimism, it often seems as if the money fairy smiles on them. In fact, provided they have a sound idea, some solid Phlegmatics to do the routine work, a couple of Melancholics to take care of the details and watch for trouble and a Choleric to lead them on when they show signs of wandering off track, their businesses do do well. Since they present such a wonderful image, love to please and can inspire their clients and customers to dream, people love to work or do business with them and their business grows.

The best way for a Sanguine to save is to have the money diverted to a savings account at source. They rarely keep a running record of what should be in their cheque account: such details are too tedious for them. Instead they will simply either buy what they want and worry about paying the bills later (Stage I) or look at what's in their purse, available on their credit card or in the bank and buy if the money is available (Stage II). Only a Stage III Sanguine will give more serious thought to their purchases. If it's there, it's for spending is the Sanguine's attitude, and unless they are very mature it is probably best *not* to give them a credit card. If the money isn't there, well, they can entertain themselves in different ways. In the meantime, their savings account can be growing quietly each week – but don't tell them.

Stage III Sanguines usually provide for their future, though the future is not something to which they give much thought. Equally, they are often loved by their family and in old age are cared for by family and friends who have received much from them during their lifetime. Children are usually happy to have elderly Sanguine parents staying with them and the grandchildren love them.

The Sanguine and Time

Sanguines find it extremely difficult to keep track of time and to be on time. If there is something they passionately want to do, however long it will actually take, the Sanguine is easily able to believe that there is plenty of time to do it, and off they go. The moment is all.

The Sanguine housewife will rarely have meals ready on time: there are too many possibilities for interruptions between the idea and getting the meal on the table. When the food does arrive, however, it will have been worth waiting for – not because she is necessarily a good cook, though she may be, but because it is beautifully presented and there will be her usual laughter at the table. Meals may even be unusual, due partly to her lively imagination and partly to the fact that she didn't allow enough time for shopping, didn't plan what the meals would be or had too little time to cook what she had planned. You may not have had sardines and

Roquefort cheese on spaghetti with a grated parsnip salad before, but by the time she has dressed it up with flowers from the garden and added lemon juice to the parsnip you will almost certainly pronounce it delicious.

In business the Sanguine would do well to have a Phlegmatic secretary to keep them on time, or a Melancholic who likes to see schedules running perfectly. If they have a truly creative job they may get away with it under the heading of 'artistic tolerance' but being late for meetings rarely goes down well. If you are organising a conference and have a Sanguine speaker you had better check with them beforehand to make sure they have remembered the arrangements. They may cause you some headaches in this regard, but are likely to be popular with the audience.

In the performing arts the Sanguine is likely to be temperamental and to keep other people waiting, partly due to their lack of respect for time and partly to gain attention. But again, when they do get going the result is usually worth it.

They may often run over time at meetings, to the irritation of their organised colleagues with trains to catch, but if you stay behind with them afterwards the drinks at the pub could lead on to a good dinner.

It is rarely constructive to ask a Sanguine how long they will take to do something. If you drop a Sanguine child off with friends, a Sanguine wife off at the shops or a Sanguine husband at a meeting and expect to pick them up at a predetermined time, you could be in for major frustrations. The Sanguine child who asks to be picked up in an hour could have rushed off to a new venture just as you pull up. Your Sanguine wife, or friend, will have absolutely no idea how long the shopping will take as she moves from counter to counter and shop to shop as each new thing catches her eye. Your Sanguine husband will move from idea to idea in the meeting, may even move from office to office as he follows the development of the discussion. They will all be totally surprised at the way time has passed. It's not that they are unaware of time, rather that what they are doing is just too interesting for such a mundane thought, and somehow time, in their minds, seems to expand and contract in a way that doesn't happen for other temperaments.

With maturity comes a greater degree of orderliness – but don't ever expect them to stick to the clock if it will ruin a good story or spoil the occasion.

The Sanguine in Love

Sanguines make wonderful lovers – at least if you want romance, excitement, great erotic charm and a willingness to experiment, even the extreme extroversion of being willing to have group sex or swap partners. When it comes to long-term staying power with one single partner, however, there may be problems.

The Sanguines are only really happy when they are in love, and they can fall in love easily, suddenly and passionately. They will do so on the spur of the moment and with little consideration of the consequences. Once they do, other aspects of their life can fade into insignificance. They may become so besotted or involved they may risk their job, their friends, their family, anything. Why not? After all, each time they fall in love, this is *it*, this is the one, this is their perfect mate . . . at least until the next time. The world is well lost for love and the loved one becomes an all-consuming passion.

For the Stage I Sanguine the need to be in love may be so great it can overcome their common sense and they may even create a fantasy around their lover. They may meet someone they like, build up a picture of them as the ideal soulmate and fall in love with this fantasy. This will last until their lover is seen as an earthbound human being with faults and weaknesses, or they fall in love with someone else or some other fantasy. The current liaison then becomes an unwanted tie, a shackle to be lost. Rather than face up to the denouement and the emotional scene that parting may precipitate, they tend to disappear, to fade away and to announce the end of the liaison simply by being absent. The easy way out is quickly taken, particularly by the immature Sanguine.

The young Sanguine will focus on love, want to be in love, and may well create a love affair where it would not otherwise exist, just so that they can be in love. Their hunger for love may be such that they latch on to the most likely partner, imbue them with all the qualities they most desire and then fall in love with this image. They can fool the person, they can fool their own friends and they can even fool themselves.

Sanguines can be interested in all sorts of people, but frequently lack discrimination and are often unable to tell the true friend from the sponger who hangs around like a moth around a flame. They can fall in love unwisely and get hurt all too easily. Yet that too passes as they pick themselves up and move on.

Because Sanguines can suit their mood to the company they are in, they can take on the colours of their environment and the people they are with. They can fool themselves into feeling they are at home with a most diverse group of people and friends. A female Sanguine may be madly in love with an artist and convince herself that art and artists are her milieu. Later she may fall in love with a mechanic and be all too ready to give up the paint-filled attic for the outdoor life of a racing driver, and convince herself that this is what she was really meant for. Then comes the businessman and the corporate cocktail parties: again she will fit in, will even come to 'realise' that this is her true setting.

Sanguines hate to be alone, hate to be single, hate to waste time when they could be experiencing the glory of a love affair. Their fear of being out of love may be so strong they will hold on to an old affair, long past its use-by-date, until such time as they can find another relationship to move to, like an inexperienced swimmer going from one handhold to another rather than pushing out into deep water.

Sanguines usually have a clear idea of the type of person they like. Since much of this is based on appearances and external factors, such as the way they behave and how fun they are to be with, little time may be spent, in the initial stages, on finding out what the person is like inside, as a unique individual. When they meet someone of the general type they like, they are likely to fall in love instantly without ever finding out more about that particular individual. When the person fails to live up to their expectations the Sanguine is likely to feel let down and betrayed and to move swiftly on to the next affair.

Sanguines, who like to look good, also want their partner to look good, yet the definition of this can alter radically, as they are apt to see their lover through rose-coloured glasses. It is hard for the Sanguine to understand why other people are not as besotted as they are with their latest love.

Sanguines not only are tall and slender, but they often want the same thing in their lover. Not for them the stolid Phlegmatic or the slow-moving and introverted Melancholic. They may well love and admire the strong Choleric or be swept up in the fantasy created with another Sanguine.

When you first meet a Sanguine they will tell you wonderful stories of who they are and what they have done. Most of it will be somewhat true, or have a basis in truth; very little will be totally accurate and much may be embellished. Some may well be totally false. As in other spheres of life, again they do not mean to lie. They are simply telling you how it seemed to them: the aim, after all, is to make a good impression. This is particularly true when they have just met the new love of their life and are out to impress or attract. This love of fantasy and a good story may get them into trouble occasionally, but even when their lover sees through them they may still be captivated.

The female Sanguine must guard against earning a reputation for promiscuity and superficiality. To others it may seem that she flits from lover to lover having one casual relationship after another. To her this is ludicrous. In her own eyes each affair was one of great passion and depth and, while it lasted, *the* one true love.

The Sanguine man has an easier time of it. He is likely to be thought of as the romantic, the young Lothario, the man of the world, the experienced lover, much admired by his more reserved and shy friends. He almost certainly had his first sexual affair, certainly his first passion, younger than his friends, leading them, rather than being a follower in this as in other aspects of his life.

Because of his liking for a good time, his good looks, his extroverted and dynamic nature, his ability to create enthusiasm wherever he goes and to turn the dullest event into an exciting party, he is likely to be the centre of attraction with a number of girls all longing for a chance to be his particular girl. He can pick and choose, and will do so regularly and frequently. He is fun to be with but do not expect fidelity and, above all, do not try to tie him down. He will be off on his butterfly wings the moment rings, parents, babies or wedding bells are even hinted at. Even the idea that they are 'going steady', a 'couple' or a 'unit' may be enough to scare him off and send him looking for the next conquest. The Choleric hates to be boxed in because he wants to be in control. The Sanguine hates to be boxed in, period.

To many Sanguines the contest is the best part, a game to be played with the full force of their imagination and charm. The search, the chase, the victory – this is the exciting part. After that the routine can set in, and routine is anathema to the Sanguine. If you have set your cap at a Sanguine, man or woman, keep them guessing: they will be yours until they have conquered or can take you for granted. If you relax once you are living with them or married to them you could lose them. They may not choose divorce – they are often realistic enough to know that other relationships could also become routine, and may even like the excuse of being married to avoid other entanglements – but they will certainly look for additional pleasures elsewhere. If you keep surprising them and keep the excitement alive they will be yours.

In crowds it is the Sanguine who has eyes all round his head. He will notice every pretty woman and even some that are not so pretty. His delight in an attractive pair of legs, a warm smile, glowing hair and a trim figure will lead him to be constantly on the look-out for them, always aware of them and frequently moved to comment on them. If he is with his current lover he may well comment to her, expecting her to share his enjoyment in the beauty of others, and be surprised if she gets jealous. He will then, if the present affair is at its height, insist that these comments in no way affect his present lover and this will indeed be true, at least in his mind. He is simply expressing his appreciation of beautiful things. But be warned, he will also remember these women when the present affair cools, and will certainly have an extensive little black book of names and numbers to call when the time is right to move on.

Some Sanguines, male or female, will be hanging on to a worn-out affair until another lover turns up, but frequently they will have done automatic groundwork and have a number of prospects in mind, almost without consciously planning it.

Female Sanguines may be somewhat more faithful than the males, but that is sociological rather than inherent: they too crave excitement and variety.

Marriage

Marriage is likely to come after a whirlwind romance. *This* time, they tell all their friends, this is the real thing, isn't it wonderful, love at first sight, they just know that this is Mr or Miss Right so why wait? And before you know it, they are married. You have heard it all before and seen other relationships wither. All you can do is cross your fingers and hope that this time it will last. Do not advise them against the move. You will not deter them and you may lose their friendship.

Once married the Sanguines can make wonderful partners, keeping the excitement alive in spite of the mortgage and the routines. In fact they have to do so for their own sakes. If you are married to one and are not one yourself, pay attention to these needs unless you want your partner to stray. The Sanguine still needs the romance, variety and excitement, although romance for the Sanguine is a much more light-hearted affair than the soulful romance of the Melancholic. Surprise treats, intimate dinners with flowers and candles – even if they are in a toy-littered family room – mean a lot. A bunch of flowers, a spontaneous small present and being constantly reminded that they are loved and wonderful is meat and drink to a Sanguine. They love presents and will thank you with a warmth that may seem overwhelming: it is not necessarily the present that has thrilled them, but the fact that you bothered. Use any occasion you can. If you buy something you know they need and want, don't simply give it to them – wrap it up, make them guess what it is, even hide it and give them elaborate clues. Never, ever take them for granted or they will not be there.

The men, particularly in Stage I, will often stray, they may divorce and they may have several marriages. Or they may not marry, simply having a long string of affairs. While married they may be unfaithful regularly and often, and cause a considerable amount of pain in the process. They need the reassurance that they are still admired and wanted and they are still in constant search of excitement. Typical Don Juans, they will be thrilled by the intrigue and the clandestine.

As he grows older, the need of the Sanguine man to be reassured that he is still in demand grows too. He will continue to need the flirtations, and that may well be all they are, yet they will still be important to him. An elderly, Stage I Sanguine man in constant search of his lost youth and vitality can be a sorry sight.

By Stage II they may still be straying, but only temporarily. They will be coming to recognise their own nature and be endeavouring to be more constant. Yet rather than keep the affair secret they may well come home and tell their wives, again insisting that these forays mean nothing and do not put the marriage at risk. The sensible wife will recognise that he needs these successes to reinforce his desirability and reassure himself that he is not losing his touch, that he is not becoming old and staid, and she will believe him for, indeed, it is true. He does need the excitement, but he probably knows himself well enough to realise that he also values the home he has and recognises that swapping wives will still not quench his thirst.

If he has reached Stage III he will be a lot more mature, more sure of himself and more willing to play a responsible role in the relationship, sacrificing his desire for change to the happiness of his partner.

If caught and threatened with divorce he will promise to reform, and may do so for a while for he does not like to hurt the other person knowingly. But as so often, his promises are made to be broken. Sooner or later his need for an audience, for new experiences, will surface.

If you are married to such a man you would be wise to laugh at his peccadilloes, and recognise that that is all they are, at least until such time as he tells you otherwise. In return you have an exciting partner who will, in all probability, stay with you. He will make the home a place of joy and sparkle: never the dull and routine for you, life will be full of surprises. He delights in treats and in giving, so be content to be the happy receiver. The alternative is a divorce and either another Sanguine with a similar scenario or a much duller life.

If your Sanguine husband has an activity or job, or a selection of hobbies and leisure pursuits in which he is passionately interested and about which he gets excited daily, then new romances may lose their interest for him. It's even better if you share his interests, his delights and his joys.

Sanguine women are also inclined to have affairs even after marriage, though somewhat less often than the men. Certainly they will flirt. They love to be told they are attractive and fun, they love to bathe in the admiration of other men. They also like their husband to notice that they are in demand and are popular. In time, or even from the start, the flirtation may be sufficient and the need for the sexual act with another person will fade. At the same time the other men in the room will be envying the Sanguine's husband, thinking him a lucky man to have such an exciting wife. If he is wise he will lap this up, knowing that his marriage is indeed much more fun than theirs.

If you are having an affair with a married Sanguine and they tell you they will leave their partner and pair up with you, don't believe them. They will constantly make promises they cannot keep. The affair is just that to them: an affair. It is their desire to please and keep you happy that drew the promise from them in the first place. They hate to hurt people and would rather promise the earth than face up to and tell you the truth.

Sex

Sanguines are great lovers with erotic skills that can send you spinning. They are kind and endlessly fascinating. What more could you ask of an affair that will delight your days and give you something wonderful to remember? Ultimately they can surprise you by being remarkably faithful to their wife or husband. This may be due to strong feeling or the desire not to hurt their existing partner. Enjoy them for themselves and take all they say with a pinch of salt.

Female (as well as male) Sanguines expect to experience full sexual satisfaction, and usually do. They enter into the spirit of things completely, focusing all their attention on the present and on full physical and emotional gratification. Unlike the Choleric whose intellect may get in the way, the Phlegmatic who feels she must do her duty or the Melancholic for whom the subtleties of the emotions are important, the Sanguine is in there, with every nerve cell excited and involved. They give in to the moment, let go, respond enthusiastically and are vocal and demonstrative in expressing their own needs and requirements as well as in meeting those of their partner.

Their interest in sex continues through the years; so does their love, warmth and affection. As long as there is sufficient excitement at home and you keep their interest you can have a wonderful marriage with a Sanguine.

The Sanguine at Home

Sanguines are restless creatures, so their homes are often temporary and they know it – and want it that way. However, they like to be in pleasant surroundings. Caring more for the look than the substance, they are happy to make do. Their first home could be a flat with limited furniture but inventive use of bricks and timber for shelves and storage, and hooks and dramatic fabrics to create hiding places for clothes.

When they want something they want it now, so they are more likely to make do with the materials they have to hand, or rush out and buy the nearest thing that is available, than to plan and purchase what they need for future construction. Of course these are only temporary measures, but somehow they never get round to changing them. They're too busy with the next project. They will see the glamour of it as they intended it to be, and will be surprised when a more meticulous Melancholic points out the deficiencies. Yet because their sense of colour is so strong the results are often effective and striking.

At first they will be totally enamoured of their new home and, convinced in their own minds that it is permanent, just as they believe each new love is *it*. They will spend love and care on it while friends are saying 'Why bother? You won't be here all that long, it's only rented'.

Later, when the spirit takes their fancy or a better home becomes available, they will up and off, leaving all their creative work behind them with an alacrity that will stagger their friends who can only see what they are leaving behind. The Sanguine, however, can only see what they are moving towards, and not even the reality of what they are going to, but their fantasy of it. The Sanguine could have lavished love and care on a garden, created the most beautiful studio room with paints and fabrics, covered the walls with murals and have it just right when the most beautiful, absolutely the most beautiful, attic flat becomes available. No matter that it is draughty, the roof leaks and the floorboards squeak, the Sanguine can see instantly how fabulous it would look with a little love, care and attention – and wouldn't living in an attic be romantic? In no time it will be transformed, at least on the surface, into a place that all visitors love. They won't, of course, see that the leaks have been dealt with by strategic bowls of flowers to catch the drips, that the draughts are kept out by nothing more substantial than hanging Persian rugs, and that only the constant music and laughter drowns out the floorboard cacophony.

Sanguines are artists and craftspeople. There is likely to be a lot in their home that they have made or created themselves, by hand, as well as a lot that they have designed and created by virtue of the choices they have made.

With maturity the Sanguine will settle somewhat more permanently, though they will never be one to let their home shackle them when there is a chance to move on. As their income grows and their sense of security and financial worth rises, they strive for a home that not only looks good on the outside but is solid on the inside. They are disinclined to deal with the details themselves so will probably get outside help. Theirs will be the ideas; others, as usual, will be called on to put them into practice.

In general, Sanguines favour unusual homes: very old or very modern, at the top of hills, with an unusual history or a sense of originality. Not for them a copycat house in a suburban street. They care little for the good address in a solid suburb. Certainly they want to have their house in a place where they can be admired, but they are not averse to living in a converted barn or garage, a penthouse over a city office block, or a boat on the river. Wherever they live they will dress the place up so that it is unusual and interesting and rises above its surroundings.

Maintenance may be minimal. Time is too short for housework and making the beds. Why put clothes away when you'll be wearing them again in a day or so? Why make the bed when you will be sleeping in it again in a few hours? Ideally the Sanguine will find a domesticated partner, male or female, or hire a housekeeper and gardener. Someone else can see to the routines and the in-between maintenance. They may, for instance, take a passionate interest in growing roses for a while, but there should be someone around to take over or the effort of preparing the ground and nurturing the young plants could be wasted as their interest moves on to building and developing a rockery.

A Sanguine's home is likely to be full of people and activity. They will organise many social events. They also love to have friends drop in unexpectedly, and their friends know this and love to do it for their welcome is so warm and the activity they will find there is so appealing, if somewhat chaotic. It might be wise to phone first, though, as your Sanguine could be out on the town. Do not expect meals on time when you visit a Sanguine friend, but do expect to find interesting people and chat, and always expect the unexpected.

The Sanguine Parent

Sanguine parents can be a delight for the children, but they can also create some problems with regard to discipline, or the lack of it, and the security that discipline can provide.

The Sanguine father is likely to leave the disciplining to the mother. Dad will be the playful and loving parent that comes home at the end of the day bringing light and laughter into the home. He will play with the children, bring them presents or surprises and help them in their latest games or endeavours. The children will be looking forward to the excitement of his return and he will rarely let them down in this, provided he does come home. With his own

Sanguinity to cope with, of course, he may suddenly go off and do something else for the evening, even forgetting to let his family know. But when he does come back, however late, he is likely to waken the children and reward them with hugs and play and be totally forgiven, by the children at least.

He will let the children do more or less what they want, feeling that they have the right to self-expression. He will encourage them to come and go as they please and keep open house for all their friends without vetting or criticising them. As they grow up he will assist them in their goals, lend them his car – even give them one, if he can afford it – feeling that they should have the best possible start in life. In his mind this means that, since life is for living, and youth is the best part, they should have as much fun as possible at this stage. More than most parents he is likely to retain their friendship through the teenage and early adult years as they give him their confidence, feeling that he understands them and relates to their view of the world. They are encouraged in this attitude by the fact that he rarely lectures them or tells them what to do but gives every impression of trusting their judgement.

If Mother is Sanguine she is likely to take much the same view. If she is working, the scenario will be much the same as with Dad, although Mother is somewhat more likely to have favourites than Father. If she is at home all day she is more likely to spend time playing with the children rather than doing the housework. Housework may even become a game that the whole family plays. Rather than make a chore of it she prefers to laugh her way through the dusting, with even the smallest child helping, even if the end result is not all that impressive and an ornament gets broken as they pretend to be birds, darting around. She likes to be with her children instead of doing the job quickly and efficiently herself (not easy) and achieving clean surfaces while leaving the children segregated in their room.

When Father comes home the house will be echoing with laughter as they all tumble through a wet and splattered bathroom in which they have been busy playing battleships. If Father is Sanguine he will join in. If he isn't, he may be dismayed at the wet footprints along the hall and irritated by the noise and untidiness of discarded clothes and toys when all he wants to do is relax after a long day. He may then be frustrated when told that dinner is either not ready or not going to be available because the shopping was not done correctly. A somewhat dismayed Mother may have trouble explaining why the colour of the tins was more important than the contents, but with her usual flair she will probably create an alternative with what they do have, and if he is wise he will appreciate the real warmth of the welcome she gives him.

If the Sanguine parents are such fun from the children's point of view, where is the problem? The problem comes when the child wants security and boundaries. Children like to know the limits to their world. They gain security from knowing they can go just so far and no further. They can be a little bit late but if they are very late they will be in trouble. Not only does this ensure their safety, it also lets them know their parents care what they do and are making rules that will protect them. Children like the freedom to speak their mind, but if they know they can say anything and not be reprimanded they may fail to learn manners. A child may want to do well at school but if the parents don't encourage their studies and hard work they may not only fail but feel let down.

As children grow through their teens some of them become embarrassed among their friends by a parent who is young, at least at heart, who is a friend and still tries to join in their games.

Stage I parents may be the gypsies who take their children from one school to another as they move on in their own lives. They may fail to provide a stable home, and may exhaust the children by letting them stay up till midnight. Their own unreliability may create insecurities for the child. The possible infidelities in the home may cause further problems.

All in all, however, Sanguines can make wonderful parents, be good companions and stay friends with their children, especially if they have matured to Stage II or III.

The Sanguine in Old Age

Sanguines hate to grow old; they even hate to grow up. Youth is the best time of their life and they frequently take it into old age with them, maturing it gently as they do so but always staying young at heart and much younger than the other temperaments.

A mature Stage III Sanguine is a delight. They have steadied somewhat and developed depth. They have made something of their life and brought happiness to others. They usually have a large circle of friends and a lot of loving relatives. They will be much in demand for babysitting, which delights them as they continue to love children and relate well to them. The grandchildren love them in return, recognising that they provide games and excitement with fewer demands for proper behaviour than their parents are apt to impose.

They enter easily into the child's world, getting just as excited as the children over fairy stories or games with toys. They are easily moved to tears when the child is hurt and just as easily laugh again when 'kissing it better' has done the trick.

The Stage III Sanguine is full of ideas which they will happily share with others. Since they age a lot more slowly than their years, they are often at their peak in old age with ideas to give and the maturity to let others take over and enjoy the limelight. The ideas may relate to work, either their own or the work or careers of others, or to their hobbies, projects or other interests, of which they still have many.

They may also, at this stage, be mature artists or craftsmen. They still love to entertain and be entertained and they still love to travel, health permitting. They may set off on the most unlikely tours at an age when the other temperaments are content to stay at home and settle down.

Mature Sanguines will help others, though not in the way the Melancholic does. Sanguines will give of what they have to spare – money, clothes, goods, even their own time – but only up to a point. If the deserving or needy make too many personal demands or are not interested in the advice the Sanguine has to give, the Sanguine will move on, looking for others to help. The Sanguine will cast pearls before the needy, but stop if the advice is ignored. They are less likely to hold someone's hand and listen to sorry tales, or not for long. In any case, when the moment has passed and the story is over they won't remember the details, content in the knowledge that the sufferer has had the chance to unburden themselves and that no further action is needed from the Sanguine.

Stage I Sanguine men in old age are a sorry sight. They have failed to mature and continue to insist they are young and one of the lads. The women may continue to wear clothes and make-up that denies their years but looks out of place. They will try to join in with younger people, not recognising the age difference but in defiance of it. They may seem silly and be an embarrassment to their family and friends. They are not happy themselves.

To avoid this, if you are Sanguine, and recognise yourself as

Stage I, it is time to mature. You can then be a delight, at any age and in any setting.

Health and the Sanguine

Young Sanguines take their health for granted. Life is too short for them to contemplate getting colds or spending time in bed with equanimity, and with their natural exuberance they make light of minor afflictions, unless they are craving for more overt care and affection than they are receiving.

Sanguines operate on their nerves and should take some time out to relax. This is not easy for them. Their Melancholic counterparts love to lie down and spend a relaxing hour or two while someone else massages them and eases out their cramps and tensions. The Sanguine is too impatient for this: why waste a precious hour of their time willingly doing nothing? Yet it would benefit them to learn to relax.

Their energy and activity tend to keep them slim. They usually eat well but are often impatient to be away from the table and getting on with the latest activity. They may be picky eaters, they can easily develop a sweet tooth and if their genes dispose them to poor health and their early childhood eating patterns provide inadequate nutrition they can suffer, through poor nutrition, from a weakened immune system and frequent infections.

They tend to drink alcohol, possibly to excess, but otherwise may not drink sufficient fluids. They should pay attention to this, drink more water, herb teas, fruit juices or coffee substitutes, all of which, unlike tea and coffee, are non-diuretic drinks. Sanguines should take care of their kidneys.

As the eternal optimists, adult Sanguines, if healthy in childhood, assume their health will never deteriorate, their body will not let them down and they can live the life of Riley without fear of the consequences.

Stage I Sanguines may abuse their body with social, recreational or highly addictive drugs, and assume they can get away with it. They may smoke, drink, stay up late, party, womanise, and generally raise Cain. They will have hangovers the next day but few regrets and will focus on where to find the next party. They may readily become addicted and they may go downhill, for their body is not, in fact, all that strong. This can be a particularly deadly combination if they are in some of the high-stress, glamorous occupations where drugs are freely available.

They are causal about the routines of life, about food, about having good-quality, nutritious meals, at regular intervals and every day. They are more likely to grab a quick snack on the run, as they flit from one activity to another. They may leave work, go to the gym for a quick workout, down to the pub to catch up with friends and off to a late-night movie or club. They may then keep their stomach quiet with peanuts, a bag of chips or a quick hamburger: not a good way to stay healthy. If their Stage I immaturity leads them to nightly wining and dining in expensive restaurants they may still suffer as they choose the most exotic and colourful meals rather than the most nutritious.

This is somewhat counterbalanced by their natural tendency to activity. While they do not like heavy work Sanguines do enjoy their body, delight in its suppleness and dexterity and so can be found playing tennis, swimming, skiing, running up stairs and darting around. All this activity helps to keep them slim. Even if they don't exercise they are still quick in their movements and will dance rather than fight, run rather than walk, and so burn up the calories.

The exception to this occurs when things go wrong. The unhappy Sanguine, lacking the inner depth that could have helped them through the problem, can turn to food for comfort. Then the weight will go on. With their butterfly nature they find sticking to anything, including a diet, difficult, and so the weight may stay on.

If they fall, are thrown from a horse or suffer a similar accident, their natural dexterity gives them a good chance of landing safely and delicately, somewhat like a cat. If the fall is bad their long and slender bones may break or their loose joints may suffer sprains.

Mature Sanguines will take better care of their health. They may have learnt to eat for nutrition as well as for looks – the looks do still have to be there. All in all they are taking better care of their health than their Stage I counterparts.

In general, they will ignore minor signs. They are too keen to get on with life to want to spend time in waiting rooms and discussing their symptoms. When a visit to a doctor is necessary they will want to be given a quick fix, a prescription or remedy that will cure the problem in one hit and won't interfere with their lifestyle. The more mature they are the more willing they will be to make appropriate and significant changes. If they are confined to bed they will rebel: they make poor patients. Since they are popular the sickroom will be filled with visitors at all hours, and since they have many interests their bed will be covered with signs of multiple activities.

They should be careful of the consequences of their excesses. As for everybody else too much smoking will affect their lungs, too much drinking their liver, and a poor diet can have many and varied consequences, but the Sanguine will never believe it and of all the temperaments is likely to over-indulge. They should also watch their nerves as they can be highly strung and emotional.

The Sanguine When Things Go Wrong

Sanguines are inherently happy. They like to look on the good side of things and ignore the bad. They tend to overcome minor problems by ignoring them or by assuming that they will, if left to themselves, simply disappear. Often this happens. But if problems persist there can be trouble. Living on the surface and lacking inner resources, the Stage I Sanguine can collapse when times get really tough.

It is the Sanguine's love of fantasy, their imagination and their tendency to superficiality that can get them into trouble. If they do not mature through Stages I, II and III, but become stuck in Stage I, they may feel that life is leaving them behind, that they are missing out. Rather than make the effort to mature they may tell more and more outrageous stories and weave ever more imaginative fantasies, all in an effort to be liked and loved. They will do almost anything to get back into the limelight.

If they lose their job or their partner leaves them they may first try drowning their sorrows in alcohol, escaping into drugs or embarking on a hectic round of parties and social activities, pretending all is well. But when reality hits they may fall apart. They may stop bothering. They may refuse to get up, or to dress properly, or to shave or put on make-up. They may even shun their friends. This Sanguine can become selfish, take for granted whatever help is given them and fail to say thank you. They may become petty, like a spoilt child. They will grumble that life is not worth living and become snappy and irritable. They will become temporary Melancholics. They will then be staggered that their friends desert them, not recognising that they were attracted initially by the fun the Sanguine could provide. The wealthy jet-setter who runs out of funds or happiness, and finds his or her acquaintances were hangers-on rather than friends, is a classic.

Many well-meaning people have tried to change the stuck Stage I Sanguine, to help them grow up and mature. They may try to restrain the Sanguine, to discipline either by advice or by force, or by their authority. This rarely works. The moment you try to restrain a Sanguine, to insist that they change and conform, you are lost. The Sanguine will resort to deceit and lies, telling you what they think you want to hear, to keep you happy, while they continue to live their life as they want to. Give them a long lecture on the dangers of exaggerating, the triviality of superficiality or the stupidity of frequent swapping of jobs or lovers and they will wait until you have finished and then leave, forgetting everything you have said, and get on with their plans. They know that you and what you recommend are dull and boring. The sort of pressure that can be applied in this way can backfire seriously. The Sanguine's whole nature may be warped. They may become so superficial that they laugh at things that anyone should take seriously; they may lose all touch with reality.

The opposite action can be almost as bad. Sanguines hate to be ignored, and if, instead of trying to force them to make changes you ignore their erratic behaviour, and in so doing ignore them, then their imagination may come in to play again. They will behave more and more outrageously in an effort to get, if not your approval, at least your attention.

Mentally, when things go wrong, they can wander off into a dream world. They may indeed become superficial, even to the point of losing all touch with reality and becoming lost in their own fantasy. It is likely that they will make light of serious things and reduce their life to a meaningless puff.

They may start to believe that the rules do not apply to them. They can steal – after all, they are too quick and smart to get caught, or so is their reasoning. They can cheat on their tax returns: the taxman will never find out. They don't call it cheating or stealing, of course, they are simply borrowing, or taking what is rightfully theirs. After all, they have so much to offer, the world owes it to them. They will cease to do what they're told. They are confident that their brilliance will make it impossible for the boss to consider sacking them and losing the benefits they bring to the job, and that their popularity will make it impossible for their partner to insist on a divorce, since they are such an asset to any home. They are totally surprised when the sacking or the divorce does come.

In time the Sanguine's optimism and cheeky confidence may return as they show their uncanny ability to make things come right for them. If this doesn't happen they can degenerate badly. They may take to drink or gambling, to prostitution or theft. They can become tricksters and swindlers.

When they do go insane they are likely to be subject to hallucinations, delusions of grandeur and popularity and exhibitionism. They may become schizophrenic or develop split personalities.

What the Sanguine Can Teach Us

Sanguines are wonderful people. They are fun, exciting, optimistic and extrovert. They can show other more serious mortals the wonders of the world. They bring light, life and enthusiasm into situations, show other people the positive possibilities and the light at the end of the tunnel.

If you want to be cheered up, find a Sanguine. If you want to find something positive to believe in, find a Sanguine. If you don't know what to do because your world is dull and boring, it will doubtless be a Sanguine who shows you the possibilities. If you are in need of ideas, if you need creative input into a project, talk to a Sanguine. Their ideas may not be sound, and they will rarely flesh them out with details – that is your job – but the Sanguine can plant the seed and show you the way.

The Sanguine does not know that certain things are impossible so they steam straight ahead with 'what if . . .' and look at the outcome. Things you would not, for a moment, consider, the Sanguine does spend thought on, and out of that come many new ideas, innovations, inventions and breakthroughs in the way we think and live.

Their art is on display in galleries, performed on stages and heard on the radio. Where would your soul be without it? Even if they do not make the world stage or your local craft shop, the paintings done for the family and the impromptu performances they put on at Christmas will give endless pleasure.

Because they are interested in so many things it is often a

Sanguine who starts several different projects going in a company, who opens up your mind sufficiently for you to consider that some of these 'impossible' ideas could even become reality. The other temperaments will then have the job of working out the 'how to' and converting the Sanguines' fantasies into reality.

Sanguines provide hope. When all is lost, it is the Sanguine who can ignite the spark and convince you that life is not all bad, in fact not really bad at all, and that with a little application you will rise up again. The Sanguine does this not only because they genuinely want you to be happy for your own sake, but because they also want all the people around them to be happy rather than sad so they can be happy themselves. They also do it because they genuinely only see the good. If the bad and depressing do penetrate their mind or their experience, it is only briefly. Sanguines will give you little chance and certainly no encouragement to focus on a negative past. Convinced that the future is all good, they will lead you toward it generating hope along the way.

You can live vicariously through the Sanguine. If you would love to go sky-diving but haven't quite got the courage, you can watch the Sanguine do it. If you would like to risk all and succeed in some outrageous behaviour, let the Sanguine do it for you. The Sanguine can give you the thrills and delights you might never create for yourself. In a dull world of wars and recessions, of starvation, drought and despair, Sanguines pull the clouds aside and let the sun and blue skies show through.

PART III:

Taking the Temperaments a
Step Further

CHAPTER 14

Love and Compatibility

Now that you have an idea of which temperament you are, wouldn't it be wonderful if you could use the knowledge to ensure you end up with the right person, certain the relationship would provide all you need and that you could count on it being satisfactory and continuing for the rest of your life? Unfortunately it's not that simple. For a start you will probably meet your partner when they are in Stage I, possibly Stage II. A lot will depend, for your future happiness, on whether they mature and develop the better aspects of their temperament or remain stuck or even deteriorate. Your own development will also, of course, affect the relationship.

You might think that, since opposites so often attract, Melancholics should marry Sanguines and Cholerics marry Phlegmatics. This commonly does happen as the individual sees in their proposed partner the characteristics they feel they lack in themselves. Yet as soon as it happens each of the people involved then tries, almost inevitably, to change their partner to be more like themselves. Equally, many happy marriages are made when you marry someone just like yourself. Does this mean that if you are Phlegmatic you should marry another Phlegmatic, or if you are a Choleric you should marry another Choleric? Possibly. It all depends on what you want.

When Opposites Attract

So often, people are attracted to someone who is entirely different to themselves. The quiet Phlegmatic may be fascinated by the courage and daring of the Choleric, the Melancholic captivated by the fun and laughter that surrounds the Sanguine. Alternatively the excitable Choleric may appreciate the calm of the Phlegmatic and the superficial Sanguine may value the depth of feeling displayed by the Melancholic. In all these examples the person concerned, aware of the characteristics they lack, looks for them in their partner, and finds them in a partner of the opposite temperament.

All too often, however, once the couple is married it is just these differences that each of them tries to change. The things you loved about the other person during the 'getting to know you' phase become the things you try to change when you spend time with them, live with them and try to incorporate the other person into your own life and lifestyle. It's a bit like eating: you may love the food for its taste, texture and colour but, once you have eaten it, you have to destroy these facets of the food, you have to digest the food and make it into a part of your own body. If you fail to do this, indigestion results.

The quiet Phlegmatic may expect the exciting and strong Choleric to calm down once they have married and settle into the quiet Phlegmatic routine of married life. The Melancholic may expect the attention of the lively Sanguine to focus on their own problems and be dismayed when they find their partner still wants to go out and be the life and soul of the party. The fiery Choleric may find, with time, that the calm of the Phlegmatic stops being peaceful and becomes stifling and boring and they start to berate them for having no get up and go – the very attributes to which they were attracted in the first place. The fun-loving Sanguine may get bored with the Melancholic's absorption with their feelings and try to cheer them up; always a mistake, as we have seen.

If you are attracted to someone because of the differences you observe in them then don't try to change them. If you try to make them more like you, you will lose what attracted you, and the person you met and fell in love with will have gone. You can't have it both ways. If you marry someone who is different, then preserve these differences, respect them, enjoy them and appreciate them. As you observe them and value them for what they are you can learn much about other ways of living, feeling and thinking. You may have a stormy time and an exciting time. You will certainly have an interesting time.

When You Meet Someone Just Like You

If you are attracted to someone who is like you your life is more likely to be predictable. What you see is what you get and you know about it already because you are the same way.

But what happens when you think you have found someone who is like you and then find out your mistake? If you are quiet and the other person is too, you might feel you have found another Phlegmatic soulmate only to realise, on better acquaintance, that the person you met originally was a Melancholic in their most cheerful phase and that now their Melancholic nature is showing through. Then you could be in for trouble.

It is so easy to know that when you behave in a certain way it means so and so, and easy then to assume that when someone else behaves in the same way it means the same thing. Often this is not the case. When the Melancholic gazes into your eyes and tells you you are divine they probably mean it and you could have the basis of a long and monogamous relationship. When the Sanguine does the same thing it may be true for the moment, but you may be the third person they have told that evening. If you give them your heart on only this guarantee it will almost certainly be broken. When the Phlegmatic says they will do what you have asked you can rely on them. If one of the other temperaments says the same thing you should not be so sure.

You may well have assumed that when the other person does or says something it means what you would mean. When you spend limited amounts of time with them you may not recognise your mistake. When you live with them it may become all too obvious. By knowing the temperament of the person you are about to marry or live with you can understand them a great deal better and can improve the odds on making the right decision and making the relationship work.

How the Temperaments Can Help You to Make Your Choice

A knowledge of the temperaments can help you choose your friends, your short-term lover or your long-term partner. You can never fully know another person. This may not matter in the creating of friendships and relationships with colleagues; in fact it may add to the interest. When it comes to the person with whom you plan to live for the rest of your life, then the more you can know about them before you make your choice, the better.

Knowing their temperament can help you in this quest. It will help you to understand the person better now, in the present, and to know more accurately how to interpret their moods, their behaviour, their words and their emotions. It will also help you to predict what the years ahead will be like. It will give you an idea before you make your choice as to how they will feel about children, about discipline and rules within the home, the balance of home to outside interests and about careers. You will know better how they are likely to react to money matters, to financial crises, to spending sprees. You may still make the same choice, or you may decide to save yourself from a painful mistake.

If your choice is already made, this knowledge of the temperament of your partner can help you to improve your present relationship and to understand the person you live with in a deeper way. Knowing another person's temperament, understanding your own, and recognising how the two can interact can make an enormous difference if you want to improve the relationship you have, to understand the other person better and to know how to bring out the best in them and in the relationship. We have seen the ways in which a person can be led from Stage I to Stage II, and on to Stage III. Often this role is taken, at least in part, by the person's partner as each of you helps the other to develop and mature. Knowing how to provide this help in the best possible way can enrich the relationship. Not knowing could be the cause of much disharmony and possibly of separation.

In any relationship there is room for friction and misunderstanding. There is also the possibility of great riches. Once you understand the different temperaments and how enormously different people can be, whole new worlds can open up. It is easy to say that, of course, people are different. It is worth repeating that, consciously or unconsciously, much of the time we continue to expect other people to be like ourselves. I see so many patients in my practice in pain and suffering because of damaged relationships. Frequently the problem is based on such comments as 'I wouldn't do that to someone I liked or loved, so how could he do it to me and still call himself my friend?' or 'If I did that to someone I could no longer expect them to respect me. I feel so ashamed each time I see her, yet she doesn't seem to care. Perhaps she doesn't value my opinion of her.' These and countless other comments betray the unconscious assumption that other people are just like us. All too often this leads to confusion and heartache.

As you apply your knowledge of the temperaments in detail, and truly come to recognise the differences, you may be able to watch and observe other people, recognise that their actions and words do not always have the meaning you would give them and see an exciting new world opening up before you.

Your road is not their road. What is right for them is not necessarily right for you. What may be exciting for you is dull for them. This applies in all walks of life; above all it applies in the close relationship you have with your spouse or partner.

Which Temperament Is Your Perfect Partner?

There is no one temperament that is the perfect partner for you. Whatever temperament you are you can have either a wonderful or a horrendous relationship with someone of each of the other three temperaments. Keep in mind too, that no one is solely and only one temperament all the time. Some people may be one temperament most of the time, but there are always exceptions, even if they last only briefly, and the various combinations of temperaments lead to different combinations of relationships.

The way to use the information here is to decide what it is you want in life and in your love relationship and then to assess which temperament is most likely to provide this. You could also consider the things you absolutely don't want in a relationship and decide which temperament or temperaments to avoid to achieve this.

If you want a gentle romantic relationship with much soul searching, long periods of tender loving care and quiet introspection then choose a Melancholic. The negative side of this is that you may find that, just when you want to go out and have some fun, they are too depressed or languid to move and they refuse to make the effort to accompany you. Just when you want to be up and doing things around the house they want to discuss the details of a Shakespearean sonnet or the meaning of life and, when you don't adapt to them, they sulk.

If you want someone who is steady and reliable, who is likely to be faithful and loyal, someone who will come home from work, regular as clockwork, or who will keep a tidy home for you, then choose the Phlegmatic. Don't complain if they protest when their routine is disrupted or if you sometimes find your life seems monotonous or dull and you want to put a bomb under them.

If you want someone strong and independent, someone you can depend on and who makes a success of their life then choose a Choleric. Don't complain when they insist on doing things their way and on making the decisions, and when they take it for granted that you will recognise their wisdom and their right to dictate. Be willing to let them have their way some of the time and stand up to them at other times. Do not expect an easy, expressive and close relationship but do recognise the depth and strength of their emotions.

If you want to live the jet-set life, on the crest of the wave, socialising every evening and with a large circle of friends, if you want to dream dreams and then live them, choose a Sanguine. Enjoy the fun and the laughter, follow their expressive lifestyle. But don't be surprised when you find they have been unfaithful or when some of the promises they have made do not come true. What do you want – the dream *and* the reality?

Couples

What follows is by no means intended to be a comprehensive comment on each of the pairs indicated. Far from it. It is designed to be read in conjunction with the rest of this book, not only with the four sections of each of the temperaments in love but with the whole book. It is intended simply to highlight a few pertinent points.

The Choleric Man and the Choleric Woman

Two Cholerics can make for a dynamic couple. Life will never be dull. Together they can accomplish much. They can inspire each other and have great times together. Cholerics have to respect the person they love and they will find much to admire in each other. Inevitably there will be rows as their ideas and their wills clash, for they both want to lead and be the stronger. Yet even in these clashes they can express their respect for their partner. There can also be enormous strengths. Inevitably the Choleric man will feel that he should dominate. He may have to fight hard to do this as she too will feel she has a right to her own way.

There may be a certain lack of domestic bliss. She may leave much to be desired in the running of the home, though not always, for if the home is her chosen career she can be very successful there. If she chooses another career, which is a strong possibility, there may often be clashes as their individual careers and needs come into conflict.

When they pull together they can enjoy the adventure of life. They may well be the adventurous couple that other people admire and hold in awe, going out and doing things the rest of the world only dream about.

This combination is probably the only one where the Choleric woman can feel she has found a man to whom she can surrender. A man she can look up to and admire in all respects, and with whom she can have a fully satisfactory sexual relationship in which there is a meeting of the minds as well as of the bodies: something they both desire.

The Melancholic Man and the Melancholic Woman

Romeo and Juliet. These are the soulful lovers, lost in themselves and in each other. They may be tragic lovers or they may be wonderfully together, each searching for their own identity and, together, exploring their mutual relationship. They may spend hours in quiet talk and mutual introspection as they share their feelings. They are articulate and expressive and will use this to create and explore their relationship, almost as if they are developing a third identity, the one they create by coming together.

In the early stages of their relationship, if it is close, there may be little room for outsiders or other friends. Individual Cholerics, Sanguines and Phlegmatics have trouble fully understanding a single Melancholic at the best of times. For them to try to understand the love relationship between two Melancholics is even more difficult. They may see its surface, but rarely its depths, its intricacies and its subtleties. They fail to comprehend fully the absorption of the players in the relationship itself.

The Melancholic couple will assume, sometimes wrongly, that they are thinking, feeling and acting as one. If this is not so then the discovery of the illusion can be painful. However, they are usually too much in tune with each other for this to occur.

If they are both in Stage I there can be problems: both will want centre stage as they recount and dwell on their own problems. By Stage III they can give each other the nurture and care they both want to give and receive. They may work together in a caring situation, perhaps as house parents for retarded or unwanted children, in a medical setting, or as missionaries.

The Phlegmatic Man and the Phlegmatic Woman

This may look like a very dull relationship from the outside, but do not discount it. There is a high probability of quiet companionship and peace. Other couples, particularly those in strife with each other, will look longingly at the tranquillity and companionship of this relationship.

It may be slow to get started, but they both know that this is how it should be. You can't rush these things. Neither will be unduly expressive or demonstrative. They may even pay each other backhanded compliments as if afraid to come out in the open and tell their partner they love them or think the other person is terrific. They may declare their love once and expect that to suffice for years.

This is the couple you will see sitting in a restaurant on their anniversary in near total silence, but enjoying quiet companionship. If asked later, they will assure you they were very happy and had a wonderful evening.

In their desire for peace they may push problems under the carpet and refuse to look at them. This can work or it may lead to a destructive festering. They hate to have rows, thinking arguments are stupid and cause unnecessary pain, though they can happen. I once commented to the man in a Phlegmatic–Phlegmatic couple of my acquaintance that, just in the past few months, they had begun to argue a lot. From then on the arguments stopped. Eventually I commented on this and asked what had made the difference. 'I thought about what you had said and discussed it with my wife. We both realised you were right, we just hadn't noticed the drift, so we decided to stop, not to argue any more.' A truly Phlegmatic response and action.

Phlegmatics prefer to avoid change, including the change engendered by divorce and separation. Since they are tolerant and uncritical it is relatively easy for them to stay together. If they have chosen well and matured together it is likely that they will live out a long, quiet and loving relationship, caring for each other at the end as much as, or even more than, at the beginning.

Together they will be the pillars of their society and their local community. Do not expect dramatic changes or innovations from them, but they will be the ones who arrange and support community events. Their home and garden will be neat and tidy. Their friends will know what to expect and the couple will be quietly popular. They will have a routine social life, doing the same things at regular intervals.

The Sanguine Man and the Sanguine Woman

These are the beautiful people, the high-flying, jet-setting social couple. They will be enormous fun and do all sorts of exciting, if somewhat irresponsible, things. Invite them to your party and it will go with a zing. Or they may be the interesting and arty couple living an unusual life.

They will have fallen passionately in and out of love many times before they come together. Their coming together is exciting as both realise this is *absolutely* 'it' this time – as opposed to all the other times. You can expect a marriage within weeks, if not within days, of their meeting.

Their wedding will be unusual – in mid-air, on the top of a mountain, in a train or at some other exotic or trendy venue. They may wear white but might also dress up in an outrageously staged performance. They carve their names on trees, plan exciting and romantic surprises for each other and declare their passion to the world.

Problems may occur when the dust settles, the excitement wears off and they each look around for something new. If they mature to Stage III, all may be well. If they stay in Stage I they may both be unfaithful and this wonderfully romantic and passionate relationship of a few short years, or even months, earlier, may suddenly, to the surprise of all their friends, fall apart.

To help it stay together they should plan surprises for each other and do all they can to keep the excitement within the relationship. They should also, of course, do all they can to mature. Introvert Sanguines show affection more by action than by words and should make the effort to tell as well as to do, particularly if their partner is one of the more common extrovert Sanguines.

The Choleric Man and the Sanguine Woman

In many ways this is an ideal relationship. She is beautiful, elegant and much admired by his friends. He is proud to have won her and to show her off as his wife. As always in the Choleric make-up, particularly in the case of the male, there is an element of ownership involved, at least in his mind. She is unlikely to mind this, knowing he can give her the good time she enjoys. He will love buying her clothes and jewellery; she will love showing them off. She won't keep house too well but he will be happy to provide the wherewithal for someone else to take care of the details, and together they will entertain and be much sought after socially. However, she should curb any tendency to roam as he hates to have his authority and ownership questioned.

The Sanguine Man and the Choleric Woman

Love relationships are difficult for the Choleric woman. If she fails to find her ideal mate among the strong Cholerics she may choose a Sanguine for the fun he can bring into her life. He, in turn, will be drawn by her strength and self-confidence, recognising that she does not need others to endorse her but is confident within herself, whereas he needs the compliments and the positive feedback of his friends and acquaintances to reassure him.

If they want to build successfully they should continue to appreciate their differences. He can bring her out of her more serious side and soften some of her tendency to seem unfeeling and excessively strong. She can bring a depth and stability to the relationship and to his life that he would otherwise lack.

At first she may think he is her ideal and then come to realise his lack of depth. If she is disappointed in the relationship she is likely to throw herself into her career instead – something she may do anyway, even in a happy relationship. He may be overwhelmed or intimidated by her strength and success and feel his own intellectual inadequacy. His escape is to find another woman who worships him. If he is unfaithful he should take care. While historically it has been more acceptable for the man of a couple to be unfaithful but not for the woman, this pattern is changing and she is nearly as unlikely as her male counterpart to accept this disloyalty.

The Choleric Man and the Phlegmatic Woman

This is probably a better partnership for the somewhat more introverted Choleric. His Phlegmatic wife will provide him with the home and background he wants and against which he can go out and conquer the world. Knowing he has a stable base to come home to he can take the risks, run the business and deal with the crises at work. When he chooses to entertain he knows she will provide a predictable event. It may not be spectacular but, provided she has been given warning, things will be prepared and ready when he brings guests home. He can also be sure that his children will be well and reliably cared for, their clothes cleaned and mended. He should take care not to treat his home as a hotel: there when he wants it but not intruding on his attention when he is away.

In turn she can be sure that he will provide, although she may be somewhat overwhelmed by the risks he takes and his outgoing and possibly fiery nature. She may wish they could be closer and that he shared more with her. She may also wish for a more peaceful and settled life, that she could be sure what time he would be home and that they could plan more things in advance rather than doing them on the spur of the moment. However, she is usually happy to have someone who takes control, makes the decisions and tells her what needs to be done. In general, she will defer to his wishes, often for the sake of peace, and also for the feeling of security this generates.

They will have good times together. He will also have friends, mostly male, and find companionship outside the marriage, among colleagues or at the clubs to which he belongs. She will spend time with other wives and mothers. Each will be happy that this is so.

He may well be faithful. Having decided on a partner, he does not like to announce that he has made a mistake by looking for another. He also takes responsibility for his own actions, provided he has matured, and will blame himself, rather than her, for any inadequacies in the relationship.

The Phlegmatic Man and the Choleric Woman

This partnership is that of a strong and outspoken woman with a quiet and placid man. He may be attracted to her initiative and get-up-and-go. She may be attracted by his calm nature as a haven in her life of high activity and drive.

If they do not try to change each other she has found a man who, while he cannot match her as could a Choleric partner, will at least let her go out and have her career. He in turn has found a woman who brings excitement into his life and provides some of the drive he may feel he lacks. His will probably be the less demanding career; he may even do a major share of the child rearing, working more predictable hours than she does.

This is one of the relationships where the partners would do well not to try and change each other after they come together. If they succeed they will lose the best of both of them. She will become a subdued Choleric and he will be forced out of his comfort zone.

If they do try to change each other they will almost certainly fail. She may get impatient with him when he does not respond or react as she wants. When she is angry with someone or about something and he sits there calmly refusing to get excited about it she may simply get more cross, and with him now as well as the original cause of her irritation. She will do and say more and more in an effort to get a response out of him, a response that is foreign to his Phlegmatic nature. He is calm and disinclined to fight, not out of fear – his calm is part of his nature – but because he feels that things will work themselves out in the end and that there is no need for him to get excited. To the outsider he may even seem the typical henpecked husband subdued by a female termagant who is trying to change him, to make him 'be a man'. If he tries to change her, which is the less likely scenario, he will try and tie her down to his routine and quiet lifestyle. This will cramp her style and may eventually drive her away through boredom and frustration.

The Choleric Man and the Melancholic Woman

If he wants to be adored he could do worse than choose a Melancholic woman, for she is apt to be blind to his flaws. She in turn has a husband whose strength she can appreciate yet may not understand.

However, he may find she lives at too slow a pace for him and that she is too dependent and may even be clinging. He may be impatient with her needs, her willingness to pick up, as he sees it, lame ducks and help everyone in the neighbourhood. He may also get impatient with her desire to explore their relationship and delve into his feelings. When he wants quick and energetic sex after a long day at the office, and then to be able to roll over and go to sleep, she may be hurt by this and want long slow lovemaking with many emotional declarations both before and after. With less she may come to feel, in her worst moments, that he is a heartless brute.

She may find he is too strong and unfeeling for her. He can be sarcastic or cutting and his words may hurt her. In general he is likely to express his love logically and intellectually, whereas she wants to experience the feelings and may wonder if, by her standards, he has any.

Together, in their community and among their family and friends, he will provide the strength and she the caring. He will be strong and admired, he may be asked to provide support because of his capabilities, people may go to him for advice which, when given, will be intellectual and informative. On the other hand, people will go to her when they need a shoulder to cry on, a place to pour out their woes. They will go to her when they want comfort and understanding.

The Melancholic Man and the Choleric Woman

He will take his time wooing her and may be surprised to find, on many occasions, that she has become impatient and moved on. The Choleric woman is, in general, looking for someone she can respect and look up to. None of the temperaments fully understands a Melancholic and the Choleric woman is particularly at sea here. If she wants the relationship to work she may be telling herself that his silences are profound and his gentle ways indicate a deep nature, as indeed they do. Many of the emotional events that fill his life will pass by her unnoticed. In this she may be able to respect the unknown. Certainly she will not be able to admire his overt strength and independence, for these are not in his nature. In fact she may become the dominant player in the partnership.

If they do not try to change each other he may be able to bring out her softer and more caring side. It is there, but it does tend to get lost among her strengths and her inability to be fully in touch with and express her feelings. She should not try to make him independent but be willing to offer support and lend him her strength when he needs it.

The Melancholic Man and the Sanguine Woman

This is definitely a case of opposites attracting. He was probably attracted initially by her extroverted sense of fun and her liveliness. He probably saw her as someone who could lift him out of his moods and sombre feelings and bring some fun into his life. Many Sanguines, particularly in Stage I, are unhappy with what they see as their lack of deep feelings. So she probably saw him as someone who could help her find a more stable base for her emotional life and could help her to settle down and gain deeper emotional values.

To a certain extent each of them is right, but if they try to change each other too much they will both lose. Instead they should try to continue to appreciate and value their differences. He would be wise to let her bring some fun and happiness into their life while at the same time accepting her lack of emotional depth. She would be wise to recognise his deep concerns about things that, to her, seem unimportant. She should not, of course, try to cheer him up with assurances, in her happy Sanguine way, that everything will be all right. He does need her to understand, or at least to be willing to try to understand, and certainly to respect, his concerns.

They may come together in a shared common interest in the arts, although he will be interpreting them whereas she is more inclined to be creating.

The Sanguine Man and the Melancholic Woman

This is a somewhat easier combination than the above, although it is still a case of opposites attracting. In this relationship he is able to be the outgoing one, setting the pace of their social life while she is the nurturing homemaker. This provides somewhat more traditional roles than the reverse relationship.

He will be inclined to roam, especially when he is looking for a good time and is finding her moods too heavy. If he does roam and she is in Stage I she may accept the situation and blame herself, saying it is no wonder he has found someone else, she is no good and he'd be better off without her. If he insists the relationship is still important to him she will probably accept the pain as part of life and be willing to continue.

If she is attracted to someone else it may well be another Melancholic, someone who can understand her, someone with whom she can share her feelings, and quite possibly this will be a platonic relationship. It may even be with another woman, a friend to whom she can confide and who will commiserate with what she is experiencing.

Again, they would be wise to appreciate each other and not to try to change each other.

The Melancholic Man and the Phlegmatic Woman

The Melancholic man will appreciate her quiet calm. This is not someone who will ride roughshod over his concerns but someone who will sit quietly and listen to all he has to say. He will have a chance to unburden himself, to explore and discuss the problems of the world. He will also be able to explore his relationship and discuss their marriage, the family, their friends and so forth. She may not have a lot to say, and may not be giving him her full attention, but he will feel she is part of the conversation.

She will provide a stable home for him, one with few disasters or crises. She will not jolly him along or expect him to be more cheerful than he feels like being. When he brings home people he wants to help she will provide the practical wherewithal to do this while he provides emotional support.

Their life may not be exciting but it can have a quiet depth and companionship.

The Phlegmatic Man and the Melancholic Woman

This relationship will be pretty similar to the above. Here it is his turn to be the solid and stable support providing emotional stability for her. His role may be more in the community than in the home and in domestic matters, but otherwise it is similar. He will provide the home where she can perform her role in helping others.

If he comes home and she has been lost in what she is doing that day, be it dealing with her own mood or helping other people, and there is no meal on the table, he will take this in his stride. He will either order a meal in or will get a meal together for the family. If the children are still up or need to be bathed he will down tools and help out. Calm, and above all routine, will be restored. Since he rarely brings work home or stays late at the office he has the time and the inclination to do this.

The Phlegmatic Man and the Sanguine Woman

The Phlegmatic man is a traditionalist and enjoys routine. He may also, as a bachelor, have felt that his life was rather staid and dull. He may have looked on in admiration and envy as his friends had an exciting time while he followed his routine lifestyle. The Sanguine woman, when he first met her, may have been a beacon of fun and light, someone he admired. He may have felt that to win her was a real feather in his cap.

Once married, things could change. He will expect her to conform, to live by the rules – not an easy thing for her to do. As she becomes a part of his life and he feels that the way she behaves reflects on him, he may become disturbed by her more flamboyant behaviour and, as he sees it, some of the more outrageous things she does. He may even find she embarrasses him when they are in public. He may want her to settle down and lead a quiet life with him.

At some point in their life together he may want them to move to quieter surroundings, to live in the country, or to do something that would reduce her chance for extroversion, for creativity, for social enjoyment. If this happens he will expect her to fit in, and be surprised when she feels restricted and confined by this and is not happy.

She, on the other hand, may grow to feel he is a boring old stick-in-the-mud. She may behave more and more outrageously in an effort to stir him up and bring some fun into their life. She would do well to recognise that his quiet and Phlegmatic ways are not signs of stupidity or laziness but reflect a deep inner calm and acceptance from which she could learn, just as he could learn from her to lighten up a bit.

The Sanguine Man and the Phlegmatic Woman

It is likely that, initially, he was attracted to her calm and her depth. This depth may have been real. On the other hand it may have been imagined. He may have observed her quiet steadiness and taken it for depth, a depth and stability that he, as a, possibly immature,

Sanguine felt he lacked. Many Sanguines are happy with themselves but there are also many that are uncomfortable with the way they flit from occupation to occupation and from one hobby or interest to another. To the latter, the stability of the Phlegmatic has great appeal.

All may be well for a while, but in time the Sanguine man may grow restless for new activity, for change and variety, and his Phlegmatic wife will be unable or unwilling to keep up with him. He may want to socialise more than she does or to bring friends home and entertain. If she is a typical Phlegmatic she will go along with this, will provide the food and so on, but it is unlikely that she will be the life and soul of the party. If he wants to travel or to change jobs she will fit in as best she can, but will not be comfortable.

If they have both reached Stage II or III it is possible that she will enjoy the excitement he brings into her life, even though she will still be more audience than participant, and he will enjoy the background she provides, against which he can go out and do all his Sanguine things, happy in the knowledge that he can return to a stable home.

Being Phlegmatic she will do all she can to fit in with this. She will endeavour to be, as she sees it, a proper wife. But, especially if they have both stayed in Stage I, she may also find it disturbing and he may begin to find her tedious and think of her as spoiling his fun. This restlessness may lead him into affairs even if he still loves his wife. She may find out about them but decide to tolerate them for the sake of the relationship or the family. In fact, he may be one of the Sanguine husbands who comes home and tells her about them, insisting that they are unimportant and that they don't threaten the marriage. If she is a full Phlegmatic she may recognise the truth of this and be willing to tolerate the situation.

So who will you choose? Who have you chosen? It is easy to see why opposites attract. It is also easy to see why troubles come about. If you give it a little bit of thought, with the knowledge you have now acquired, you can turn this situation around and appreciate and build on the positives.

CHAPTER 15

Combining the Temperaments

There is always a danger in categorising anything, and this is particularly so when it comes to categorising people. People are infinitely varied and infinitely wonderful, in the literal meaning of the word. Putting them into four groups, you may feel, is too restrictive. You could even say there are, or should be, as many categories as there are people, for at times it seems that different people behave almost as if they are from different species. You can doubtless think of people who live and behave in ways entirely foreign to you, ways that you would never copy or duplicate and even in ways that you can entirely fail to understand. There are huge ranges in human behaviour and personality.

To try to reduce the whole of the human race into four types, made up of the temperaments as they are described here is, at one level, to try to do the impossible. Yet at the same time we do have to make some sense of the world around us, of the people we meet and with whom we interact.

In this book the description of each temperament has been given as if the person concerned is made up wholly and solely of that temperament. This is necessary so that you can become familiar with each temperament in its pure or archetypal form. In practice there are indeed some people who are 100 per cent a specific temperament. More often, however, you will find there is some blending.

Double Combinations

The simplest combination to consider is the mixing of two temperaments. You may, for instance, be a lofty Sanguine, but if you combine this with a measure of the steadiness of Phlegmatic you can bring many of your imaginative ideas to fruition. You may have the drive of a Choleric, but if this is combined with some Melancholia you could become either moody and difficult, or more sympathetic to the needs of others, especially those you are trying to control.

The Eysenck Circle

There is a helpful way to consider this blending of the temperaments in pairs, as a first step. One of the questionnaires that has been used in the past to determine a person's personality type is the Eysenck questionnaire. As described earlier, Eysenck studied two continuums, one from introverted to extroverted and the other from stable to unstable. When these two are plotted on lines lying at right angles, as shown in the accompanying diagram, four quadrants result. Eysenck has suggested that each quadrant may represent one of the four temperaments.

Eysenck further subdivides the quadrants into a number of subtypes indicated by the words around the circle. We have not used his questionnaire here as it is not based on an approach that starts with the concept of the four temperaments, but with different subdivisions. Further, the results people obtain using his questionnaire often lead to a different outcome to the results they get from the questionnaires used in this book, questionnaires that are based more firmly on the concept of the four temperaments. None the less his circle is useful.

If you start at the top left at the centre of the Melancholic quadrant you will notice that they are 'Sober', a word implying a certain amount of passivity and steadiness in body and mood. By the time you move clockwise slightly towards the Choleric quadrant, you will see that the energy of the Choleric combined with the Melancholic generates a degree of anxiety and tension. The Melancholic moodiness then gives way to a Choleric touchiness as the degree of activity and extroversion increases.

At the centre of the Choleric arc are 'Excitable' and 'Changeable'. Moving towards the Melancholic side is 'Aggressive' with heavier tones than the 'Changeable' found on the Sanguine side. As you move on, clockwise, the influence of the Sanguine on the Choleric becomes obvious with such terms as 'Impulsive' and 'Active'. These are clearly related to the Sanguine influence and are quite different from the Melancholic influence.

Within the Sanguine arc the Choleric influence maintains the extrovert nature and the person is 'Sociable' and 'Outgoing'. The pure Sanguine influence is found in 'Talkative', 'Responsive', 'Easy-going' and 'Lively'. Once the Phlegmatic influence comes in there is a degree of relaxation and settling down. 'Carefree' is more relaxed than 'Responsive' or 'Talkative', and by the time you approach the Phlegmatic quadrant, through 'Leadership', you are into the calm. This Leadership is not the dynamic demand of the Choleric to be in charge, but is the quiet and mature leadership of the Phlegmatic that has developed with time and as people come to depend on the stability of the Phlegmatic. It is somewhat enlivened by the extroversion of the Sanguine influence.

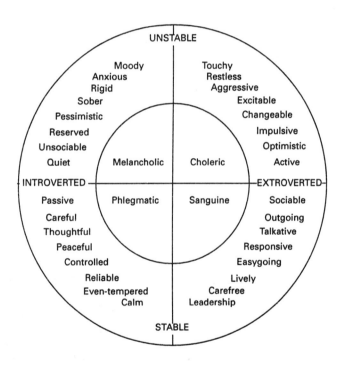

As the degree of Phlegmaticness is increased and the Sanguine influence is diminished, the mood settles down to 'Calm', 'Even-tempered' etc., and increased passivity. As we go back into the starting, Melancholic, quadrant we have the combination of Phlegmatic and Melancholic which provides someone who is indeed 'Passive', 'Quiet', and 'Unsociable'.

Triple Combinations

Triple combinations are more apparent when you look for the one that is missing rather than for the three that are present.

If the Choleric temperament is missing you have someone who is a combination of Melancholic, Phlegmatic and Sanguine. They lack the strength and drive of the Choleric but show signs of the melancholic gentleness and sensitivity, the fun and liveliness of the Sanguine, tempered by the calm and reliability of the Phlegmatic.

If the Melancholic temperament is missing you have someone who is a combination of Phlegmatic, Sanguine and Choleric. This person will be a happy optimist, only rarely getting depressed and even then only for short periods of time. Otherwise they have the strengths of the Choleric, the liveliness of the Sanguine and the steadiness of the Phlegmatic. They may be somewhat short of deep feelings and emotional sensitivity.

If the Phlegmatic temperament is missing you have someone who is a combination of Choleric, Melancholic and Sanguine. They do not like routine or the humdrum. Their moods may swing between the Melancholics sensitivity and tendency to pessimism and the Sanguines butterfly happiness, and they have many of the strengths of the Choleric.

If the Sanguine temperament is missing you have someone who is a combination of Choleric, Melancholic and Phlegmatic. They are unlikely to be the happy optimist. In fact they may be quite the opposite. They combine the strengths of the Choleric with the steadiness of the Phlegmatic, tempered by the sensitivity and possible pessimism of the Melancholic.

Obviously these four thumb sketches are just that, very brief indications of what the four possible triple combinations are like. The details will depend on the proportions within the combinations and the degree of maturity of the individual.

When the individual is mature and can draw by choice on the different aspects of their nature, these combinations can be particularly powerful. If, on the other hand, there is uncontrolled oscillation between the opposite temperaments, between the Choleric and Phlegmatic components or the Melancholic and Sanguine components, then a very changeable personality can result.

Variations with Time

People are not limited to a blend of characteristics that are fixed in regard to time. It is possible that a little bit of each temperament is present in all of us but that the minor ones are normally swamped and hidden by the actions of the major temperament or temperaments.

You may, as a happy Sanguine, spend very little time feeling depressed or melancholic. Yet when something sad happens the Sanguine can indeed display their Melancholic aspect. It is simply that Sanguines are inherently much more optimistic than true Melancholics and so, when something does upset them, they are likely to cheer up and bounce back much faster than the other temperaments and get on with their life.

You may be a caring Melancholic, not much given to laughter and frivolity, but when you are reassured that everyone understands that problems do exist, and when you feel safe with friends you may, from time to time, become quite extrovert, talkative and cheerful.

A calm Phlegmatic can, when pushed and when an emergency requires it, become extremely aggressive and active. But once the emergency is over they will relax and retire into the background far faster than the true Choleric.

Similarly the Choleric can, when situations demand it, settle down and endure in a way that is more usually found in the Phlegmatic. But when the situation changes they will be among the first to get up and get going.

You may normally live in a chaotic mess but then find, when things suddenly get too much, that you have a sudden urge to spring-clean and tidy everything up. The quiet mice may, when goaded, suddenly stand up for themselves.

Every time you do something that is somewhat out of character you are letting one of your minor temperaments show through.

Variations with Place

Some people find that their behaviour changes with the circumstances. If, for instance, you feel you are a combination of Choleric and Phlegmatic, you might find that your Choleric part is active at work and the Phlegmatic part takes over when you get home and relax. You might be a quiet Melancholic at home yet draw on your Sanguine side when out socialising. You might be an active Sanguine but for some reason get trapped in a job requiring monotony and routine. Provided there are some Phlegmatic characteristics in your make-up you will be able to draw on these to see you through the boredom.

Watch other people as their nature seems to change and then look for other subtleties to help you in your relationship with them. You might, for instance, meet someone at a party who seems like a happy outgoing Sanguine, and then wonder why they are regaling you with stories, albeit seemingly funny on the surface, of everything that went wrong for them that day. As you get to know them better, instead of being confused and puzzled by this seeming dichotomy, you may come to realise that, when not at parties, this person really is quite Melancholic. The best way to relate to them, therefore, is as a Melancholic and not as the Sanguine you seemed to be meeting at the party.

There is enormous power, freedom and a wealth of resources in understanding yourself and the people around you. Allow your new knowledge of these temperaments and their combinations to guide you to a better understanding of people. I was reminded of this recently when an acquaintance phoned and kept me on the phone for ages, talking about things that were happening in her life. Then I suddenly thought, 'Wait a minute, she must be a Melancholic, I need to lead this conversation.' So at each pause I asked a question that led her on to another topic. Very quickly all her topics had been exhausted and, as she was about to hang up she said, 'This is marvellous. Usually I find I'm on the phone for hours, but I seem to have covered everything with you that I wanted to and now I'll have enough time to write some letters.'

If you are not sure of the temperament of someone you meet you might want to use a process of elimination. The acquaintance discussed above was clearly neither Sanguine nor Choleric – she was much too quiet and softly spoken for that – nor had she ever displayed the typical Phlegmatic traits, so, although she was rarely depressed, I figured that that meant she had to be a Melancholic. As I thought about it further, and as the conversation continued, I realised that indeed she was.

Clearly, knowing the dominant temperament of the person you

are relating to can help both of you. Do not let it lead you to force people entirely into one box or another. If you recognise that someone has many Choleric traits and interpret *all* their actions as being Choleric you may miss their sympathetic Melancholic qualities. Recognising specific combinations, and the ways in which they can change with time and place, can help you further.

We have made a wonderfully rich language with twenty-six letters, but you do not need that many. Four, combined in infinite proportions, will help you understand the huge tapestry of human nature that you can experience daily.

CHAPTER 16

The Sub-Types of Each Temperament

If you have had fun so far and are enjoying what you have learnt, with no desire to make it more complex, this chapter is not for you. If, on the other hand, you want to delve deeper, to understand the different aspects of the Choleric or Phlegmatic temperament, the extremes of the Sanguine or Melancholic, to develop a more detailed understanding of individual people, then this chapter will enable you to do this. It will give you a start and, at the end there are some suggestions for further reading and exploration.

It is possible to divide each of the four temperaments into four sub-types, giving sixteen groups in all. As a result you can obtain a more detailed analysis and understanding of your temperament and your nature than that derived from simply determining your dominant temperament(s). This can be useful if you are working closely in a field where you can apply the results. However, few people can recall the details of sixteen character types and keep them constantly in their minds and few people, except those professionally involved, want to try. That is why this chapter has been set aside, after the end of the main book. For those who do want to explore further, read on.

Sub-Categories

The four temperaments have been around for centuries and even millennia. As mentioned earlier, the ancient Greeks spoke of them in some depth and they are still terms and concepts in use today.

Modern psychology has taken this concept even further by dividing the four categories or temperaments into four sub-types of each. This is not done arbitrarily, but by a logical format based on certain characteristics. It is exemplified by the Myers–Briggs questionnaire and analysis. This questionnaire is lengthy and complex and is usually administered by professionals. It divides people into sixteen categories based on four contrasting pairs of character attributes or types.

As you will recall, no judging is implied during the description of each of the temperaments and their stages of growth and development. No temperament is better or worse than another. This avoidance of value judgements also applies to the following groups. This way of looking at people's characteristics differs from many other psychological questionnaires and divisions. Measuring IQ, or mental alertness, or doing aptitude tests are obvious examples of situations in which you are, or could be considered, better than or less good than someone else, based on how well you score. Each type of temperament has good and bad points, positive and negative aspects, strengths and weaknesses. The end result of the group of characteristics within each type depends on how the individual uses their characteristics and how they develop and mature them.

To determine the sixteen categories or types, questions are asked that segregate people on the basis of four pairs of categories.

The four pairs are:

(a) Introverts   or Extroverts I or E
(b) Sensors   or INtuitors   S or N
(c) Thinkers   or Feelers   T or F
(d) Judgers   or Perceivers J or P

When the full questionnaire is completed and analysed, the result shows the relative amount of I or E, S or N, T or F and J or P in the person's make-up. Sometimes the results are clear and you might be, for instance, an INTP or a ISFJ or an ESTP etc. On the other hand, you might clearly be an I, S, F but hover with about equal amounts of J and P.

In addition to the full Myers–Briggs questionnaire, some quick ways have been devised for getting an idea of which sub-set you fall into. Although these quick methods of testing are less rigorous than the full questionnaire they do seem to provide pretty reliable results. Here is one that has been elaborated by Tad James in his NLP (Neuro Linguistic Programming) trainings.

1. When it's time to recharge your batteries do you prefer
   (a) to be alone   I
   (b) to be with people   E

2. If you are going to study a certain subject are you
   (a) interested solely in the facts and their
       application to the present   S
   (b) interested in the ideas and relationships   N
3. Which of the following are more important to you, to be
   (a) fair, caring and sensitive   F
   (b) reasonable, logical and practical   T
4. If we are going to do something together would you prefer that
   it be
   (a) planned, orderly and sequenced   J
   (b) unplanned, open-ended and flexible   P

You may find that your answer to each question is obvious. You may be totally an Intuitor and not a Sensor, totally a Judger and not a Perceiver. Alternatively you may be able to say that you do have some of either characteristic: perhaps you are partly introvert and partly extrovert, but dominantly extrovert. In that case use the initial of your dominant type, in this case 'E'. Or you may feel that you are a nearly equal blend of another two, such as Thinker/Feeler. In that case consider the description of both types; you will probably find you have some characteristics of each.

How does this relate to the temperaments?

There are sixteen possible combinations, four within each temperament, and they are as follows:

Cholerics are all iNtuitive rather than Sensors and Thinkers rather than Feelers.

Thus Cholerics all have **NT** in their set of initials.

There are four possible combinations:
   ENTJ, ENTP, INTJ, INTP.

Melancholics are all iNtuitive rather than Sensors and Feelers rather than Thinkers.

Thus Melancholics all have **NF** in their set of initials.

There are four possible combinations:
   ENFJ, ENFP, INFJ, INFP.

Phlegmatics are all Sensors rather than Intuitors and Judgers rather than Perceivers.

Thus Phlegmatics all have **SJ** in their set of initials.

There are four possible combinations:
   ESTJ, ESFJ, ISTJ, ISFJ.

Sanguines are all Sensors rather than Intuitors and Perceivers rather than Judgers.

Thus Sanguines all have **SP** in their set of initials.
There are four possible combinations:
ESFP, ESTP, ISFP, ISTP.

The following discussion will give you a brief idea of the variations we find within each temperament. Whole books have been written on the subject so this discussion is extremely brief and is only intended to be an introduction.

Introverts and Extroverts

Before we start you will notice that all the temperaments can be either extroverts or introverts. Neither the E or the I is an essential component of any one temperament. So far we have considered the Cholerics and Sanguines to be extroverts and the Melancholics and Phlegmatics to be more introverted. This still holds. You will rarely find a full Phlegmatic who is consistently as extrovert as the average Sanguine, or a Choleric who is consistently as introverted as a full Melancholic. However, within the range of behaviour of a Phlegmatic some are more extroverted than others, and within the range of behaviour of a Choleric you will find some who are relatively introverted.

Melancholics are indeed relatively introverted and wish to focus attention on themselves, but they also want other people's attention drawn in with them in such a way that the other people enter the Melancholics' world and focus on their problems, concerns and ideals. Melancholics like to be the centre of their own individual universe. Melancholics are not concerned with what other people think or feel of them; they do like to please others but they are not interested in making an impression like a Sanguine. They are focused on themselves and the way they feel. They are often content to be by themselves, contemplating their inner world. But they also want the other person's attention focused on them. Equally, and particularly as they mature to Stage III, they are concerned about other people and their needs, and in this way they can be extroverted.

Phlegmatics are also relatively introverted but for them other people are not needed. Phlegmatics live in their own world, taking pleasure in the job at hand, being left on their own to pursue their own thoughts and actions, withdrawing from their surroundings and getting on with the job. The less they draw other people's attention to themselves, the better. Yet they also care about their community and about contributing to it, and in this regard you will find extroverted Phlegmatics. They simply express their extroversion in a different way, for instance, to the Sanguine.

Sanguines, in contrast to the Phlegmatics, are extroverts, and most of them are turned totally outward, needing, if not demanding, attention from other people. Sanguines turn their attention outwards, focusing on other people and outer activities with little thought to their inner life. Their reality is the reflection they get from their audience. They live for the show, for entertaining a crowd, for fun and laughter. Yet even Sanguines can have an introverted side.

Cholerics, also extroverts, do not need attention to establish their identity. They are concerned with the outside world to the extent that they can challenge it, modify it and adapt it to their will. The Cholerics desire to conquer the environment and become the hero. They are less concerned with other people's opinion of them than with their own, yet their attention is dominantly outward. A few, a very few, introverted Cholerics do occur, only 2 per cent of the population in all.

The Sub-types

INuitors are likely to be have the highest intelligence, which means that, taken as a group, those with the Choleric or Melancholic temperament are generally more intelligent than the Sanguines or Phlegmatics. Sanguines and Phlegmatics, on the other hand, are good with their hands and are often artisans or craftspeople.

Cholerics

Cholerics are all iNtuitive rather than Sensors and Thinkers rather than Feelers. Their four possible combinations are therefore:
ENTJ, ENTP, INTJ and **INTP**.

ENTJs (5 per cent) are typical Cholerics. They are the real leaders, they take charge, create structures and provide shape and direction.

They are practical and structured, they plan and shape the future, working towards goals they have already clearly defined. They anticipate and welcome a challenge and a good fight. They usually win, but if not will either beat themselves up (if immature) or respect the victor (if mature). They have little respect for those that fear them, and can be impatient and intolerant.

They focus more on career, usually corporate, than on home and family. They will take leading roles in the community, in their work and at home. They are more interested in their society, in the structure, in the overall good, than in the individual. Reason and logic are more important than feelings.

ENTPs (5 per cent), the perceivers rather than the judgers, are more interested in the broader ideas and concepts. They are the mental leaders and are often teachers or researchers. They are intelligent, analytical, verbally adept and excellent conversationalists. They enjoy following complicated ideas and arguments through to their conclusion.

They are sure of themselves and their ability to cope or make do. They are creative nonconformists, striving to make things happen in new ways and generating interesting results in the process. They understand the complex relationships that exist between objects, ideas, things and people. They thrive on competition and will often create it if it doesn't exist.

They hate to be manipulated by others, avoiding this wherever possible, and they hate routine and monotony. They are better tempered than the ENTJ: gregarious, outgoing and usually popular. Life with them is likely to be fun, lively and exciting, but you must let them lead. They are likely to have a variety of interests, centred more on adults than on their children – who may get erratic attention from them.

INTJs (1 per cent) More introverted than the previous two, INTJs are supremely independent, self-confident and successful. They are logical and theoretical, living in a world of ideas, wanting to know and taking in the overall big picture. They are surrounded by books, read extensively and create new ideas. They enjoy challenges and brainstorming and strive to complete projects and overcome difficulties. They may be scientists or work with natural and human resources.

They can be single-minded, focusing on the current project and working long hours to achieve their goals. As a result they can seem cold, aloof and unemotional, yet they are sensitive to slights and can easily be hurt by those they love, though they will keep this hidden. Certainly they have difficulty expressing their emotions. When they find someone they can fully love, trust and respect then, and often only then, they will let their deep emotions show.

At home they like things to be organised and peaceful. They are devoted to their children but prefer to allow them freedom to develop rather than exercise authority and control. They expect their children to become independent rapidly and successfully.

Less sociable than their more extroverted counterparts (though this may change as they age) they are less likely to welcome friends dropping in without invitation and interrupting their activities. They dislike idle chatter and may offend by refusing to participate in the social platitudes that oil the wheels of human relationships.

INTPs (1 per cent) are also leaders and intellectuals. With these people there is likely to be an emphasis on philosophy, maths and the sciences. They value intelligence and may become intellectually arrogant, belittling people who do not keep up with them, and whom they readily call 'stupid'. They think conceptually and want to understand their world, a world that must be consistent and logical.

They delight in solving intellectual problems. They create ideas and projects, possibly losing interest once the creative phase is over and the problem-solving has been done. They then leave others to make them happen, and often to take the credit as well. These are the teachers who set high standards and work best with the bright students. Absentminded professors, they have the ability to concentrate totally on the ideas of the moment.

They are devoted to their family though somewhat uninvolved emotionally, are usually faithful to their spouse but may not put a lot of energy into the relationship.

Melancholics

Melancholics are all iNtuitive rather than Sensors and Feelers rather than Thinkers. Their four possible combinations are therefore:

ENFJ, ENFP, INFJ and **INFP.**

ENFJs (5 per cent) care strongly about their relationships and will invest much time and energy in them. They relate well to other people, may seem to get inside their skin and know what they are thinking and feeling.

Their intuitions are usually sound and they commonly and accurately recognise the underlying motives and intents of the people around them. They take on other people's burdens and seem to assume some responsibility for them, feeling guilty if they cannot make a difference in the other person's life. When help is needed people often turn to ENFJs, expecting them to know what to do and being willing to follow their lead. Thus ENFJs make good leaders, not so much because they desire it as by common consent.

They are good verbal communicators, particularly face to face, good at social and interpersonal relationships and usually popular. They like harmony around them and they like to please. They are perfectionists and like to have some degree of organisation in their life. They like to plan and know where they are going. They like to create organisations and projects that will help people and be good for them, often feeling that they know best what others need. Any criticism, conflict or even mild questioning of their actions is taken personally and makes them depressed or bitter.

They have a strong and reliable intuition and should make decisions on this basis rather than on logic, where they may fall down. At the same time they are good at juggling complex data.

ENFPs (5 per cent) Being Ps rather than Js these Melancholics are very perceptive: they like to observe life and look for meanings, rather than plan and organise. They like to find out what makes people tick, and to encourage self-expression. They like to please and pay compliments and may do so to such an extent that they seem to be insincere, pleasing the other person being more important than the truth – whatever that is.

They expect the best, so they often bring out the best in people. They have a keen intuition and readily understand people's motives and desires. Combined with their preference for observing and watching this means they are the group least likely to enjoy the categorisations we are making here.

They are dynamic, emotional, warm and fun to be with. They place a high value on intense emotional relationships. They expect these to be perfect and in them are often excessively and inappropriately self-critical, feeling that if they themselves tried harder the relationship could be even better. In this they filter out their positive input and find the negatives that they expect to find. In other respects this group is usually the most positive of the Melancholics. They may have trouble settling for a single relationship, feeling that the perfect and sublime one is still out there somewhere waiting for them.

They search out possibilities and meanings and look for new opportunities. They are initiators, preferring to let other people complete the projects they themselves have designed and started.

In their search for meaning they may live in the clouds and seem impractical; they may have many of the luxuries of life while still lacking the necessities, choosing to buy a book of poetry when food is needed.

INFJs (1 per cent) are intuitive and psychic. Like all Melancholics they live in their feelings and like to please. However if, when committed to a particular ideal, they meet resistance they may become stubborn. They are artistic and creative, but if there is no extrovert around the results of their idealism, intuition and planning may remain within them and be lost to others.

These introspective judgers have great depths and are intuitively aware of the depths in other people. They are also alert to and aware of the needs of others, possibly even seeming to be psychic. They have a strong desire to help people in trouble and are the carers and nurturers. They make excellent therapists and counsellors. Being Js they do this in a structured and organised way.

Introspective, they are dreamers and may seem shy and very private. When working with people they like to deal one to one rather than with groups or crowds; they might tutor, for instance, rather than lecture. Undemonstrative, they are not easy to get close to, but they are sensitive and easily hurt.

INFPs (1 per cent) are idealistic and honourable. They are caring and may espouse causes whereby they can do good and provide benefit for the world at large, especially places and people in need. While they are easygoing and like peace and tranquillity, their idealism may make them stubborn or aggressive if you push them too far or challenge the things that really matter to them.

They have their own set of standards. Their code of honour is based on their own values, and they adhere strongly to this, at least for themselves. As introverts they feel little need to impose this on other people as they tend to follow the 'live and let live' edict.

They often seem shy but usually form a few strong relationships about which they care deeply.

Phlegmatics

Phlegmatics are all Sensors rather than iNtuitors and Judgers rather than Perceivers. Their four possible combinations are therefore:
ESTJ, ESFJ, ISTJ and ISFJ.

ESTJs (13 per cent) are very masculine, the most typically male of all the sixteen types. Their nature is composed of the elements commonly thought of as male: being extroverted rather than introverted, practical rather than intuitive, thinking and logical rather than swayed by their feelings, and judging and organising their world rather than being content to explore and perceive, or waiting to see where their future takes them. Life is more difficult for the women of this type.

As the most practical, thinking and judging of the sixteen types, these people are reliable and responsible. They are the pillars of society in which they live, they support their community, they do the right thing and they evaluate and judge others by standard procedures. They prefer the established and traditional way of doing things to the new and innovative, and prefer to support the existing institutions and routines rather than create new ones. They are uncomfortable with unconventional behaviour and expect people to obey the rules.

They live by the rules themselves, and make good administrators and organisers. Jobs should be done thoroughly, properly and with full attention to detail. They are logical thinkers but tend to form opinions and judgements perhaps somewhat too quickly. They are practical, outgoing and firm. Since they have earned their position within the family, their social group or at work, by applying their own traditional values they feel secure, confident they are right and willing to tell you the way things are and must be. They may seem conservative and stick-in-the-mud, but you can rely on them to be consistent and strong in their beliefs.

They enjoy parties and often have a well organised social life. They enjoy a good joke but it may be macho, sexist or racist, even coarse. The man's man, swapping ribald stories at the bar, is an example of this type, but these stories would not be told at home, it is simply not done.

ESFJs (13 per cent) are much more emotional than their thinking counterparts (ESTJs) and are more gentle. This is a somewhat motherly type and one in which it is easier to be female than male. They want harmony in their lives and will do a lot to achieve it. They are sentimental, emotional and need to be loved. They also want to be appreciated and are sensitive but, as extroverts, their emotions show and they are easily hurt.

They are the most sociable and caring of the Phlegmatics and this takes the form of being good hosts and providing for others. Life centres round their home. Outgoing, they like to serve others, are conscientious, co-operative, obedient, eager to please and orderly. At social events they will be seeking out the lonely and making sure they have someone to talk to, whereas the ESTJ will be checking that things are properly organised.

They are still the traditionalists and are conventional and they, too, like routine and established procedures. They often choose careers that involve teaching or serving and supporting people, institutions or companies.

ISTJs (6 per cent) are quiet, private, very self-contained and will do a lot to avoid the limelight. They focus on their thinking rather than their feeling and can spend much time in quiet thought. They are the least likely to share these thoughts with others.

They are dependable, persevering, practical and sensible. They are totally honest and trustworthy: if they make a commitment they will honour it, if they say something is so, then it is. Duty is important and they will always try to do what is right and what should be done. Like other Phlegmatics they are traditionalists and follow the proper and established procedures. They support their community and institutions, usually from behind the scenes.

They are more interested in facts and data than in ideas, and in procedures and rituals than in people. They make good accountants and auditors and are ideal for maintaining safety and security arrangements, for setting standards and seeing they are maintained.

ISFJs (6 per cent) These are the introverted version of the feeling ESFJs. Like their counterparts they like peace and harmony and will put up with a lot to achieve this rather than assert themselves or make demands. As introverts they would rather be behind the scenes than visible, though they do appreciate praise for their efforts, even when they seem to be embarrassed by it.

They do their duty, are serious-minded and obedient. They do not like to be in positions of authority or control. At home they will insist that their partner looks after the money or makes the decisions. At work they choose to be secretaries or assistants and to be told what to do rather than act for themselves. Once told and shown what to do they are reliable, persevering and thorough. They work well for their boss and are loyal – but do not ask them to take the initiative. If they have to make a decision they will find out what other people have done and follow that.

They are patient and self-effacing, will put their needs second and be content to wait until you have time for them or there is a task that you want them to perform. They stand back in queues or in crowds and may seem to let others take advantage of them.

They are caring and like to serve others, again usually from behind the scenes, often seeming to let others make use of them or garner the praise. They like to keep working and doing things and are disinclined to relax, have fun or let others look after them. It is easier for these people to be female than male and they are excellent homemakers and make caring wives and nurturing mothers.

Sanguines

Sanguines are all **S**ensors rather than i**N**tuitors and **P**erceivers rather than Judgers. Their four possible combinations are therefore: **ESTP, ESFP, ISTP and ISFP.**

ESTPs (13 per cent) are extrovert and fun-loving. However, they tend to be more aware of the feelings, motivation and moods of other people than ESFPs. They love an audience and perform for it, seeming to pick up on minimal clues and to know what others are thinking and wanting, all the time playing to them and checking for their response.

They are active and dynamic; they make things happen, they can even make the dull and commonplace seem exciting and interesting. They love action and fun and sharing these with others. They know their places to go and the things to do.

They take risks and love excitement. They make good entrepreneurs and negotiators. They solve problems, at least in concept:

rarely in detail, of course. They like to solve the problem, create the solution and then move on to exciting new pastures, leaving others to deal with the details. They can be active in corporate takeovers, taking risks that would stop other people sleeping for weeks. If not channelled to positive goals they can become criminals and racketeers.

While ESFPs are more involved with their feelings, ESTPs are the thinkers, and this adds an edge to their good time. They make things happen more than the ESFP and use their brains and their intuition to help achieve the outcome they want. They start ventures, bring people together, negotiate, make things happen. They are diplomats and can sell ideas. They are also pragmatists, feeling the end justifies the means, and are rarely worried by their conscience as they move on to the next activity.

They are practical and impatient, wanting to do things, not read the manual, plan or consider the concepts, and they will only do things that are immediately interesting. Otherwise they will move on to the next activity that catches their attention, even in the face of authority. They are willing to play truant or ignore established procedures.

ESFPs (13 per cent) are typical Sanguines. Positive optimists, they are fun-loving, warm, gregarious, generous, witty and charming. Living for the enjoyment of the present they display the most light-hearted of the Sanguine characteristics. They are realists, yet at times their passion for fun and the sensations of the moment lead people to think of them as empty-headed and refuse to take them seriously. If this Sanguine fails to mature they can become the superficial social butterfly.

They are concerned more with their feelings than with thinking, happy to have and share the good times and wanting to please others and thus be loved in return. Live and let live is their attitude: they are more interested in being on good terms with you than in judging you. They enjoy life and make it possible for you to do the same.

Where the ESTPs ignore their conscience, these ESFPs ignore anxieties. They have a low threshold for worry so they turn their back on problems and refuse to see, think about or worry about things that could go wrong.

They hate to be bored. They know they only live once, and they intend to enjoy every minute of it. Provided all is going well they will share all they have and adapt to their surroundings, converting them into the paradise of stimulating activity and emotions they crave.

ISTPs (7 per cent) The introversion of these Sanguines can make them seem shy, aloof and withdrawn. Their activity and desire for the new and the interesting take place internally rather than overtly, and they often wait to see where a conversation or activity is going before jumping in and becoming involved. This is somewhat countered by their willingness to explore and find out what will happen, which can make them seem more spontaneous than they are. They are unpredictable, being both fun and reserved, but this makes their company all the more exciting.

They are also impulsive and quick to pit themselves against a challenge, ignoring the odds and willing to take risks and enjoy the thrill. They may even be thrill-seekers, seeming to thrive on adrenalin. They will try anything once and will accept almost any dare. They do things for the doing of them, not for the end.

Their creativity is more physical and practical than that of the ISFPs. They work best with tools, and their sports are likely to involve rackets, sticks or bats. They enjoy their dexterity in managing machines and equipment. The normal Sanguine extroversion of expression is channelled inwards and then comes out in what their hands can do or create. If not channelled positively their tools may be weapons. They may once have been highwaymen and could now become hired hit-men.

They focus on what they are doing, hating to waste time and preferring to get on with their current passion. Being particularly good with their hands, with sensing and crafting, they will plunge into fixing things without searching out the book of instructions. If help is needed they will only ask about the specific aspect of the task; they don't want the whole picture or the broad concept.

ISFPs (5 per cent) are relatively introverted for a Sanguine. Their involvement with their emotions and their enjoyment of the sensory lead them into artistic creativity with their hands and their bodies. They create in a variety of media: pottery, dance, sculpting, gymnastics, crafts etc., but are looking for the sensory pleasure of the moment rather than the deep significance of the artistic Melancholic (INFP being the equivalent).

As introverts they let their medium, on which they focus, do their talking for them and, although it is done indirectly, they do delight in expressing themselves. They give by their actions rather than by their words. Like all Sanguines they tend to live in the present. If they seem to practise endlessly it is because of present enjoyment and is not a disciplined action of will to prepare for a future perfect presentation.

Like the ESTPs they are keenly aware of other people and what is going on under the surface, but unlike ESTPs, who love the crowds of the cities, you may well find the ISFPs in the relative solitude of the country, in which they delight. They are unconventional, not to be different, but because they have frequently figured out a better way of doing things than the normal way. It is another, indirect, form of expressiveness.

They are enormously kind, wanting others to be happy, just like their extroverted counterparts. But since this is tempered both by their own introversion and by their focus on feelings rather than thought, it is done by attempting to create harmony rather than by performing for an audience. They want harmony, and this extends to animals. No conflict and no cruelty, that is their preference.

Summary of Sub-temperaments

Temperament	%	Brief description
Cholerics	**12**	
ENTJ	5	commanding leaders
ENTP	5	like excitement and challenges, inventive
INTJ	1	self-confident builders, scientists
INTP	1	like problem-solving and designing solutions
Melancholic	**12**	
ENFJ	5	caring, persuading
ENFP	5	authentic, affirming, commentators
INFJ	1	provide inspiration, welfare of others
INFP	1	idealistic
Phlegmatics	**38**	
ESTJ	13	responsible administrators
ESFJ	13	providers and carers, create peace and harmony
ISTJ	6	dependable, honest and reliable
ISFJ	6	service and duty, conservation
Sanguine	**38**	
ESFP	13	live in the present, impulsive, performers
ESTP	13	resourceful, practical, promoter
ISFP	5	in tune with the world, creative, fine arts
ISTP	7	daring and excitement, crafts

In the table below you will find a summary of some aspects of the four temperaments. You might like to add to the table yourselves as you develop your understanding of the four temperaments.

	CHOLERIC	MELANCHOLIC	PHLEGMATIC	SANGUINE
MIND AND EMOTIONS				
Disposition	Ruling Superior	Heavy Self-absorbed	Quiet Inferior	Happy Pretentious
Mood	Enthusiasm Enthusiastic	Pessimism and soul-searching Depressed	Pessimism leading to caution Steady	Happy optimism Variable
Emotions	Spirited	Depressed	Dutiful	Joyful
Thinking	Extrovert Self sufficient	Introvert Needs others	Introvert Self sufficient	Extrovert Needs others
Imagination	Practical imagination	Imagines things to worry over	Practical No imagination	Fantasy Imagination
In love	The boss	Tragic/intense	Steady	Romantic
Sex Stage I	Conquering Angry/intolerant	Suffering/expressive Depressed	Accepting Dependent	Passionate Restless
Stage III	Patriarch/matriarch	Serving	Understanding	Inspiring
Positive	Benevolent	Understanding/caring	Loyal	Exciting
Negative	Tyrant	Depressing	Self-focused	Superficial
Insanity	Violence	Suicidal	Catatonic	Schizophrenic
BODY				
Height	Short/medium	Medium/short	Medium/tall	Medium/tall
Width	Muscular	Average	Flabby	Slender
Stance	Upright	Drooping	Heavy	Elegant
Movements	Strong	Needs support	Clumsy	Light
Walk	Striding	Dragging	Plodding	Dancing
Skull	Strong	Average	Thick	Delicate
Hair	Dark/thick	Dark	Medium/mousy	Blonde/soft
Eyes	Direct	Discontented	Expressionless	Alert
Nose	Strong	Thin	Thick	Retroussé
Mouth	Firm-lipped	Drooping	Slack	Mobile/soft
Complexion	Ruddy	Pale/wan	Pasty	Clear
Hands	Square	Drooping	Large	Slender
System	C.V., blood	Bones	Glands	Nerves
Organs	Heart	Lungs	Liver/growth	Kidneys/activity

	CHOLERIC	MELANCHOLIC	PHLEGMATIC	SANGUINE
PRACTICALITIES				
Self worth based on	Achieving their aims	Self-realisation/ caring for the needy	Doing their duty/ supporting the community	Having fun/ being popular compliments
Desire for perfection	To be in control/ avoid criticism	Fundamental need	To do what's right	Unimportant as long as they get compliments
Work	In command	Accepting	Obeying	Creating
Time	Thinks of future	Lives in past	Present, introvert	Present, extrovert
Money	Generous	Indifferent	Honest/saves	Spendthrift
Clothes	Useful, comfort, practical, habit	Soft colours, materials, own style	Classic, functional, plain, quiet colours	Bright, stylish, flamboyant
Goal	Functional/smart	Personal statement	Classic, unobtrusive	Compliments
Writing (fact) (fiction)	Technical Action with information	Biographies/history Deep and meaningful, exploring emotions	Reports and records Conveying information	Quick notes Fairy stories, rich fantasies
At a picnic	Discuss work/ lead adventures	Worry about children/ discuss meanings	Find jobs to do/ tidy up	Play games/ have fun
Offer of a drink (alcohol)	Takes control/ plays host	Will it make me feel good?	Is it the right time?	What fun!
The arts	Active audience	Interpretative	Passive audience	Performing/ creative
Motivation		Finished goal To feel everything		Present pleasure To do everything
Teaching	Lecturing, to bright students Exciting	Nurturing, young children Patient, understanding	Maintaining society through the traditions of education. Serious	Performing and showing off their knowledge. Fun
Phone calls	Short and to the point	Lengthy discussions	Ordered, point by point	Chatty, may forget the purpose
Ending the call	Have a good day	Take care	Be good	Have fun
Home	Their castle, status	Background for their relationships	Security, a stable base	Display, for fun and parties
Greek gods	Apollo	Prometheus	Epimetheus	Dionysus
Seasons	Summer	Autumn	Winter	Spring
Elements	Fire	Earth	Water	Air
Ancient fluids	Yellow bile	Black bile	Phlegm	Blood

Further reading

Type Talk by Otto Kroeger and Janet M. Thuesen (Delacorte Press, New York, 1988)

Please Understand Me by David Keirsey and Marilyn Bates (Prometheus Nemesis Book Company, 1978)